MW01255004

GREAT PREACHING ON

COMFORT

GREAT PREACHING ON

COMFORT

COMPILED BY
CURTIS HUTSON

SWORD of the LORD
PUBLISHERS
P. O. BOX 1099, MURFREESBORO, TN 37133

Printed and Bound in the United States of America

Preface

There is no question we ask more often than, "Why?"

Hundreds of graves need to be explained. Hospitals for those in pain and misfortune, institutions for the insane and blind—things now utterly unexplainable—God will clear them all up someday.

Bartimaeus will thank God that he was blind; and Lazarus, that he was covered with sores; and Joseph, that he was cast into the pit; and Daniel, that he was in the lions' den; and David, that he was driven from Jerusalem; and Dorcas, that she could only get a few pence for those beautiful handmade garments; and that invalid, who for twenty years could not lift his head from the pillow; and that widow, that she had such hard work to earn bread for her children.

It is reported that a minister chose as his text one Sunday morning this phrase: "And it came to pass," and he gave it this development: (1) "It came" and (2) "It passed."

Times of trial and blessing come to all of us—but they also pass. No affliction in this world but that "it comes" and "it also passes." Our heavenly Father is keenly aware of just what each of us can bear.

One often sees on the approaches to bridges some such sign as LOAD LIMIT TEN TONS or LOAD LIMIT FIVE TONS, as the case may be, so that trucks with burdens that would endanger the safety of the bridge may not be driven over it.

Although Christians carry no visible signs, God knows the "load limit" of every one of us, and He will never permit that load limit to be violated or overtaxed.

When our cross seems heaviest, when it seems that our life has neither plan nor purpose, when it seems that we are being pushed about by a blind and merciless fate, what comfort to remember that in every valley of affliction, our hand is in His! And with our hand in His, we are forever safe. His omnipotent hand will hold us; His affectionate hand will guide us.

We have diligently searched through 2,600 issues of THE SWORD OF THE LORD magazine for the best messages we could find to comfort the weary, the sad, the burdened. Here are the best. Though many of these giants represented here have passed on to their rest, they continue to speak powerfully to us through the written message.

May this volume of 19 messages bring to many thousands of you spiritual strength in heaping measure.

Curtis Hutson, Editor
THE SWORD OF THE LORD

Table of Contents

JOHN R. RICE
1895-1980

ABOUT THE MAN:

Preacher. . . evangelist. . . revivalist. . . editor. . . counselor to thousands. . . friend to millions—that was Dr. John R. Rice, whose accomplishments were nothing short of miraculous. Known as "America's Dean of Evangelists," Dr. Rice made a mighty impact upon the nation's religious life for some sixty years, in great citywide campaigns and in Sword of the Lord Conferences.

At age nine, after hearing a sermon on "The Prodigal Son," John went forward to claim Christ as Saviour. In 1916, with only $9.35 in his pocket, he rode off on his cowpony toward Decatur Baptist College. He was now on the road to becoming a world-renowned evangelist, although he was then totally unaware of God's will for his life.

There was many a twist and turn before Rice rode through the open door into full-time preaching—the army, marriage, graduate work, more seminary, assistant pastor, pastor—then FINALLY, where God planned to use him most—in full-time evangelism.

Dr. Rice and his ministry were always colorful (born in Cooke County, in Texas, December 11, 1895, and often called "Will Rogers of the Pulpit" because of their likeness and mannerisms)—and controversial. CONTROVERSIAL—and correctly so—because of his intense stand against modernism and infidelity and his fight for the Fundamentals.

Dr. Rice lived and died a man of convictions—intense convictions. But, like many other strong fighters for the Faith, Rice was also marked with a sincere spirit of compassion. Those who knew him best knew a man who loved them. In preaching, in prayer, and in personal life, Rice wept over sinners and with saints. But there is more. . .

Less than seventy-one hours before the dawning of 1981, one of the most prolific pens in all Christendom was stilled. Dr. John R. Rice left behind a legacy in writing of more than 200 titles, with a combined circulation of over 61 million copies. And through October of 1981, a total of 24,058 precious souls reported trusting Christ through his ministries, not counting those saved in his crusades nor in foreign countries where his literature has been translated.

And who but God knows the influence of THE SWORD OF THE LORD magazine which he started and edited for forty-six years!

And while "Twentieth Century's Mightiest Pen"—and man—has been stilled, thank God the fruit remains! Though dead, he continues to speak.

I.

The Heavenly Language of Flowers

JOHN R. RICE

(Written in 1957 after Dr. Rice suffered a skull fracture)

"Consider the lilies. . . how they grow. . . ."—Matt. 6:28.

For eighteen days I have lain flat on my back with a skull fracture and concussion, after having fallen down a flight of stairs at my office. Now I am propped up in a hospital bed in my bedroom, with a dictating machine on a bedside table.

I find such a fragrance about these days which include suffering, being shut in and limited, waiting on God for healing and strength, that I have someway associated it all with beautiful flowers which have perfumed my room these two and a half weeks.

David the Psalmist was inspired to say, "The Lord will strengthen him upon the bed of languishing: thou wilt make all his bed in his sickness" (Ps. 41:3). And I tell David today, "The Lord certainly did tell you something there!"

Never, in the last forty-five years of my life, have I spent as much time in bed as these last eighteen days. Yet how sweet and blessed these days have been! God has certainly strengthened me upon my bed of languishing. He has made all my bed in this sickness. It is better to be sick in the will of God than well outside His blessed will.

As I look on the great array of flowers adorning my room, I realize there is a language of flowers. Sometimes lovers think more about them than anyone else. Every rose, violet, carnation or forget-me-not has some sweet meaning to those in love.

Surely God has some language of flowers, too.

There is a vase of great cut roses sent by Drs. Bob Jones, Jr. and Sr. How dark the color, how big the bloom! I remember the roses sent by one of my staff—a language of friendship, devotion and prayer.

Beside my bed is a potted plant, the big "Maid of Orleans," with clusters of tiny roses. Then a big vase of cut flowers, another vase of asters brought by a daughter and grandchildren. A Sunday school teacher and her class of boys selected a big pot of pale blue hydrangeas. The big clusters of blossoms are each six or seven inches across. Then there is another new pot of giant pink hydrangea blossoms from my sister Jimmie.

Another pot of hyacinths was delivered; soon the spears expanded gorgeously into great blue plumes of flowers. A big plant with lily blossoms came from our beloved printer of THE SWORD OF THE LORD. Another employee and his family, Rev. and Mrs. Charles Vradenburgh, sent another pot of lilies; members of Calvary Church here in Wheaton sent more yet.

Then there was the huge bowl of fifteen giant carnations from Mr. Bill MacLeod in our advertising department. How sweet have been the suggestions they brought to mind every time I have looked about me.

As people have entered my room, all have noticed the sweet odor of lilies, of roses, of carnations, hyacinths and hydrangea.

I have just looked into the heart of a dozen lily blooms near my bed. Who could make anything so delicately pure as the inside of a lily blossom! And the delicacy of the blossoms, the sweet faintness of the perfume, speak of God. No wonder Jesus said, "Consider the lilies... how they grow." Doubtless He has considered them countless times and has rejoiced in their beauty and fragrance.

Let us see from Scripture what the heavenly language of flowers is.

I. FADING FLOWERS PICTURE MAN'S FRAILTY AND BREVITY OF LIFE AND OPPORTUNITY

In Psalm 103, after naming particularly the five greatest blessings which ought to move us to thankfulness and grateful remembrance, God says:

"As for man, his days are as grass: as a flower of the field, so he flourisheth. For the wind passeth over it, and it is gone; and the place thereof shall know it no more."—Vss. 15,16.

No wonder God pities us, saying, "For he knoweth our frame; he remembereth that we are dust," in verse 14 here. Our days are as the grass of the field. Men fade as a wild flower. Only one abrupt, harsh wind, and the delicate flower is broken and dead. Only one touch of frost, and the flower is killed. Such a striking illustration is this of the uncertainty, the brevity, the passing opportunity which man's life here affords!

That thought is expressed again in James 1:9-11:

"Let the brother of low degree rejoice in that he is exalted: But the rich, in that he is made low: because as the flower of the grass he shall pass away. For the sun is no sooner risen with a burning heat, but it withereth the grass, and the flower thereof falleth, and the grace of the fashion of it perisheth: so also shall the rich man fade away in his ways."

It is addressed particularly to "the rich" because a rich man dies as soon as a poor man. That truth is brought out vividly in the story of the rich man who died and went to Hell, and the beggar at his gate who went to Heaven. Riches cannot put off sickness and death.

Isaiah 40:30 tells us that "even the youths shall faint and be weary, and the young men shall utterly fall." Youth guarantees no more time. Strength, education, position—none can guarantee one extra hour of opportunity which we may have let slip.

Whoever reads this and boasts in the strength of youth, in a robust body, I beg you to hear this: One day your limbs will be as frail as those of old men; one day your brilliant mind will be as doting and senile as that of old age, unless cut off before that time.

God has given me a robust body and, with enormous labors and burdens, I have felt compelled to guard my health. God has maintained my strength, and I can now do more work than ever before. But it is not hard to see, yea, it is even blessed to realize that my hair is growing gray, my steps are not as quick as they once were, and even the limitations that other men have are now my limitations.

By the flowers in my room I am reminded that life itself is a fading business. Who knows but that I may never preach another sermon, may never write another article. I may never again have the privilege of family worship, as we do each morning now, nor a circle of prayer with my wife and children; for my life is "as a flower of the grass" that passes away. The sun withers it; the flower falls.

"As a flower of the field" I have flourished. But some wind of God will pass over me, perhaps very soon and certainly not very late; and I will be gone, "and the place thereof shall know it no more."

But in this heavenly language of flowers is there any sadness, any defeat? Must I grieve that my strength is not that of a young man, that my days may be suddenly cut off? No indeed! Rather, like the Apostle Paul, I shall "glory in my infirmities, that the power of Christ may rest upon me." I remember also how Paul said in II Corinthians 4:16-18:

"For which cause we faint not; but though our outward man perish, yet the inward man is renewed day by day. For our light affliction, which is but for a moment, worketh for us a far more exceeding and eternal weight of glory; While we look not at the things which are seen, but at the things which are not seen: for the things which are seen are temporal; but the things which are not seen are eternal."

All the afflictions of a Christian are light compared to the eternal weight of glory awaiting us. And though the outward man perish, we can so enjoy God's favor and constant spiritual renewal that we can say "the inward man is renewed day by day."

Paul continues in II Corinthians 5:1-4:

"For we know that if our earthly house of this tabernacle were dissolved, we have a building of God, an house not made with hands, eternal in the heavens. For in this we groan, earnestly desiring to be clothed upon with our house which is from heaven: If so be that being clothed we shall not be found naked. For we that are in this tabernacle do groan, being burdened: not for that we would be unclothed, but clothed upon, that mortality might be swallowed up of life."

The frailties of this old body will be completely conquered one day! And so I long, not to be unclothed but to be clothed upon with a glorified, resurrected body which God Himself will give. Then it will be no more fading like a flower or withering by a wind, displaced and forgotten so people will know it no more.

Sweet indeed is the heavenly language of flowers. Flowers tell me that life is short, the body weak and that God has better things later on!

May we do today what ought to be done today. If there are any you should win or warn, any blessing you should pass on, any labor yet to do, thank God for the opportunity and do it today.

James 4:14 warns, "Ye know not what shall be on the morrow. For what is your life? It is even a vapour, that appeareth for a little time, and then vanisheth away." Yes, life is a vapor or a fading flower; so let us not be found boasting of tomorrow.

The beautiful spires of the blue hyacinth rear themselves grandly by my bed. But in a few days they will droop. Though my wife tied up the big spears of flowers to a central stick, the decay continues; and soon they will wither.

The big bowl of giant carnations was lovely. But the fifteen have withered one by one until only two remain.

One blossom on the big pot of Easter lilies is already turning brown and is limp. So do all flowers of the earth. Thank God, something is better for man than this life!

II. FLOWERS PICTURE HOW SWEET WE ARE TO THE LORD

In the Song of Solomon human love is used as a type of the love between Christ and His church, the saved. Flowers are sometimes used in the Song of Solomon to picture the Lord Jesus, but more usually these flowers picture a Christian in God's sight.

For example, 2:1 says, "I am the rose of Sharon, and the lily of the valleys," indicating that the one speaking is the bride of Solomon, who here pictures the child of God. To Jesus Christ, then, I am the rose of Sharon, the lily of the valleys. The rose may be flamboyant and spectacularly beautiful; the lily of the valley may be the most modest, shy, tiny flower growing in the shade: a Christian is like both to the Lord.

If a reverent heart reads chapter 4 of the Song of Solomon, he will find the Bridegroom speaking, picturing Christ speaking to the Christian.

"How much better is thy love than wine! and the smell of thine ointments than all spices! Thy lips, O my spouse, drop as the honeycomb: honey and milk are under thy tongue; and the smell of thy garments is like the smell of Lebanon. A garden inclosed is my sister, my spouse; a spring shut up, a fountain sealed."—Vss. 10-12.

Then Christ, the Bridegroom, continues, likening the Christian, the bride, to

"Spikenard and saffron; calamus and cinnamon, with all trees of frankincense; myrrh and aloes, with all the chief spices: A fountain of gardens, a well of living waters, and streams from Lebanon."—Vss. 14,15.

Then the Bridegroom calls to the north wind and the south, "Blow upon my garden, that the spices thereof may flow out." We are God's pleasant garden, the fragrant flowers which He loves, the incense which delights His heart.

True, we poor, frail sinners are tainted, fallen and corrupt. True, "The heart is deceitful above all things, and desperately wicked," as Jeremiah 17:9 says. True it is of all of us, as it was of Paul, that "when I would do good, evil is present with me." But there is planted in us a heavenly, a divine life. We have been made into sons of God. Not only are we friends of Christ, but brethren. "For both he that sanctifieth and they who are sanctified are all of one: for which cause he is not ashamed to call them brethren" (Heb. 2:11).

One day the Lord, who sees in us such beauty ascribed to us by His grace and mercy, will find that beauty and fragrance made perfect. One day we will actually be like the sweet flowers to which Christ now compares us.

How blessed that the Lord loves sinners and wants to save them! It is even more blessed that He delights in our presence, our fellowship; that He thinks us beautiful, as a bridegroom delights in his bride and is blessed by her love!

Then let us who are born of God rejoice in that we are made into children of God and are precious to our Lord.

As the father loved the prodigal and ran to meet him and wept on his shoulder and prepared for him a feast and delighted in his boy's return, so God delights in us.

As the one lost piece of dowry money was precious to the woman who lit a candle, swept the house and searched diligently until she found it, so dear, so precious are we to God.

As the shepherd, who thought one lost sheep of more worth than the whole ninety and nine safe ones, went to such length and labor in the night to seek and find the sheep and carry it home on his shoulder, so are we worth more than gold to our Saviour.

As I look about me and smell the scented flowers, provided by loving hands as tokens of love, I know that God loved me, too, and planned all the flowers for my delight. And to Him, I, too, am a rose of Sharon, a lily of the valleys. To Him I am a garden of spices. This pictures how dear we are to Christ.

And how does God reward our prayers? These are to Him bowls of sweet incense in fragrance, perfume that delights His heart. That is part of the language of flowers described in the Bible.

III. FLOWERS REMIND US OF CHRIST'S GLORIOUS MILLENNIAL REIGN

Flowers are so beautiful, so beyond the power of man to imitate, that they surely seem fitted for a better world. And they are. One day flowers will come into their own.

Now the earth is cursed. If a rose garden is left unattended, weeds and briars choke it. Even the roses themselves have thorns. There is a curse upon the ground, a curse upon nature. Flowers seem to dwell so insecurely in this sad world. One touch of frost, one step of a careless foot, one whipping gale or beating rain or hail, and the delicate bloom is gone. Or it will wither in the sun.

But this will not always be so. Great blessings are in store for this earth itself. When God deals with sinful man, when the last rebel against Christ and God is taken from the earth, and when all have received new bodies and have banished forever this curse of sin in our nature, then the earth also will feel the touch of eternal springtime. Then flowers also will come into their own.

Lions will eat straw like oxen. Cows and bears will feed together, and their young will lie down in harmony. The child shall play upon the cockatrice' den, and they shall neither hurt nor harm in all God's holy mountain. For then the earth shall be filled with the knowledge of the Lord as the waters cover the sea. Then nature will reach the glory it had in the Garden of Eden before sin brought the winter blasts of death to earth.

Ten short verses in Isaiah 35 tell of the marvels of the kingdom age, when the Lord shall return with all His saints and angels and reign on David's throne in Jerusalem. And we are told:

"The wilderness and the solitary place shall be glad for them; and the desert shall rejoice, and blossom as the rose. It shall blossom abundantly, and rejoice even with joy and singing: the glory of Lebanon shall be given unto it, the excellency of Carmel and Sharon, they shall see the glory of the Lord, and the excellency of our God."—Vss. 1,2.

The desert shall rejoice and blossom as a rose! I want to see the Sahara in Africa when it is filled with blooming flowers. I want to see the Arabian Desert, the Gobi Desert in Mongolia and every other sun-baked, dried and barren area of the earth, when flowers make glad forever the land of God!

I once drove across the desert from Arizona to California just after a most remarkable rain. I found that here, where there had not been for many years a wild flower but only cacti, lizards and Joshua trees, there were acres upon acres of wild flowers. The unusual rain which had blessed the desert had sprouted seeds which had lain dormant for many years. But the hot sun soon withered these flowers; now the desert waits again for some unusual watering, some unusual smile of God.

One day the desert areas of the world

"shall blossom abundantly, and rejoice even with joy and singing: the glory of Lebanon shall be given unto it, the excellency of Carmel and Sharon, they shall see the glory of the Lord, and the excellency of our God."

IV. FLOWERS ILLUSTRATE GOD'S LOVING CARE

The heavenly language of flowers is so sweet as I think on them lying here in my sick bed. The flowers in my room—Easter lilies, hyacinths, roses, hydrangeas, asters and carnations—all are so beautiful for the eye and soul. Each has a distinctive shape, color and odor; and all came from loving hearts.

My office is in prayer for me after working hours each day, and others are praying for my recovery. How touching is this all to me! And the many messages I have received have been so comforting.

Heavenly language! Every word of God translated into flowers is sweet.

One of the most loved and enjoyed passages about flowers is that with which we began this message—Matthew 6:28-30, where Jesus said:

"And why take ye thought for raiment? Consider the lilies of the field, how they grow; they toil not, neither do they spin: And yet I say unto you, That Solomon in all his glory was not arrayed like one of these. Wherefore, if God so clothe the grass of the field, which to day is, and to morrow is cast into the oven, shall he not much more clothe you, O ye of little faith?"

Why should we take thought for raiment? We should, instead, "consider the lilies of the field, how they grow." The Lord had no doubt noted them many and many a time on the hillsides in Galilee. He remembered that the flowers did not work, did not spin wool or linen, did not weave, and they did not buy garments. Yet these flowers were dressed even better than Solomon in all his glory. Why? Because the supreme Dressmaker and Clothier, the God who created them, clothed the flower of the field.

If God so clothes the grass of the field, shall He not much more clothe us? How little is the faith of a Christian who cannot depend on God for his need!

When he made his stately ascent into the Temple, Solomon was dressed so wondrously that the Queen of Sheba declared the half had not been told her of Solomon's glory. But Solomon had on only sackcloth compared to the silken riches of the lilies of the field! Solomon had on only garments made by frail human hands.

But lilies of the field have garments made in Heaven by the hand of God and sprinkled with the pearls and diamonds of His dew! And the odor of all the flowers is the breath from another world! Oh, He who clothes the lilies will clothe us also!

"Behold the fowls of the air: for they sow not, neither do they reap, nor gather into barns; yet your heavenly Father feedeth them. Are ye not much better than they?"—Matt. 6:26.

God feeds the birds. They don't sow wheat crops, put binders or combines into the field, thrash grain and store it in barns. No. The fowls of the air are fed from God's larder, from God's barns. A loving Father says not one sparrow falls to the ground without His attention.

God loves birds; but does He not love us better? Is not a child of God, made into a new creature and destined for Heaven, far better than the grass of the field which withers tomorrow? Oh, the little faith of those who fret about clothes and food!

That God loves flowers is made very clear in many ways. They are mentioned often in the Bible.

There were flowers and buds on the golden lampstand in the Tabernacle of God. There was lily work in the great laver which He had Solomon make for the Temple. Pomegranates and palm trees were just a part of the Temple's decoration.

Of the millions of wild flowers on the desert, very few are carefully examined by human eye. Very few are ever appreciated. They are trampled by the cattle or eaten with the grass. They are killed by frost, beaten by hail or whipped by gales. Few know or care when a flower blooms and sheds its fragrance, then drops its petals and withers. But God sees every one and delights in each. Oh, our beauty-loving God!

In his "Elegy Written in a Country Churchyard," Gray has these remarkable lines:

Full many a gem of purest ray serene,
The dark unfathom'd caves of ocean bear;

> **Full many a flower is born to blush unseen,**
> **And waste its sweetness on the desert air.**

But those gems unseen in dark ocean caves are seen by the God who made them. And every desert flower, unseen and unsmelled by man, is seen; and the sweet odor is enjoyed by the delighted God who made these things of beauty. God loves His flowers.

But does He love them more than He loves His saints? In the Old Testament law it is written: "Thou shalt not muzzle the ox that treadeth out the corn" (Deut. 25:4). But Paul tells us that God's care was not just for oxen but was a type of God's preachers who should be rewarded and provided for by those to whom they minister.

So it may well be that He made infinite billions of flowers primarily to illustrate to the beloved children of Adam, whom He had made, that He loves and cares for them.

Oh, may every Christian heed that sweet command of Jesus: "Consider the lilies of the field, how they grow," and remember that He said He would so clothe us, too.

The Saviour continues on this matter in Matthew 6:31-34:

"Therefore take no thought, saying, What shall we eat? or, What shall we drink? or, Wherewithal shall we be clothed? (For after all these things do the Gentiles seek:) for your heavenly Father knoweth that ye have need of all these things. But seek ye first the kingdom of God, and his righteousness; and all these things shall be added unto you. Take therefore no thought for the morrow: for the morrow shall take thought for the things of itself. Sufficient unto the day is the evil thereof."

We are to neither fret nor worry about what we eat or drink, or how we will be clothed. Heathen worry about these things, but no child of God needs to. Instead, we are to seek first the kingdom of God, and all these things shall be added unto us.

As I dictate, my heart is touched. For more than thirty years I and my family have learned to depend on God to care for us. Thirty-one years ago I gave up my life insurance, gave up all regular salary for the rest of my life, to depend solely on God. I have proved again and again and again, and ten thousand times more, that one can safely trust things with God and seek first His kingdom and His righteousness.

The money for college for my six daughters; the money for voice lessons, piano lessons, clothing and weddings—there has always been a sufficient supply. There has never been one hour of fret about paying college bills or music bills or clothing bills. We run no charge accounts anywhere, and we do not buy on credit; yet we are never in need. Praise be to our God!

Since I have been laid aside for awhile, my heart has been cheered not only by the huge stack of greeting cards, the letters, the promises of prayer, the daily prayer meeting of my beloved workers for my health, but also because God has put it into the hearts of a number to send gifts. When the doctor's bill is in and when the X-rays and medicine bills come, there will be money at hand to meet every need.

Blessed be God who, in the language of flowers, tells us not to fret about clothing or food—or anything else!

V. FLOWERS TEACH THE INDESTRUCTIBLE, ENDURING QUALITY OF THE WORD OF GOD

Isaiah 40:6-8 is another message in God's heavenly language of the flowers:

"The voice said, Cry. And he said, What shall I cry? All flesh is grass, and all the goodliness thereof is as the flower of the field: The grass withereth, the flower fadeth: because the spirit of the Lord bloweth upon it: surely the people is grass. The grass withereth, the flower fadeth: but the word of our God shall stand for ever."

All flesh is grass, and all the goodliness of mankind is like the flowers of the field that wither. God's Spirit blows on the flower and it fades. People will, at the breath of God, lose their strength, their health and pass off this scene. But in contrast to mankind and to the withering flower is the Word of God which "shall stand for ever."

The above Scripture is referred to and quoted in the New Testament, in I Peter 1:23-25:

"Being born again, not of corruptible seed, but of incorruptible, by the word of God, which liveth and abideth for ever. For all flesh is as grass, and all the glory of man as the flower of grass. The grass withereth, and the flower thereof falleth away: But the word of the Lord endureth for ever. And this is the word which by the gospel is preached unto you."

No one can be saved without the incorruptible Word of God. The Holy Spirit uses the Word planted in the heart—the Gospel—and as that Word sprouts into life eternal when a sinner trusts Christ, we are reminded of the eternal values of this Word.

So we are told, "For all flesh is as grass, and all the glory of man as the flower of grass. The grass withereth, and the flower thereof falleth away."

Man, in the flesh of this life, is temporary; but the Word of God is eternal. Man fails and withers like grass and flowers, but the Word of God endureth forever. And we are solemnly exhorted to remember the wonderful truth, "And this is the word which by the gospel is preached unto you."

The Word of God, then, is eternal. Let everyone who looks upon a flower and sees it wither know that all flesh, all human instruments, ways and values wither also.

But the Word of God is not like that. Here we have the blessed truth that, while man in the flesh is like grass, the new nature, which God implants in a human being through the Gospel and saving faith, is as eternal as the Word of God.

The Lord, too, said it was eternal, that it would never pass away. Read His words in Matthew 5:17,18:

"Think not that I am come to destroy the law, or the prophets: I am not come to destroy, but to fulfill. For verily I say unto you, Till heaven and earth pass, one jot or one tittle shall in no wise pass from the law, till all be fulfilled."

Jesus did not come to destroy the law, that is, the Mosaic books, the Pentateuch. He did not come to destroy Isaiah, Jeremiah and the other prophets; for He said, "Till heaven and earth pass, one jot or one tittle shall in no wise pass from the law, till all be fulfilled." Again Jesus said, "Heaven and earth shall pass away: but my words shall not pass away" (Luke 21:33).

Even Agur, by divine inspiration, knew the perfection of the law and was inspired to write, "Every word of God is pure" (Prov. 30:5). That meant inspiration, eternal verity.

Again in Psalm 19, the first six verses talk about this universe—the starry heavens, the planets, the sun. These are wonderful. But one day the heavens will be rolled up like a scroll, and the earth shall melt with fervent heat. All things material are subject to change. The curse on this earth and universe will be removed; then we will have a new heaven and a new earth. But we will not need a new Bible, for after the six verses about this universe which declare the glory of God and the firmament which shows His handiwork, David was inspired to write, "The law of the Lord is perfect, converting the soul. . ." (vs. 7).

The sun is not perfect; neither is the earth. But the Bible is perfect. That is why it works a miracle of regeneration to one who hears the Gospel and trusts in Christ. Jeremiah said:

"Thy words were found, and I did eat them; and thy word was unto me the joy and rejoicing of mine heart: for I am called by thy name, O Lord God of hosts."—Jer. 15:16.

I wish I had time to expound the wonderful 119th Psalm with its 176 verses—all about the Bible. David said, "For ever, O Lord, thy word is settled in heaven" (vs. 89). David could say, "O how love I thy law! it is my meditation all the day" (vs. 97).

The Bible describes the Word of God as a sword, as a fire, as a hammer. It is sweeter than honey and the honeycomb. Oh, the sweet, blessed, eternal Word of God!

Flowers fade, daily reminding us that all things human, all things under the curse of sin, fade. But that is not true about the Word of God. In God's heavenly language of flowers, every flower tells us that the Word of God will never fade, will never change, but will last forever!

VI. FLOWERS PICTURE BEAUTY AND FRAGRANCE OF OUR LORD

In the heavenly language of flowers, we are shown that flowers fade. The Bible uses that to show the frailty, the vanity, the shortness of human life. Flowers also show how sweet we are in Christ's sight. Then flowers remind us of Christ's millennial reign when the desert shall blossom as the rose. Flowers illustrate God's loving care for His own. He who clothes the lilies will clothe those who trust Him. And flowers show that the eternal Word of God never passes away.

Now we are happy to see that in God's heavenly language flowers picture the beauty and fragrance of the Lord.

In the Song of Solomon 2:2, the heavenly bride speaks about the heavenly Bridegroom: "As the lily among thorns, so is my love among the daughters." I understand this statement to be about the Lord Jesus.

Again in Song of Solomon 2:16, the heavenly bride, picturing the saints of God, speaks of the heavenly Bridegroom in these words: "My beloved is mine, and I am his: he feedeth among the lilies." A similar statement is in Song of Solomon 5:13: "His cheeks are as a bed of spices, as sweet flowers: his lips like lilies, dropping sweet smelling myrrh."

This mystical and picturesque book has many beautiful statements referring symbolically to the Lord Jesus. Here we see again and again that He is likened to sweet flowers—the lilies. He is as a lily among the thorns. In fact, He is the only pure, good Man in a race of sinning men. The Scripture says, "He feedeth among the lilies."

"His cheeks are as a bed of spices, as sweet flowers," says the spiritual Christian. Back in the first chapter of this book Christ is mentioned thus: "A bundle of myrrh is my well-beloved unto me," and again, "My beloved is unto me as a cluster of camphire in the vineyards of En-gedi" (vss. 13,14).

How fitting that the Lord should be pictured in the heavenly language of flowers. And that is not surprising. One who studies the Bible is certain to be impressed with the many beautiful, suggestive and descriptive names of the Lord. He is the Seed of the woman, the Seed of Abraham, the Seed of David. He is the Son of man, Son of God. He is a Priest forever after the order of Melchizedek. He is the Lion of the tribe of Judah, the Alpha and the Omega, the Beginning and the End. He is the Lamb of God, the fairest of ten thousand and altogether lovely.

One of the sweetest sermons I have read is "Pearls of Paradise" by Clinton N. Howard. This sermon is made up of the wonderful pearls which make a chain of pearls—that is, the scriptural names of the Lord Jesus.

Jesus is like a lily, like a garden of spices. We know that the Tabernacle, the priesthood, the Tabernacle furniture, the offerings, the Mosaic law, all pictured the Lord Jesus Christ. We know that sweet incense was specially prepared and burned on the altar of incense, picturing the fragrance of Christ. And on some other offerings to be burned with fire there was frankincense, picturing the heavenly fragrance, the perfume of the Lord Jesus.

The golden candlestick or lampstand pictured Christ as the Light of the world. As it burned olive oil, it particularly pictured the ministry of the Lord Jesus filled with the Spirit. And that light was never to go out.

Here is a suggestive and beautiful thought. On that golden candlestick were carved branches and buds and flowers! Even that gold lampstand pictured the Lord all the better because of its engraved flowers and buds.

In Exodus 25:31 Moses was commanded: "And thou shalt make a candlestick of pure gold: of beaten work shall the candlestick be made: his shaft, and his branches, his bowls, his knops, and his flowers, shall be of the same."

When Solomon built the Temple, he received divine instruction: "And he carved all the walls of the house round about with carved figures of cherubims and palm trees and open flowers, within and without" (I Kings 6:29).

The pillars of the house of Lebanon which Solomon built were rich and beautiful. And on the top of these great pillars were "chapiters," or capitals. And I Kings 7:19 says: "And the chapiters that were upon the top of the pillars were of lily work in the porch, four cubits." And again, "And upon the top of the pillars was lily work: so was the work of the pillars finished" (vs. 22).

Then Solomon made "a molten sea," a great wash basin of brass, standing upon twelve molded oxen; and here the priests offering the sacrifices were washed. And we are told, "And it was an hand breadth thick, and the brim thereof was wrought like the brim of a cup, with flowers of lilies: it contained two thousand baths" (vs. 26).

Here is something sweet and beautiful. Of Christ Himself it is said, "His lips like lilies, dropping sweet smelling myrrh" (Song of Sol. 5:13). It is said, "As the lily among thorns, so is my love among the daughters" (Song of Sol. 2:2). Again still, "My beloved is mine, and I am his: he feedeth among the lilies" (Song of Sol. 2:16).

Again and again the one flower named as picturing Jesus is the lily! He is like lilies, He feeds among the lilies, His lips are like lilies. On the golden stick were flowers, and on the chapiters or heads of the columns of the great Temple was lily work. Round the great molten sea was lily work engraved! And all of it pointed to the dear Lord Jesus!

I particularly enjoy this heavenly illustration because here before me are three beautiful potted lily plants. Upon them are twelve beautiful flowers with other buds beginning to open. I do not wonder that people prefer lilies for Easter. Lilies are intended to picture the Lord Jesus. Their purity, their sweet odor, their reference to the resurrection in the minds of multitudes, make them suitable reminders of Jesus Christ.

Dear reader, is Jesus fragrant as a flower to you? Is His presence like the fragrance from a garden of spices? Do you know Him well enough, do you have fellowship with Him so you can perceive the beauty, the purity, the lily-whiteness and the faint lily fragrance of His personality?

My beloved, the Saviour is like the flower. In the heavenly language of flowers, the Bible reminds us that Jesus is the fairest of ten thousand. He is altogether lovely. All the good things you can say about pomegranates and spices and myrrh and incense are not enough to picture the beauty, the fragrance, the sweetness of knowing the Lord and dwelling in His presence!

If one reads this who is not born again, then you will never know the Lord Jesus in His fragrance until you trust Him as Saviour. I beg you, go to Jesus now and beg Him for mercy. Believe that He does forgive you as He promised. Take Him as your own personal Saviour now and forever!

One day I shall see Him. To awake in His likeness, oh, how sweet! Paul was right when he said, "To depart, and to be with Christ . . . is far better"!

I remember that the Scripture says that "whether therefore ye eat or drink, or whatsoever ye do, do all to the glory of God" (I Cor. 10:31). Surely then every Christian who looks into the heart of a flower, who delights in a sweet fragrance, who looks on a prairie of Texas Blue-bonnets or sees dandelions on the lawn or sees florist flowers sent to a wedding, a funeral or a sick room, should remember the heavenly language of flowers.

Flowers bring us a message from God. Flowers say that man is frail, that days flee away, that opportunity passes. But flowers say also how sweet we are to the dear Lord Jesus and how He covets our fellowship. Flowers remind us of Christ's millennial reign when the desert shall blossom like a rose. And flowers prove and illustrate God's loving care for His own, so we need never fret about clothing or food. And frail, fading flowers remind us that the Word of God, sweeter than flowers, never fails, will never pass away. And flowers point to the dear Lord Jesus Christ, the fairest of ten thousand to my soul.

Bless His name forever. Amen!

HAROLD B. SIGHTLER
1914-

ABOUT THE MAN:

Dr. Sightler was born in St. George, South Carolina on May 15, 1914. He was converted at age 12 or 13 at East Park Baptist Church in Greenville, South Carolina.

Dr. Sightler has often said that Paul's admonition to Timothy to make full proof of his ministry was a lifelong responsibility. Dr. Sightler has been doing that since his surrender to preach in 1940. From his first revival meeting held on the front lawn of a dear saint of God's home to revival meetings each week, year after year, he has been making full proof of his ministry.

In 1943, he started The Bright Spot Hour radio broadcast on area stations at a cost of $24.00 per week. Today, God has allowed The Bright Spot Hour to be heard on five continents at costs of $25,000.00 per month. In 1951, tragedy struck. A fatal automobile accident took the life of his oldest daughter and threatened the lives of his wife and baby girl. It was out of this tragedy that God led him to start Tabernacle Baptist Church in 1952. By 1957, the church had over 1,200 members and at this time erected one of the largest Baptist church auditoriums in South Carolina with a seating capacity of 1,500.

Following his leadership, the church started a Christian day school in 1960, a children's home in 1963, a Bible institute in 1963, a Bible college in 1975 and a place where some of the church widows could stay in 1982. Throughout the years, the missions outreach of Tabernacle has been its life's blood. Supporting some 400 missionaries, the mission budget for home and foreign missions exceeds $1,000.00 per day above its other ministries.

As the oldest Baptist pastor in continuous service in Greenville county, this "Prince of Preachers" continues to make full proof of his ministry for his Lord and Saviour, Jesus Christ.

II.

The Ministry of Tears

Why Does God Allow His People to Weep?

HAROLD B. SIGHTLER

In Revelation 21:4 we find a blessed promise which assures us of a day when God shall wipe away all tears.

"And God shall wipe away all tears from their eyes; and there shall be no more death, neither sorrow, nor crying, neither shall there be any more pain: for the former things are passed away."

In the meanwhile, all of us have the experience of tears. Our hearts have been and are being broken as we pilgrimage upon the earth. From our souls we each have cried, WHY? *Why does God allow me to weep?* Sometimes we have seen the very finest and most consecrated of Christians with broken hearts. Why does God allow this?

Full well do I recognize the impossibility of knowing fully the motives behind our weeping. However, I feel there are some things which we can understand. The Bible will tell us much about the tears of God's people along the way.

I. FALSE IDEAS ABOUT TEARS

May we note some common false ideas about tears. There is the idea that

All Tears Are the Result of Personal Sin.

To be sure, sin produces much weeping. However, there are Bible examples of God's people weeping who were not guilty of personal sin. Job is an example. The very first chapter of the book of Job tells us the kind of a man Job was: just, upright, perfect; and he despised evil. He walked before the Lord as holy as he knew how to walk. Yet no man ever had his heart broken as did Job. Certainly no man would dare accuse him of sin because of the trouble which plagued his life. There can be no doubt but that his weeping and suffering were for God's glory and for our encouragement.

Again, there is Hezekiah. In Isaiah 38:1-3 we read:

"In those days was Hezekiah sick unto death. And Isaiah the proph-et the son of Amoz came unto him, and said unto him, Thus saith the Lord, Set thine house in order: for thou shalt die, and not live. Then Hezekiah turned his face toward the wall, and prayed unto the Lord, And said, Remember now, O Lord, I beseech thee, how I have walked before thee in truth and with a perfect heart, and have done that which is good in thy sight. And Hezekiah wept SORE."

Here is an example of a man of God suffering and weeping sorely. No man would dare charge him with sin. He called upon God to "remember" three things about his life: "I have walked before thee in truth. I have walked before thee with a perfect heart. I have done that which is good in thy sight."

There is no record that God denies any of these three things about Hezekiah. We must conclude, therefore, that they were true things. Yet note the pitiful four last words of verse 3, "And Hezekiah wept sore." Again, we see an example of weeping where there was no personal sin to produce it.

Then in John 11 we read the story of the death of Lazarus. Perhaps no chapter in the Bible records as much weeping as does this one. In verses 33 to 36 we read:

"When Jesus therefore saw her weeping, and the Jews also weep-ing which came with her, he groaned in the spirit, and was troubled, And said, Where have ye laid him? They said unto him, Lord, come and see. Jesus wept. Then said the Jews, Behold how he loved him."

These four verses record the weeping of Martha and Mary as well as the Lord Himself. Note also the weeping of the Jews. Is it reasonable to conclude that the personal sin of any of these, including Lazarus, produces this weeping? No. Here is another example of God's people weeping but not because of personal sin.

Again I say, sin does produce weeping. Sin always produces per-sonal suffering. However, there can be no doubt but that some suffer-ing and weeping are for other reasons.

There is the idea also that

It Is Never God's Will for His People
to Suffer or Weep.

It is the common message of many so-called "faith healers" in these days that God does not will any of His to suffer or weep or to be sick. They proclaim the idea that, if one suffers or weeps, it is because of some sin or faithlessness.

I have just reminded you of three instances in the Bible of weeping and suffering. In none of the cases was the suffering and weeping the result of sin or faithlessness. It is reasonable to conclude that in the three instances it was God's will that these saints suffer. It was for His glory that they suffered. I shall show you later in the message JUST HOW God receives glory from the suffering of His saints.

Too, there is the false idea

That Jesus and Salvation Make Life Easy
for the Believer.

All without exception have been exposed to the idea that Jesus is the answer to all experiences of life. This new "Hollywood" slant on religion has deceived the masses into believing that to become a Christian is to drift into Heaven on a flowery bed of ease. Such an idea is far from the truth and far from experience.

Well do I know that there is joy in the Lord. However, with this joy sometimes comes heartache. The truly born-again person can never become adjusted to this world. He can never settle down. He can never so live until he isn't pricked by the thorns of this journey.

In Luke 12:49-53 Jesus forever explodes this false idea of a life of ease for the believer.

"I am come to send fire on the earth; and what will I, if it be already kindled? But I have a baptism to be baptized with; and how am I straitened till it be accomplished! Suppose ye that I am come to give peace on earth? I tell you, Nay; but rather division: For from henceforth there shall be five in one house divided, three against two, and two against three. The father shall be divided against the son, and the son against the father; the mother against the daughter, and the daughter against the mother; the mother in law against her daughter in law, and the daughter in law against her mother in law."

God deliver us from the sin of desiring an easy way! My prayer is for grace to meet every need.

Another false idea about suffering and weeping is

That God Cannot Get Glory From Such.

Much do I believe that God delights in mercy toward His children. However, God can and does receive glory through the sufferings of the saints.

Look for a moment at Paul. In II Corinthians 12:7-10 we read:

"And lest I should be exalted above measure through the abundance of the revelations, there was given to me a thorn in the flesh, the messenger of Satan to buffet me, lest I should be exalted above measure. For this thing I besought the Lord thrice, that it might depart from me. And he said unto me, My grace is sufficient for thee: for my strength is made perfect in weakness. Most gladly therefore will I rather glory in my infirmities, that the power of Christ may rest upon me. Therefore I take pleasure in infirmities, in reproaches, in necessities, in persecutions, in distresses for Christ's sake: for when I am weak, then am I strong."

In no uncertain words these verses reveal the truth that God can and does receive glory through our infirmities. God says, ". . . for my strength is made PERFECT in weakness." Unless there is a personal infirmity and a personal weakness and trial, the strength of God to give GRACE can never be made perfectly evident.

Nothing so brings glory to God and nothing so demonstrates the sufficiency of God's grace as the suffering Christian with his head lifted, giving praise to Jesus. Nothing so brings glory to God as the weeping Christian with a look of Heaven upon his tear-stained face.

II. BEYOND THE TEARS: WHAT?

Now we come to a second thought: beyond the tears—WHAT? A wise man has declared that "life is a vale of tears." Sooner or later in each life will come a tragedy or sickness or disappointment which will produce the tears.

What Ought Be Our Attitude?

Will we accuse God foolishly? Shall we miss His deep purpose in allowing these tears and these disappointments and tragedies?

Life is beautiful, inspiring and good. The loveliness of nature all about us defies the description of human words.

What is more thrilling than the rainbow wrapped around the neck of a dying storm?

What is more beautiful than a blond-haired baby, with deep blue eyes, with soft-colored complexion and deep dimples, smiling at his mother?

What is more blessed to sacrificing parents than to see a son or a daughter with cap and gown receiving the sheepskin in his or her hand, signifying honor and achievement?

What could fill the heart of a father or mother with more pride than to see a son return from battle decorated by the President for courage and valor beyond the call of duty?

Yes, life is beautiful and good and inspiring.

But it is also true that life is not all sunshine and roses. There are clouds and thorns and ugly situations. All men meet with these clouds and tragic situations. Hours come when all the lights go out—our hearts are filled with sorrow and disappointment or despair. We are pained, we suffer.

What does one do when one's child, in good health, is cut down by polio and can no longer run and play as other children? What happens when an automobile driven by a drunken driver hits and kills your eleven-year-old pride and joy?

Suppose in the very prime of life, with apparent good health, the doctor pronounces "cancer."

What does one do when hard-earned life's savings are lost in some business reverse?

When a person becomes blind and can no longer be able to see his loved ones and the beauties of nature—to live in darkness until death— what then?

Innumerable other tragedies can produce suffering and tears, for this life is full of them.

Beyond the tragedy—what? Beyond the experience of suffering— what? Beyond the tears—what?

It is only human in the face of tears to ask why. And it is also human to be unable to see the whole picture and thus be able to get the correct answer. So we wonder and become bewildered, and the temptation is to despair and accept defeat.

As I have already said, a good percentage of our sorrows and tears are the result of our wrongdoings. These we must accept and suffer the consequences of our sins.

But what about those things which plague us for which we are not the cause and for which we are in no sense responsible? What caused them? There are only three possible answers—

First, the tragedies are purely natural and have no meaning either good or bad. We are the pawns of nature and are just unlucky to get hit.

Second, the tragedies are caused by Satan. We are living in a world of war between good and evil, God and Satan, and thus may have to suffer for this cause. This answer only pushes the problem back a bit to ask, Whence comes Satan? and, Why does God permit him to exist?

Third, the tragedies are caused by God or, at least, permitted by Him.

To conclude that nature or Satan is a satisfactory answer creates a greater problem. If there is no God, no purpose, no justice and no eternity; if we are animals and will die as animals, then nothing is really a tragedy. It has no significance; it is merely an unfortunate event coming to a body of earthly clay which will soon revert to the earth again. When we solve the problem of suffering and evil thusly, we also abolish all good, renounce all higher value, deny immortality, bury God. Thus, in reality, we have no problems—just events in a passing natural existence which will soon be over as far as we are concerned.

To adopt this attitude "beyond tears" is unsatisfying, irrational,

And Results in Hopeless Doubts.

Beyond tragedy there is another attitude. It is this: I do suffer. I am distressed. I do not understand. I cannot see the reason. I visualize only a fragment of the picture. If I could see the whole, I would know the purpose. So, although I suffer and am limited, I can believe and trust and have faith that life does have a meaning, that God is just as Paul declared:

"For our light affliction, which is but for a moment, worketh for us a far more exceeding and eternal weight of glory; While we look not at the things which are seen, but at the things which are not seen: for the things which are seen are temporal; but the things which are not seen are eternal."—II Cor. 4:17, 18.

The supreme attitude toward "beyond tears" is found in another blessed verse from Paul in Romans 8:28, "And we know that all things work together for good to them that love God, to them who are the called according to his purpose."

Will your tears make you better or bitter? richer or poorer? stronger or weaker? Will they be stepping stones to something higher or stumbling blocks to something lower?

Beyond the suffering, tears and tragedy, will you be a skeptic, a cynic, an accuser of God, or will you be a firm believer in the eternal purposes of God?

Only the last attitude can be pleasing to God. It alone offers help, solace and satisfaction "beyond tears."

So, although your tragedy does hurt and pain; although suffering and tears produce distress, throw away your doubts, your skepticism, your cynicism, and

Put Your Faith in a God Who Doeth All Things Well.

Dr. Oswald Smith, the great Canadian preacher of righteousness, received the terrible news of the awful tragedy which befell his sister, a missionary in South America. Her husband had suddenly died, blasting their hopes and ruining their plans. He wrote to her in her dark bereavement:

> **God understands your sorrow;**
> **He sees the falling tear,**
> **And whispers, "I am with thee,"**
> **Then falter not, nor fear.**
>
> **God understands your heartaches,**
> **He knows the bitter pain.**
> **Oh, trust Him in the darkness,**
> **You cannot trust in vain.**

III. WHY GOD ALLOWS TEARS

Finally, note with me why God allows us to weep.

Birds and animals do not cry. So why does God permit the human person to weep? We have already seen that tears are for a purpose. What is that purpose? If and when the suffering saint learns this truth, he has mounted high in things of the spirit. Someone has said that "tears are agony in solution."

First, the ministry of tears is to

Fit Us for the Office of Sympathy.

Under the Old Testament law the priest was consecrated for the office of sympathy. This consecration was produced by placing a drop of water on the right ear—consecrating that ear to hear the tales of woe and trouble from the people. A drop of water was placed on the thumb of the right hand—consecrating the hands to minister to the needs of those in trouble. A drop of water was placed on the toe of the right foot—consecrating the feet to go about in administering to those in need. The priest was unfit for the office of sympathy until he had thus been consecrated for the task.

Do you not see the picture for us today? No Christian can possibly know the art of sympathy until that Christian has been prepared of the Lord for the task. This preparation cannot be acquired at the seminaries. This preparation is acquired ONLY in the valley of experience.

For years as a pastor I tried to sympathize with my members when death came. I honestly did the very best I could to sympathize with each of them. I tried to say the very words which I thought would lift them in the awful hour of sorrow. Yet in all my efforts I could not really feel with those dear ones until my own heart was crushed and my own home circle broken. When death came into my own home and removed one precious to my own heart, it was then that I was consecrated to the office of sympathy.

This would, indeed, be a terrible world in which to live if there were no people in it who could administer sympathy. But, alas, God has His own all over the land who have been tried in the fiery furnace. They have trod the very valley of sorrow. They have had their own hearts broken and their own hopes banished. Through all of this, they have been consecrated to the office of sympathy.

Those who have been consecrated to the office of sympathy do not need to open their mouths to say words of comfort. Their very presence will comfort the brokenhearted. The grip of a handshake will speak volumes. A look of the eyes will provide courage.

Now, my friend, if God sees fit to consecrate you to the office of sympathy by allowing you to experience tears, will you rebel against such a high privilege? The Christian who has shed bitter tears and endured bitter sufferings is the one whom God has elected for the high office of sympathy.

May we perform our task nobly and well. May we use this office to help those around and about when they one by one enter into the valley of trial and sorrow.

The weeping Christian has been carried of the Lord to a higher plane in the journey than others. He has been brought into an inner circle of disciples. He has become a chosen vessel of the Lord, a pioneer in blazing the trail for others who come along after him.

Yes, the weeping and suffering Christian has been consecrated to the high office of sympathy.

Second, the ministry of tears is

To Lead Us to Place Our Complete Dependence Upon God.

Nothing will so destroy the arm of flesh as tears. It is the will of God for His own that we look to Him. This is no easy task. There is something about the flesh which will seek to strengthen itself. The natural man will seek to solve all the problems himself. He will spend himself to work out his own hard places.

This may sound noble and reasonable. However, it is the will of God that we look to Him. The Word says, "As the father pitieth his children, so the Lord pitieth them that fear him." Again, "No good thing will he withhold from them that walk uprightly." Again, "He delighteth in mercy."

If a valley or trial experience teaches us to "look to Him," then it is a blessing in disguise. It is only when one has come to the limit of his own strength that he will turn to God for help. The tears of this experience force us to this limit. The psalmist says, "But I am poor and needy; yet the Lord thinketh upon me: thou art my help and my deliverer; make no tarrying, O my God."

Hear the psalmist as he confesses his complete dependence upon the Lord in Psalm 18:1-6:

"I will love thee, O Lord, my strength. The Lord is my rock, and my fortress, and my deliverer; my God, my strength, in whom I will trust; my buckler, and the horn of my salvation, and my high tower. I will call upon the Lord, who is worthy to be praised: so shall I be saved from mine enemies. The sorrows of death compassed me, and the floods of ungodly men made me afraid. The sorrows of hell compassed me about: the snares of death prevented me. In my distress I called upon the Lord, and cried unto my God: he heard my voice out of his temple, and my cry came before him, even into his ears."

It is this same confession of our utter dependence on the Lord that God desires of each of us. Nothing so creates this dependence upon the Lord as sufferings and tears.

Third, the ministry of tears is

To Keep This World From Becoming
Too Attractive to Us.

The tragedy of the life of Lot was the attractions of this world. Many are the Christians who become engulfed in the things of this life. This is never pleasing to the Lord. To be sure, we are earthly creatures; but our citizenship is in Heaven "from whence we look for the Saviour."

God commands us to be heavenly minded; to lay up treasures above; to seek the things from above; to journey with our faces set toward Heaven, looking for a city whose Maker and Builder is God; to keep our minds stayed upon Jesus; to love not the world, neither the things which are in the world; to set our affections on things above. Here are just a few of many commands to us concerning our attitude toward Heaven and eternal things.

Perhaps a perfect example of this is David. Here is a man of God who became a slave to the lust of the eye. The things of the world attracted him so greatly that he committed adultery and murder.

For a moment he seems to forget God and to forget that he is God's man. He yields to this great temptation. He satisfies the lust of the flesh. For a moment there was joy and pleasure in the sin David committed.

However, the picture changes rapidly. The child born from this unlawful relation is taken deathly sick. David repents and calls upon the Lord; but God does not heal the child. He dies. Before death David was plunged into deep sorrow. The grief of his soul is felt as we read the account of it in the Word. His heart was broken for the first time. He could not be comforted.

Rest assured that David was never the same man from this experience on. God removed from him the love of this life and world. In the valley of this experience, David is heard making his vow to meet the child on the other side. He mounts from this valley to become "the man after God's own heart."

Fourth, the ministry of tears is

To Make Us Homesick for Heaven.

We are Heaven's citizens. We are headed toward Heaven's bliss.

However, as we journey we are hindered by the pull of this world. It is very easy to become satisfied in this life.

Have you ever thought that, if this life offered no hardness, no sufferings, no tears, no bitterness, no disappointments, most of us would be content to remain here?

It is the nights of this earth that make Heaven to be desired—where there is no night.

It is the tears of this life that make Heaven a delight—where God shall wipe away all tears.

It is the sufferings of this life which make us long for Heaven—where there shall be no pain nor sickness.

It is the poverty of this life that makes the riches of Heaven more desired than ever.

It is the disappointments of this life that make us long for the bliss of Paradise.

It is the heaviness of this life that makes the rest of Heaven a holy anticipation.

It is the mourning of this journey that will make the hallelujahs of Heaven blessed.

It is the loneliness of this life that makes us long for the fellowship of Jesus in Heaven.

The longer we live and the more tears we shed, the more homesick we become for Heaven. One by one our loved ones are crossing over, until soon we have more loved ones on the other shore than here. As this separating continues, so the more we desire to depart this life and enjoy reunion with loved ones who have outstripped us to Heaven's shore.

Fifth, the ministry of tears is

To Demonstrate the Sufficiency of God's Grace.

I think this is one of the most important reasons why God allows His people to weep. We cannot escape the fact that life has its hard places. Trouble, sorrow and tears are the common lot of all people. The sinner and saint suffer alike. The sinner and saint weep alike. Death comes into the homes of both sinner and saint. It has a biting sting to both sinner and saint.

Though tears, suffering and sorrow are the common lot of both sinner and saint, there is, however, a difference in the inward attitude.

We sorrow, but "not as others." To us who are saved there is a "blessed hope."

Listen to the words of Paul in I Thessalonians 4:13-18:

"But I would not have you to be ignorant, brethren, concerning them which are asleep, that ye sorrow not, even as others which have no hope. For if we believe that Jesus died and rose again, even so them also which sleep in Jesus will God bring with him. For this we say unto you by the word of the Lord, that we which are alive and remain unto the coming of the Lord shall not prevent them which are asleep. For the Lord himself shall descend from heaven with a shout, with the voice of the archangel, and with the trump of God: and the dead in Christ shall rise first: Then we which are alive and remain shall be caught up together with them in the clouds, to meet the Lord in the air: and so shall we ever be with the Lord. Wherefore comfort one another with these words."

The reason we sorrow "not as others" is because of the grace of God which begins to operate when the trials come. Just as God allowed Paul to bear the thorn in his flesh that the grace of God might be proven sufficient, so God allows us to enter into trials, tests and sorrow that His grace may be demonstrated. One can never know the grace of God apart from the trials which beset on every hand.

It is interesting to note that He never supplies grace until the test has arrived.

Sometimes we shudder at the thought of death. Need we do that? I submit that when death comes, God will supply grace.

Sometimes we fear at the thought of the loss of health. Need we do that? When health is gone and one faces the operating table, God's grace will be supplied.

You may not need dying grace, comforting grace and enduring grace just now; but as surely as the trial comes, God will delight to demonstrate His sufficient grace.

Hence, my message to you on the ministry of tears.

CHARLES H. SPURGEON
1835-1892

ABOUT THE MAN:

Many times it has been said that this was the greatest preacher this side of the Apostle Paul. He began preaching at the age of 16. At 25 he built London's famous Metropolitan Tabernacle, seating around 5,000. It was never large enough. Even when traveling he preached to 10,000 eager listeners a week. Crowds thronged to hear him as they came to hear John the Baptist by the River Jordan. The fire of God was on him as on the Prophet Elijah facing assembled Israel at Mount Carmel.

Royalty sat in his Tabernacle, as did washerwomen. Mr. Gladstone had him to dinner; and cabbies refused his fare, considering it an honor to drive for this "Prince of Preachers." To a housewife kneading bread, he would say, "Have you ever tried the Bread of life?" Many a carpenter was asked, "Have you ever tried to build a house on sand?"

He preached in all the principal cities of England, Scotland and Ireland. And although invited to the United States on several occasions, he was never able to visit this country.

HOW GREAT WAS HIS HEART: for preachers, so the Pastors' College was founded; for orphans, so the orphans' houses came to be; for people around the world, so his literature poured forth in an almost unmeasurable volume. He was a national voice; so every national issue affecting morals, religion or the poor had his interpretation, his counsel.

Oh, but his passion for souls! You can see it in every sermon.

Spurgeon published thousands of poems, tracts, sermons and songs.

HIS MESSAGE TO LOST SINNERS WILL LIVE AS LONG AS THE GOSPEL IS PREACHED.

III.

Sweet Comfort for Feeble Saints

CHARLES H. SPURGEON

"A bruised reed shall he not break, and smoking flax shall he not quench, till he send forth judgment unto victory."—Matt. 12:20.

Babbling fame ever loves to talk of one man or another. Some there be whose glory it trumpets forth and whose honor it extols above the heavens. Some are her favorites; their names are carved on marble and heard in every land and clime.

Fame is not an impartial judge; she has her favorites. Some she extols, exalts and almost deifies; others, whose virtues are far greater and whose characters are more deserving of commendation, she passes by unheeded and puts the finger of silence on her lips. You will generally find that those persons beloved by fame are made of brass or iron and cast in a rough mold.

Fame caresseth Caesar because he ruled the earth with a rod of iron.

Fame loves Luther because he boldly and manfully defied the pope of Rome and, with knit brow, dared laugh at the thunders of the Vatican.

Fame admires Knox, for he was stern and proved himself the bravest of the brave.

Generally, you will find her choosing out the men of fire and mettle who stood before their fellow-creatures fearless of them; men who were made of courage; men who were consolidated lumps of fearlessness and never knew what timidity might be.

But there is another class of persons equally virtuous and equally to be esteemed—perhaps even more so—whom fame entirely forgets.

You do not hear her talk of the gentle-minded Melancthon; she says but little of him; yet he did as much, perhaps, in the Reformation as even the mighty Luther.

You do not hear fame talk much of the sweet and blessed Rutherford and of the heavenly words that came from his lips; or of Archbishop Leighton, of whom it was said that he was never out of temper in his life.

She loves the rough granite peaks that defy the storm cloud; she does not care for the more humble stone in the valley on which the weary traveler resteth; she wants something bold and prominent, something that courts popularity, something that stands out before the world. She does not care for those who retreat in shade.

Hence it is, my brethren, that the blessed Jesus, our adorable Master, has escaped fame. No one says much about Jesus except His followers. We do not find His name written among the great and mighty men; though, in truth, He is the greatest, mightiest, holiest, purest and best of men that ever lived. But because He was "gentle Jesus, meek and mild" and was emphatically the Man whose kingdom is not of this world; because He had nothing of the rough about Him but was all love; because His words were softer than butter, His utterances more gentle in their flow than oil; because never man spake so gently as this Man; therefore, He is neglected and forgotten.

He did not come to be a conqueror with his sword nor a Mohammed with his fiery eloquence, but He came to speak with a "still small voice" that melteth the rocky heart, that bindeth up the broken in spirit and that continually saith, "Come unto me, all ye that labour and are heavy laden. . . . Take my yoke upon you, and learn of me; for I am meek and lowly in heart; and ye shall find rest unto your souls."

Jesus Christ was all gentleness; and this is why He has not been extolled among men as otherwise He would have been.

Beloved, our text is full of gentleness; it seems to have been steeped in love; and I hope I may be able to show you something of the immense sympathy and the mighty tenderness of Jesus as I attempt to speak from it.

There are three things to be noticed: first, mortal frailty; second, divine compassion; third, certain triumph—"till he send forth judgment unto victory."

Who are these bruised reeds and smoking flax?

I. MORTAL FRAILTY

First, we have before us a view of mortal frailty—bruised reed and smoking flax—two very suggestive metaphors and very full of meaning. If it were not too fanciful—and if it is, I know that you will excuse it—I should say that the *bruised reed is the emblem of a sinner in the first stage of his conviction.*

The work of God's Holy Spirit begins with bruising. In order to be saved, the fallow ground must be plowed up, the hard heart must be broken, and the rock must be split in sunder. An old divine says there is no going to Heaven without passing hard by the gates of Hell.

I take it, then, that the bruised reed is a picture of the poor sinner when first God commences His operations upon the soul. He is a bruised reed, almost entirely broken and consumed. There is but little strength in him.

The smoking flax I conceive to be a backsliding Christian, one who has been a burning and a shining light in his day; but by neglect of the means of grace, the withdrawal of God's Spirit and falling into sin, his light is almost gone out—not quite—it can never go out, for Christ saith, "I will not quench it"; but it becomes like a lamp when ill supplied with oil—almost useless. It is not quite extinguished; it smokes. It was a useful lamp once, but now it has become as smoking flax.

So I think these metaphors very likely describe the contrite sinner as a bruised reed and the backsliding Christian as smoking flax. However, I shall not choose to make such a division as that, but I shall put both the metaphors together, and I hope we may fetch out a few thoughts from them.

1. God's Promise Is to the Weak Ones

And first, the encouragement offered in our text applies to *weak ones.* What in the world is weaker than the bruised reed or the smoking flax? Let but the wild duck light upon a reed that groweth in the fen or marsh, and it snaps. Let but the foot of man brush against it, and it is bruised and broken. Every wind that comes howling across the river makes it shake to and fro and well-nigh tears it up by the roots. You can conceive of nothing more frail and brittle or whose existence depends more upon circumstances than a bruised reed.

Then look at smoking flax—what is it? It has a spark within it, it is true; but it is almost smothered. An infant's breath might blow it out, or the tears of a maiden quench it in a moment. Nothing has a more precarious existence than the little spark hidden in the smoking flax.

Weak things, you see, are here described. Well, Christ says of them, 'The smoking flax I will not quench: the bruised reed I will not break.'

Let me go in search of the weaklings—I shall not have to go far. Many in this house of prayer this morning are indeed weak. Some of God's children are made strong to do mighty works for Him. God hath His Samsons here and there who can pull up Gaza's gates and carry them to the top of the hill. He hath here and there His mighty Gideons who can go to the camp of the Midianites and overthrow their hosts. He hath His mighty men who can go into the pit in winter and slay the lions.

But the majority of His people are a timid, weak race. They are like the starlings that are frightened by every passer by—little fearful flock. If temptation comes, they are overwhelmed by it. Their frail skiff is danced up and down by every wave; and when the wind comes, they are drifted along like a seabird on the crest of the billows—weak things, without might, without power.

Dear friends, I know I have got hold of some of your hands and hearts now; for you are saying, "Weak! That I am, full often I am constrained to say. I would, but cannot sing; I would, but cannot pray; I would, but cannot believe." You are saying that you cannot do anything. Your best resolves are weak and vain. And when you cry, "My strength renew," you feel weaker than before.

You are weak, are you? Bruised reeds and smoking flax? Blessed be God, this text is for you then! I am glad you can come in under the denomination of weak ones, for here is a promise that He will never break nor quench them but will sustain and hold them up.

I know there are some very strong people here—I mean, strong in your own ideas. I often meet with persons who would not confess any such weakness as this. They have strong minds. They say, "Do you think that we go into sin? Do you tell us that our hearts are corrupt? We do not believe any such things. We are good and pure and upright. We have strength and might."

To you I am not preaching this morning; to you I am saying nothing. But take heed—your strength is vanity, your power is a delusion, your might is a lie, for however much you may boast in what you can do, it shall pass away.

When you come to the real contest with death, you shall find that you have no strength to grapple with it. When one of these days of strong temptation shall come, it will take hold of you, moral man, and down you will go; then the glorious livery of your morality will be so stained that, though you wash your hands in snow water and make yourselves ever so clean, you shall be so polluted that your own clothes shall abhor you.

I think it is a blessed thing to be weak. The weak one is a sacred thing; the Holy Ghost has made him such. Can you say, "No strength have I"? Then this text is for you.

2. Christ Does Not Destroy the Worthless Ones

Second, the things mentioned in our text are not only weak but *worthless* things. I heard of a man who would pick up a pin as he walked along the street, on the principle of economy; but I never yet heard of a man who would stop to pick up bruised reeds. They are not worth having. Who would care to have a bruised reed—a piece of rush lying on the ground? We all despise it as worthless. And smoking flax, what is the worth of that? It is an offensive and noxious thing; but the worth of it is nothing. No one would give the snap of a finger either for the bruised reed or smoking flax.

Well, then, beloved, in our estimation, many of us are worthless things. There are some here who, if you could weigh yourselves in the scales of the sanctuary and put your own heart into the balance of conscience, would appear to be good for nothing—worthless, useless.

There was a time when you thought yourselves to be the very best people in the world—when, if anyone had said that you had more than you deserved, you would have kicked at it and said, "I believe I am as good as other people." You thought yourselves something wonderful, something extremely worthy of God's love and regard.

But you now feel yourselves to be worthless.

Sometimes you imagine God can hardly know where you are, you are such a despicable creature—so worthless—not worth His consideration. You can understand how He can look upon an animalcule in a drop of water or upon a grain of dust in the sunbeam or upon the insect of the summer evenings, but you can hardly tell how He can think of you. You appear so worthless—a dead blank in the world, a useless thing. You say, "What good am I? I am doing nothing. As for a minister of the Gospel, he is of some service; as for a deacon of the church, he is of some use; as for a Sunday school teacher, he is doing some good; but of what service am I?"

But you might ask the same question here. What is the use of a bruised reed? Can a man lean upon it? Can a man strengthen himself therewith?

Shall it be a pillar in my house? Can you bind it up into the pipes of Pan and make music come from a bruised reed?

Ah! no! It is of no service. And of what use is smoking flax? The midnight traveler cannot be lighted by it. The student cannot read by the flame of it. It is of no use. Men throw it into the fire and consume it. Ah! that is how you talk of yourselves—you are good for nothing. So are these things. But Christ will not throw you away because you are of no value. You do not know of what use you may be, and you cannot tell how Jesus Christ values you after all.

There is a good woman there, a mother, perhaps, who says, "Well, I don't often go out. I keep house with my children. I seem to be doing no good."

Mother, don't say so. Your position is a high, lofty, responsible one. And in training up children for the Lord, you are doing as much for His name as yon eloquent Apollos who so valiantly preached the Word.

And you, poor man, all you can do is to toil from morning till night and earn just enough to enable you to live day by day. You have nothing to give away. And when you go to the Sunday school, you can just read; you cannot teach. But unto him to whom little is given, little is required.

Do you not know that there is such a thing as glorifying God by sweeping the street crossing? If two angels were sent down to earth, one to rule an empire and the other to sweep a street, they would have no choice in the matter so long as God ordered them.

So if God in His providence has called you to work hard for your daily bread, do it to His glory. 'Whatsoever ye do, whether ye eat or drink, do all to his honour.'

But I know there are some of you here who seem useless to the church. You do all you can, but when you have done it, it is nothing. You can neither help us with money nor talents nor time; therefore, you think God must cast you out. You think, if you were like Paul or Peter, you might be safe.

Beloved, talk not so. Jesus Christ saith He will not quench the useless flax nor break the worthless broken reed. He has something for the useless and for the worthless ones.

But mark you! I do not say this to excuse laziness—to excuse those that can do but don't. That is a very different thing. There is a whip for the ass, a scourge for idle men, and they must have it sometimes.

I am speaking now of those who cannot do it; not of Issachar, who is like a strong ass, crouching down between two burdens and too lazy to get up with them. I say nothing for the sluggard who will not plow by reason of the cold. I speak of the men and women who really feel they can be of little service—who cannot "do" more. To such of you the words of the text are applicable.

3. The Offensive Ones Christ Will Not Break or Quench

Now we will make another remark. The two things here mentioned are offensive things. A bruised reed is offensive, for I believe there is an allusion here to the pipes of Pan, which you all know are reeds put together along which a man moves his mouth, thus causing some kind of music. This is the organ, I believe, which Jubal invented and which David mentions; for it is certain that the organ we use was not then in use.

The bruised reed, then, would of course spoil the melody of all the pipes. One unsound tube would so let the air out as to produce a discordant sound or no sound at all, so that one's impulse would be to take the pipe out and put in a fresh one.

And, as for smoking flax, the wick of a candle or anything of that kind, I need not inform you that the smoke is offensive. To me, no odor in all the world is so abominably offensive as smoking flax.

But some say, "How can you speak in so low a style?"

I have not gone lower than I could go myself nor lower than you can go with me; for I am sure you are, if God the Holy Ghost has really humbled you, just as offensive to your own souls and to God as a bruised reed would be among the pipes or as smoking flax to the eyes and nose.

I often think of dear old John Bunyan when he said he wished God had made him a toad or a frog or a snake or anything better than a man, for he felt he was so offensive.

I can conceive a nest of vipers, and I think that they are obnoxious. I can imagine a pool of all kinds of loathsome creatures breeding corruption. But nothing is one half so worthy of abhorrence as the human heart. God spares from all eyes but His own that awful sight—a human heart. And could you and I but once see our heart, we should be driven mad, so horrible would be the sight.

Do you feel like that? Do you feel that you must be offensive in God's sight—that you have so rebelled against Him, so turned away from His commandments that surely you must be obnoxious to Him? If so, my text is yours.

Now I can imagine some woman here this morning who has departed from the paths of virtue; and while you are standing in the throng up there or sitting down, you feel as if you had no right to tread these hallowed courts and stand among God's people. You think God might almost make the chapel break down upon you to destroy you, so great a sinner.

Never mind, broken reed and smoking flax! Though thou art the scorn of man and loathsome to thyself, yet Jesus saith to thee, "Neither do I condemn thee: go, and sin no more."

There is some man here who hath something in your heart that I know not of—who may have committed crimes in secret that we will not mention in public. Your sins stick like a leech to you and rob you of all comfort. Here you are, young man, shaking and trembling lest your crime should be divulged before high Heaven. You are broken down, bruised like a reed, smoking like flax.

Ah! I have a word for thee, too. Comfort! Comfort! Comfort! Despair not, for Jesus saith He will not quench the smoking flax nor break the bruised reed.

4. Christ Will Yet Have Risen for These Poor Ones

There is one thought before I turn away from this point. Both of these articles, however worthless they may be, *may yet be of some service.* When God puts His hand to a man, if he were worthless and useless before, He can make him very valuable.

You know the price of an article does not depend so much upon the value of the raw material as upon workmanship put upon it. Here is very bad raw material to begin with—bruised reeds and smoking flax— but by divine workmanship both become of wondrous value.

You tell me the bruised reed is good for nothing; I tell you that Christ will take that bruised reed, mend it up and fit it in the pipes of Heaven. Then when the grand orchestra shall send forth its music, when the organs of the skies shall peal forth their deep-toned sounds, we shall ask, "What was that sweet note heard there, mingling with the rest?" And someone shall answer, "It was a bruised reed."

Mary Magdalene's voice in Heaven, I imagine, sounds more sweet and liquid than any other. And the voice of that poor thief who said,

"Lord, remember me," if it is a *deep bass voice,* is more mellow and more sweet than the voice of any other because he loved much, for he had much forgiven him.

This reed may yet be of use. Do not say you are good for nothing. You shall sing up in Heaven yet. Do not say you are worthless. At last you shall stand before the throne among the blood-washed company and shall sing God's praise.

Ay, and the smoking flax, too—what good can that be? I will soon tell you. There is a spark in that flax somewhere. It is nearly out, but still a spark remaineth.

Behold the prairie on fire! See you the flames come rolling on? See you stream after stream of hot fire deluging the plain till all the continent is burned and scorched until Heaven is reddened with the flame? Old night's black face is scarred with the burning, and the stars appear affrighted at the conflagration.

How was that mass ignited? By a piece of smoking flax dropped by some traveler and fanned by the soft wind until the whole prairie caught the flame.

So one poor man, one ignorant man, one weak man, even one backsliding man, may be the means of the conversion of a whole nation. Who knows but that you who are nothing now may be of more use than those of us who appear to stand better before God because we have more gifts and talents? God can make a spark set a whole world on fire; He can light up a whole nation with the spark of one poor praying soul.

You may be useful yet; therefore, be of good cheer.

Moss groweth upon gravestone; the ivy clingeth to the moldering pile; the mistletoe groweth on the dead branch; and even so shall grace and piety and virtue and holiness and goodness come from smoking flax and bruised reeds.

II. THE DIVINE COMPASSION OF JESUS HERE PICTURED

My dear friends, I have tried to find out the parties for whom this text is meant, and I have shown you somewhat of mortal frailty; now I mount a step higher—to divine compassion. "A bruised reed shall he not break, and smoking flax shall he not quench."

Notice what is first of all stated; then let me tell you that Jesus Christ means a great deal more than He says. First of all, what does He say? That He will not break the bruised reed.

There is a bruised reed before me—a poor child of God under a deep sense of sin. It seems as if the whip of the law will never stop. It keeps on—lash, lash, lash; and though you say, "Lord, stop it; give me a little respite," still comes down the cruel thong—lash, lash, lash. You feel your sins. I know what you are saying this morning: "If God continues this a little longer, my heart will break. I shall perish in despair. I am almost distracted by my sin. If I lie down at night I cannot sleep. It appears as if ghosts were in the room—ghosts of my sins—and when I awake at midnight, I see the black form of Death staring at me and saying, 'Thou art my prey; I shall have thee'; while Hell behind seems to burn."

Poor bruised reed, He will not break you; conviction shall not be too strong. It shall be great enough to melt thee and to make thee go to Jesus' feet, but it shall not be strong enough to break thy heart altogether so that thou shouldst die. Thou shalt never be driven to despair. Thou shalt be delivered; thou shalt come out of the fire a poor bruised reed and shalt not be broken.

So there is a backslider here this morning. You are like the smoking flax. Years gone by you found such happiness in the ways of the Lord, such delight in His service that you said, "There I would forever stay."

> **What peaceful hours I then enjoyed;**
> **How sweet their memory still!**
> **But they have left an aching void**
> **The world can never fill.**

You are smoking, and you think God will put you out. If I were an Arminian, I should tell you that He would; but being a believer in the Bible and nothing else, I tell you that He will not quench you. Though you are smoking, you shall not die. Whatever your crime has been, the Lord says, "Return ye backsliding children of men, for I will have mercy upon you."

He will not cast thee away, poor Ephraim; only come back to Him. He will not despise thee. Though thou hast plunged thyself in the mire and dirt, though thou art covered from head to foot with filthiness, come back, poor prodigal! Come back! Come back! Thy Father calls thee. Hearken poor backslider! Come at once to Him whose arms are ready to receive thee.

1. Here Much More Is Implied

It says He will not quench, He will not break. But there is more under cover than we see at first sight.

When Jesus says He will not break, He means more than that. He means, "I will take that poor bruised reed and plant it hard by the rivers of waters and make it grow into a tree whose leaf shall not wither. I will water it every moment and watch it. There shall be heavenly fruits upon it. I will keep the birds of prey from it; but the birds of Heaven, the sweet songsters of Paradise, shall make their dwellings in the branches."

When He says He will not break the bruised reed, He means more. He means that He will nourish, help, strengthen, support and glorify— that He will execute His commission on it and make it glorious forever.

And when He says to the backslider that He will not quench him, He means more than that. He means that He will fan him up to a flame.

Some of you, I dare say, have gone home from chapel and found that your fire had gone nearly out. I know how you deal with it. You blow gently at the single spark, if there is one; and lest you should blow too hard, you hold your fingers before it. And if you were alone and had but one match or one spark in the tinder, how gently would you blow it!

So, backslider, Jesus Christ deals with thee. He does not put thee out. He blows gently. When He says, "I will not quench thee," He means, "I will be very tender, very cautious, very careful." He will put on dry material so that by-and-by a little spark shall come to a flame, blaze up toward Heaven, and great shall be the fire thereof.

2. The Small Saints as Soft as the Great

Now I want to say one or two things to Little-Faith this morning. The little children of God who are here mentioned as being bruised reeds or smoking flax are just as safe as the great saints of God. I wish for a moment to expand this thought; then I will finish with the other head.

For several reasons these saints of God who are called bruised reeds and smoking flax are just as safe as those who are mighty for their Master and great in strength.

The little ones are redeemed equally with the great ones. The feeble saints cost Christ as much suffering as the strong ones. The tiniest child of God could not have been purchased with less than Jesus' precious blood. And the greatest child of God did not cost Him more. Paul did not cost any more than Benjamin—I am sure he did not—for I read in the Bible that "there is no difference."

Besides, when of old they came to pay their redemption money, every person brought a shekel. The poor shall bring no less and the rich shall bring no more than just a shekel. The same price was paid for the one as the other.

Now then, little child of God, take that thought to thy soul. You see some men very prominent in Christ's cause—and it is very good that they should be; but they did not cost Jesus a farthing more than you did. He paid the same price for you that He paid for them.

Recollect again, *you are just as much a child of God as the greatest saint.* Some of you have five or six children. There is one child of yours, perhaps, who is very tall and handsome and has, moreover, gifts of mind. Another child, the smallest of the family, perhaps has but little intellect and understanding. But which is the more your child? "The more!" You say, "Both alike are my children, certainly, as much one as the other."

And so, dear friends, you may have very little learning; you may be very dark about divine things; you may but "see men as trees walking"—but you are as much the children of God as those who have grown to the stature of men in Christ Jesus.

Then remember, poor, tried saint, that *you are just as much justified as any other child of God.* I know that I am completely justified.

His blood and righteousness
My beauty are, my glorious dress.

I want no other garment save Jesus' doings and His imputed righteousness.

The boldest child of God wants no more; and I, who am "less than the least of all saints," can be content with no less, and I shall have no less. O Ready-to-Halt, thou art as much justified as Paul, Peter, John the Baptist or the loftiest saint in Heaven. There is no difference in that matter. So take courage and rejoice.

One thing more. If you were lost, God's honor would be as much tarnished as if the greatest one were lost. A queer thing I once read in an old book about God's children and people being a part of Christ and in union with Him. The writer says:

> As a father sitteth in his room, there cometh in a stranger. The stranger taketh up a child on his knee. The child hath a sore finger;

so he saith, "My child, you have a sore finger."

"Yes!"

"Well, let me take it off and give thee a golden one!"

The child looketh at him and saith, "I will not go to the man anymore, for he talks of taking off my finger. I love my own finger, and I will not have a golden one instead of it."

So the saint saith, "I am one of the members of Christ, but I am like a sore finger, and He will take me off and put a golden one on."

"No," said Christ, "no, no; I cannot have any of My members taken away. If the finger be a sore one, I will bind it up; I will strengthen it."

Christ cannot allow a word about cutting His members off. If Christ lost one of His people, He would not be a whole Christ any longer. If the meanest of His children could be cast away, Christ would lack a part of His fullness; yea, Christ would be incomplete without His church.

If one of His children must be lost, it would be better that it should be a great one than a little one. If a little one were lost, Satan would say, "Ah! You save the great ones because they had strength and could help themselves; but the little one who has no strength, You could not save him."

We know what Satan would say, but God would shut Satan's mouth by proclaiming, "They are all here, Satan. In spite of thy malice, they are all here. Every one is safe. Now lie down in thy den forever and be bound eternally in chains, and smoke in fire!" So shall he suffer eternal torment, but not one child of God ever shall.

3. God Uses Small Saints to Save Great Ones

One thought more, and I shall have done with this head. *The salvation of great saints often depends upon the salvation of little ones.* Do you understand that? You know that my salvation or the salvation of any child of God, looking at second causes, very much depends upon the conversion of someone else.

Suppose your mother is the means of your conversion; you would, speaking after the manner of men, say that your conversion depended upon hers, for her being converted made her the instrument of bringing you in.

Suppose such and such a minister were the means of calling; then your conversion, in some sense, though not absolutely, depends upon his.

So it often happens that the salvation of God's mightiest servants depends upon the conversion of little ones. There is a poor mother. No one ever knows anything about her. She goes to the house of God. Her name is not in the newspapers or anywhere else. She teaches her child and brings him up in the fear of God. She prays for that boy. She wrestles with God. Her tears and prayers mingle together.

The boy grows up. What is he? A missionary—a William Kniff—a Moffatt—a Williams. But you do not hear anything about the mother. However, if the mother had not been saved, where would the boy have been?

Let this cheer the little ones; and may you rejoice that He will nourish and cherish you, though you are like bruised reeds and smoking flax.

III. CERTAIN VICTORY FOR CHRIST AND ALL HIS OWN

To finish up, there is certain victory. "Until he bringeth forth judgment unto victory."

Victory! There is something beautiful in that word. The death of Sir John Moore in the Peninsular War was very touching. He fell in the arms of triumph; and sad as was his fate, I doubt not that his eye was lit up with luster by the shout of victory. So also, I suppose, that Wolfe spoke a truth when he said, "I die happy"—having just before heard the shout, "They run! They run!"

I know victory, even in that bad sense—for I look not upon earthly victories as of any value—must have cheered the warrior.

But how cheered the saint when he knows that victory is his! I shall fight during all my life, but I shall write *"vici"* on my shield. I shall be 'more than conqueror through him that loved me.' Each feeble saint shall win the day; each man upon his crutches; each lame one; each one full of infirmity, sorrow, sickness and weakness, shall gain the victory. "They shall come with singing into Zion; as well the blind, and lame, and halt, and the woman with child, together." So saith the Scripture. Not one shall be left out; but he shall "bring forth judgment unto victory."

Victory! Victory! Victory! This is the lot of each Christian. He shall triumph through his dear Redeemer's name.

Now a word about this victory. I speak first to aged men and women. Dear brethren and sisters, you are often, I know, like the bruised reed. Coming events and death cast their shadows on you. You feel full of weakness and decay; your frame can hardly hold together.

But you have here some special promises: "The bruised reed I will not break." "I will strengthen thee." "When thy heart and thy flesh faileth, I will be the strength of thy heart and thy portion for ever."

Even down to old age, all my people shall prove
My sovereign, eternal, unchangeable love;
And when hoary hairs shall their temples adorn,
Like lambs they shall still in My bosom be borne.

Tottering on thy staff, leaning, feeble, weak and wan, fear not the last hour; it shall be thy best. Thy last day shall be a consummation devoutly to be wished. Weak as thou art, God will temper the trial of thy weakness, make thy pain less if thy strength be less, but thou shalt sing in Heaven, "Victory! Victory! Victory!"

Some of us could wish to change places with you, to be so near Heaven—to be so near Home. With all your infirmities, your gray hairs are a crown of glory to you; for you are near the end, as in the way of righteousness.

A word with you middle-aged men battling in this life's rough storm. You are often bruised reeds. Your religion is so encumbered by your worldly callings, so covered up by the daily din of business, business, business, that you seem like smoking flax. It is as much as you can do to serve your God. You cannot say that you are "fervent in spirit," as well as "diligent in business."

Man of business, toiling and striving in this world, He will not quench thee when thou art like smoking flax; He will not break thee when thou art like the bruised reed but will deliver thee from thy troubles. Thou shalt swim across the sea of life and shalt stand on the happy shore of Heaven and sing, "Victory," through Him that loved thee.

Ye youths and maidens, I speak to you, and have a right to do so. When the hand of God blights our fair hopes, you and I ofttimes know what the bruised reed is. We are full of giddiness and waywardness; it is only the rod of affliction that can bring folly out of us, for we have much of it in us. Slippery paths are the paths of youth, and dangerous ways are the ways of the young; but God will not break or destroy us.

Men, by their overcaution, bid us never tread a step lest we fall; but God bids us go and make our feet like hinds' feet, that we may tread upon high places. Serve God in early days. Give your heart to Him; then He will never cast you out but will nourish and cherish you.

Let me not finish without saying a word to little children. Jesus says
to you, "The bruised reed I will not break; the smoking flax I will not
quench." I believe there is many a little prattler not six years old who
knows the Saviour. I never despise infantile piety. I have heard little
children talk of mysteries that gray-headed men knew not. Ah! little
children who have been brought up in Sunday schools and love the
Saviour's name, if others say you are too forward, do not fear; love
Christ still.

> **Gentle Jesus, meek and mild,**
> **Still will look upon a child;**
> **Pity thy simplicity,**
> **And suffer thee to come to Him.**

He will not cast thee away; for smoking flax He will not quench, and
the bruised reed He will not break.

(From the book, SPURGEON'S SERMONS, Volume 2, published
by Zondervan Publishing House)

TOM MALONE
1915-

ABOUT THE MAN:

Tom Malone was converted and called to preach at the same moment! At an old-fashioned bench, the preacher took his tear-stained Bible and showed Tom Malone how to be saved. He accepted Christ then and there. Rising from his knees in the Isbell Methodist Church near Russellville, Alabama, he shook the circuit pastor's hand; and this bashful nineteen-year-old farm boy announced: "I know the Lord wants me to be a preacher."

Backward, bashful and broke, yet Tom borrowed five dollars, took what he could in a cardboard suitcase and left for Cleveland, Tennessee. Immediately upon arrival at Bob Jones College, Malone heard a truth that totally dominated his life and labors for the Lord ever after—soul winning!

That day he won his first soul! The green-as-grass Tom, a new convert himself, knew nothing of soul-winning approaches or techniques. He simply asked the sinner, "Are you a Christian?" No. In a few minutes that young man became Malone's first convert.

Since that day, countless have been his experiences in personal evangelism.

Mark it down: Malone began soul winning his first week in Bible college. And he has never lost *the thirst* for it, *the thrill* in it, nor *the task* of it since. Pastoring churches, administrating schools, preaching across the nation have not deterred Tom Malone from this mainline ministry.

It is doubtful if young Malone ever dreamed of becoming the man he is today. He is now Doctor Tom Malone, is renowned in fundamental circles for his wise leadership and great preaching, is pastor of the large Emmanuel Baptist Church of Pontiac, Michigan, Founder and President of Midwestern Baptist Schools, and is eagerly sought as speaker in large Bible conferences from coast to coast.

Dr. John R. Rice often said that Dr. Tom Malone may be the greatest gospel preacher in all the world today!

IV.

Are the Consolations of God Too Small?

TOM MALONE

(Preached in 1964)

Read Job 15:1-17

"Are the consolations of God small with thee?"—Job 15:11.

The book of Job is a dialogue between Satan and God, God and Job, and Job and his friends. The whole book is taken up with conversation. Satan talks to God; God talks to Satan. Job talks to God, and God talks to Job. Then, Job had four friends. Three are old and wise men. One is a young man. But all these four friends had much to say to him.

The book of Job is older than the book of Genesis. Some people believe that probably Moses is the author of the book of Job. No one knows. But it is the oldest book of the Bible. Bible students believe the book of Job was written earlier than any other book.

If the book of Job is the oldest book in the Bible, it is amazing that the first book God ever wrote dealt with the trials of a Christian. Even before a gospel book was written (and the book of Genesis has the story of redemption in it), this book dealing with the trials of a Christian was written.

I want to take a question out of chapter 15 of Job for our text. In verse 11 we have this question, "Are the consolations of God small with thee?"

This question was not asked by God nor by Job, but it was asked by one of Job's four friends.

Now when I use the word *friends* in relation to Job, I put a question mark beside it. When you find what these "friends" have to say to Job when he needed comfort, strength and encouragement in the hour of great trial, then I believe you too will put a question mark beside the word *friends*. You are made to wonder if they really were his friends, if they really cared about the distress of his heart and soul, if they really cared about the pain and affliction of his body.

Now listen carefully. You may not need this now, but you will need it somewhere along the journey of life: when Job listened to these four friends, this was his comment, ". . . miserable comforters are ye all" (Job 16:2). Job's friends, in the hour of his greatest test, were no help to him.

Job was a good man. The Bible, I believe, compliments Job more than any other man. God said some things about Job that He never said about Moses or Daniel or Jeremiah or Paul or Peter or John. No man was ever complimented like God complimented Job.

He said, "Job is a man that fears God." That is the beginning of wisdom. That shows that you are smart, if you have a reverential fear of God. God said, "Job fears God. He hates evil. He walks uprightly. He is a man perfect in all of his ways." That did not mean that he was not human; it meant that he was mature, feared God, walked uprightly, loved the Lord, hated evil and was mature in all his ways.

No one was ever more in the center of God's will than was Job. And right in the middle of God's will, he finds the greatest affliction that any character, outside of Jesus Himself, ever suffered.

Oh, how it came to Job! You have heard it before. He buried all ten of his children in one grave at one time. He saw his sons and daughters, his entire family, wiped out with one stroke from the hand of God. He saw in one day every material thing he owned taken away from him, until he cried, "Naked came I into the world, naked shall I return."

He lost every child he had. He lost every material thing he had. But he still had a priceless possession left—his health. Then with one stroke from the hand of God, his health was removed.

Why did all this happen? These friends thought they had the answer. But something took place behind the scenes. Job didn't see it. These friends didn't see it. Behind the scenes there was a controversy between God and the Devil.

The Devil came to God and said, "This man Job serves You because You have been good to him. You gave him a big family, thousands of head of cattle and stock, thousands of acres of rolling fields—

everything his heart has ever wanted. No wonder he can sing and praise God. You have been so good to him. You have put a hedge around him. No trouble, no sorrow, has ever come to him."

Satan challenged God and said, "Your Christian wouldn't be such a good Christian if some real tests and trials came."

God said, "I will prove to you that My child can be a good Christian in the midst of the deepest travail a human being has ever known."

So his children were taken. Every material thing was taken. Then his health was removed until the Bible says that he sat in ashes and took a piece of broken pottery and literally scraped the disease and putrefaction from his body. No one would have anything to do with him.

Finally, his so-called friends came. One of them, Eliphaz, thought he had it figured out. He said, "I am going to tell Job this great trouble has come because he has done wickedly." Here are his words: "Even as I have seen, they that plow iniquity, and sow wickedness, reap the same" (Job 4:8). This so-called friend said, "Job, you are sick, afflicted, because you have lived in sin."

That was not true, for here is the best Christian in many ways we ever read of in the Bible.

Then Bildad came in chapter 8 and verse 13 and said, "So are the paths of all that forget God; and the hypocrite's hope shall perish...." He said, "This is coming on you because you are a hypocrite."

He too was wrong. No man ever lived that was further from being a hypocrite.

Then the third man speaks, Zophar: "Should thy lies make men hold their peace?" (Job 11:3). He said, "Job, you have lied somewhere along the line. And because of your lying ways, the judgment of God has come upon you."

Here is a man who God said is upright, faithful, loyal and true. Neither did Zophar know what he was talking about.

Then there is a younger man, Elihu, who comes and says, "My words shall be of the uprightness of my heart: and my lips shall utter knowledge clearly" (Job 33:3). Elihu, this youngster, said, "Now you old grey heads don't know what this is all about. You don't know why this trouble came. You don't know why this Christian is in such affliction. But I know. You listen to me." But none of the four had the answer.

I wish I had time to deal more with the answer than with the problem, for chapter 42 of the book of Job is one of the greatest chapters in the Bible. In that chapter God doubles every blessing He withdrew from this man. He gave him ten more children, gave him double all the earthly possessions, restored his health and sat him on a pinnacle of blessing the like of which no Christian has ever enjoyed.

But in the midst of all this, there comes this question, "Are the consolations of God small with thee?"

That is a good question for a man in trouble. "Are the consolations of God too small for thee?"

I want to review that question with you in five different areas of life.

Are the consolations of God too small for you

In the Matter of Being a Christian?

A lot of Christians think they have missed something by being a Christian—I mean something good, something you would like to have. A Christian never misses any good thing. The Bible declares, "No good thing will he withhold from them that walk uprightly." We read in the Bible, "At thy right hand there are pleasures for evermore."

I read something Jesus said to people who had everything in life except one thing—Christ. They had no peace of heart and mind, no pardon and forgiveness of sin. In Luke 6:24, Jesus said, "But woe unto you that are rich! for ye have received your consolation." Jesus said, "All the consolation you are ever going to have will be in this life." He said, "Woe unto you!"

Not so with the Christian. The Christian's consolation is described in Hebrews 6:18, "That by two immutable things, in which it was impossible for God to lie, WE MIGHT HAVE A STRONG CONSOLATION, who have fled for refuge to lay hold upon the hope set before us."

That word *consolation* has two meanings in the Bible. It means something called alongside. That is a description of the Holy Spirit. Jesus said, "I will give you another comforter, another consoler. I will give you another consolation, one called alongside to help." Paul said, "We have a strong consolation. . . ."

The other meaning is a comfort, a rest, a hope, an anchor, a rock upon which to found our lives. Notice again what he said in that verse: ". . .we might have a strong consolation, who have fled for refuge to lay hold upon the hope set before us."

If you are a Christian today, review your blessings. You young people, you have not missed one good thing by being a Christian. Are the consolations of God too small for thee?

A man has his choice. He has Heaven on one hand and Hell on the other. He makes his choice. A man has two choices—the choice of peace or misery. If a man has chosen Heaven, he has chosen peace. A man has two choices—the choice of bondage and slavery or freedom. The Christian has chosen freedom.

Are the consolations of God too small for thee?

We have a refuge, thank God, because we are saved, a refuge from every storm, a refuge from every evil, a refuge in the present, a refuge in the future. This Bible says, ". . . we have a strong consolation, who have fled for refuge to lay hold upon the hope set before us. . . ."

I never saw the artist's conception of the storm, but I read the description of it some years ago. A German artist had drawn a wonderful picture of a storm. You could see the low hanging, heavy black clouds. (And they will hang low, heavy and black in your life sooner or later.) You could almost see the flash of lightning and hear the peal of thunder. You could see the trees bending in the wind. It looked like a storm would come momentarily with all of its fury.

It is said that you could see animals hurrying somewhere. You could see people going somewhere. In the direction they were going was the little log cabin home and the little log-built farm. Every animal headed for the barn. Every person headed for the home because the storm was coming.

Down underneath that artist's drawing of a storm there was one word, just one—"Refuge."

What people want in life, whether they have sense enough to know it or not, is a refuge for their souls. That refuge is only found in Jesus Christ.

Are the consolations of God too small for thee

In the Realm of Human Suffering?

This is a primary application. Think for a moment. Here is a Christian with everything gone. His wife even came to him and said, "Why don't you curse God and die and get it over with?" Job said, 'Though God slay me, yet will I trust Him.' In the midst of this suffering—I mean bodily suffering, I mean pain, I mean anguish of body and soul—someone said, "Are the consolations of God small with thee?" In other words, "Isn't God enough in the hour of trial?"

I will put the question to you this morning. When affliction, trial, distress of body, mind and soul come, are the consolations of God too small for thee?

It is amazing how much the Bible has to say about it. In II Corinthians 1:5 we read, "For as the sufferings of Christ abound in us, so our consolation also aboundeth by Christ." This Bible plainly teaches that the more the sufferings of Christ abound, the more the consolations abound.

My friends, this business of a Christian not trusting God in the dark hour of distress is something that no one can explain from the Bible. For God's Word says, "In the hour of distress, the more the afflictions, the more the consolations."

We read in II Corinthians 1:7, ". . . knowing, that as ye are partakers of the sufferings, so shall ye be also of the consolation."

I would like to use a personal illustration. I have been to see a number of times Frank Lundy. Frank had been a Catholic all of his life. He was hard to win. But the Lord came into his life.

I have never seen one suffer so much—if you will pardon the expression—"hell on earth" as this man suffered. I went into the hospital room; and if I had not known who he was, I would never have recognized him. His legs were a little stretch of skin over a rack of bones. His hair was as white as snow. His eyes were sunk far deep into his head.

When I walked up to him, he began to weep and reached up a little twisted, bony hand. I took it between mine and held it. This is what he said: "Tom, all I have left is the Lord."

You say, "That is wonderful." No. I don't like for a Christian to say that. Listen! That is all that he had to start with. That is not just what he had left. That is all the hope that he had ever had, or any Christian has ever had. The Lord is all and everything in the midst of trial or in the midst of blessing. Don't ever say, "All I have is the Lord." When you have Jesus, you have everything.

You will come to a place in your pilgrim journey of life when no human being can walk with you. It will be God or nothing, Jesus or nothing.

Are the consolations of God too small for thee?

Some of you sitting in this building are leaning on the prayers of your wife and children. You are taking the things of God lightly, and you are going as straight to Hell as a man can go.

Wake up for God's sake! It is Jesus or nothing. You have no other hope. There will come an hour in your life when no human being can walk with you. Everything I have is God's, and the same is true of you. You either have God, or you have nothing. And you will never have anything unless you have Him. Jesus said, "Without me ye can do nothing" (John 15:5).

Are the consolations of God too small for thee

In the Realm of Service?

Thank God for people who never quit! Thank God for people who are loyal! Thank God for people who are steadfast! But sometimes the best Christian in the world grows weary in the battle of Christian service. That is why God warns in Galatians 6:9, "Let us not be weary in well doing: for in due season we shall reap, if we faint not."

One of the greatest chapters in the Bible is chapter 15 of I Corinthians. It deals with every single phase of the resurrection of Jesus Christ and the human body. That great chapter closes with this statement, "Therefore, my beloved brethren, be ye STEDFAST. . . ." We need some steadfast Christians who know where they belong on Wednesday nights. We need some steadfast Christians who know where they belong on Sunday nights. ". . . be ye STEDFAST. . . ."

Strange how quickly people forget. I have seen people in this work of God, seen this church family literally turn themselves inside out for people. I have done the same thing for many a person. I have gone out of my way, by day and by night, physically, mentally, spiritually, and even sometimes financially, to do everything I could, and people forget it so soon.

I say again that one of the most wonderful things in the life of a Christian is steadfastness. Listen to it again, "Therefore, my brethren, be ye stedfast, unmoveable, always abounding in the work of the Lord, forasmuch as ye know that your labour is not in vain in the Lord." When you serve God, He will see that you are taken care of. "Your labour is not in vain in the Lord."

Are the consolations of God too small for thee in the realm of service?

Are the consolations of God too small for thee

In the Realm of Suffering Wrong?

What do you do when you are wronged? What do you do when you are mistreated? Here is the Bible answer. And I am going to tell you a story this morning, the like of which you hear but once in a lifetime. Romans 12:19 says, "Dearly beloved, avenge not yourselves, but rather give place unto wrath: for it is written, Vengeance is mine; I will repay, saith the Lord."

I noticed that expression, "for it is written"; and I said, "Where is it written?" I looked it up, and it is written in Deuteronomy, chapter 32.

One day God said to Moses, "Moses, these Egyptians slew your people by the multiplied thousands. They kept you in bondage and beat you with their whips. They starved you and killed your babies. But Moses, VENGEANCE IS MINE; I will repay." Not you, but God. And sitting today yonder on the other side of the world is a land in darkness and disease, in poverty and filth, which the hand of God is upon this very hour. God said, "I will repay." And for six thousand years God has been paying Egypt for what they did to the Jew.

I have had people say to me, "Brother Tom, why do you let some folks treat you the way they do?" God says, "Vengeance is mine." Not mine, but His. God says, "I will repay." Not me, but Him.

Are the consolations of God too small for thee when you suffer wrong? Can't you let God handle it? Can't you believe that God is big enough?

One of the men of our church whom God wonderfully saved is Emeric Kocis, a professional golfer. He was saved in this church through the witness of one of our members whose salvation is a miracle, too. Emeric has a few acres out here. He loves the woods, trees and the grass. He lives out there alone.

Some few weeks ago, a group of teenagers loaded with beer came onto his property. When he tried to put them off, they attacked and beat him. Of course, he got in a few licks himself. He defended himself. But they beat him and kicked him and stomped him. He called the police; and as so often happens, nothing happened.

But you read in your newspapers a few days ago where some murderers in a motorboat chewed the body of a twenty-year-old boy to pieces and killed him. That boy was one of the gang that attacked a Christian man. When they told me about it, I said, "God didn't wait long to get His vengeance."

Go ahead and leave God out of your life. You think you are too wise, too reserved. You don't want to be a Christian. You leave God out of your life, and when you burn in Hell someday, you will remember what this preacher said.

"Vengeance is mine...," God said.

I don't claim to have the most tender conscience in the world. But there is one thing I don't want to do, and that is to deliberately hurt some Christian. I don't want ever to deliberately wrong a human being and seek to be a stumblingblock.

Let me tell you, my friend, the consolations of God are good enough in your life when you suffer wrong.

Are the consolations of God too small for thee

In the Hour of Death?

Second Corinthians 5:1 says, "For we know that if our earthly house of this tabernacle were dissolved, we have a building of God, an house not made with hands, eternal in the heavens."

In verse 8 of the same chapter, the old apostle said, "We are confident, I say, and willing rather to be absent from the body, and to be present with the Lord."

I talked to two 83-year-old men yesterday. One of them has already gone on to be with the Lord, and one of them is the loved one of some of you sitting here this morning.

I will never forget the handshake of one of those Christians. I took a little New Testament out of my pocket, and as I began to read, that old man was sitting up on the edge of the bed pumping my hand. He just kept holding on and squeezing and shaking and pumping it.

When I started to read the Bible, he stopped. The family of the old man had said, "He wants to go to be with the Lord." There is nothing wrong with that.

The old apostle one day said, "I am torn between two opinions. I have a desire to depart and to be with Christ, which is far better. But for you it is needful that I remain."

Oh, listen! In the hour of death, are the consolations of God too small for thee? The Christian can look down at the grave—our hearts are broken, yes—but we look down at the grave, and we can challenge the grave and say, "O grave, where is thy victory? O death, where is thy sting?" I will tell you where it is. It was taken out at Calvary and defeated forever for the Christian.

A mother and her little child were out in the flower garden, and a bee was buzzing around. The little child was afraid. All of a sudden it stung the mother. The little child said, "Mother, I am afraid that bee is going to sting me."

She said, "No, it won't sting you now. The bee can't hurt you now."

"But Mama, it is still here."

The mother insisted, "It never can hurt you."

"But Mother, how do you know?"

"Because it just stung me, and the stinger is in my arm right now."

O grave, where is thy sting? It is in the body of Jesus on Calvary. Are the consolations of God too small for thee?

DWIGHT LYMAN MOODY
1837-1899

ABOUT THE MAN:

D. L. Moody may well have been the greatest evangelist of all time. In a 40-year period, he won a million souls, founded three Christian schools, launched a great Christian publishing business, established a world-renowned Christian conference center, and inspired literally thousands of preachers to win souls and conduct revivals.

A shoe clerk at 17, his ambition was to make $100,000. Converted at 18, he uncovered hidden gospel gold in the hearts of millions for the next half century. He preached to 20,000 a day in Brooklyn and admitted only nonchurch members by ticket!

He met a young songleader in Indianapolis, said bluntly, "You're the man I've been looking for for eight years. Throw up your job and come with me." Ira D. Sankey did just that; thereafter it was "Moody will preach; Sankey will sing."

He traveled across the American continent and through Great Britain in some of the greatest and most successful evangelistic meetings communities have ever known. His tour of the world with Sankey was considered the greatest evangelistic enterprise of the century.

It was Henry Varley who said, "It remains to be seen what God will do with a man who gives himself up wholly to Him." And Moody endeavored to be, under God, that man; and the world did marvel to see how wonderfully God used him.

Two great monuments stand to the indefatigable work and ministry of this gospel warrior—Moody Bible Institute and the famous Moody Church in Chicago.

Moody went to be with the Lord in 1899.

V.

Rest

D. L. MOODY

Some years ago a gentleman came to me and asked which I thought was the most precious promise of all those that Christ left. I took some time to look them over; but I gave it up, finding that I could not answer the question.

It is like a man with a large family of children who cannot tell which child he loves best: he loves them all. But if not the best, this is one of the sweetest promises of all.

"Come unto me, all ye that labour and are heavy laden, and I will give you rest. Take my yoke upon you, and learn of me; for I am meek and lowly in heart: and ye shall find rest unto your souls. For my yoke is easy, and my burden is light."—Matt. 11:28-30.

A good many people think the promises are not going to be fulfilled. There are some you do see fulfilled, and you cannot help but believe they are true. Now remember that all the promises are not given without conditions. Some are given with, others without, conditions attached to them.

For instance, when it says, "If I regard iniquity in my heart, the Lord will not hear me," then I need not pray as long as I am cherishing some known sin. He will not hear me, much less answer me.

When the Lord says in Psalm 84, "No good thing will he withhold from them that walk uprightly," then if I am not walking uprightly, I have no claims upon the promise.

Again, some of the promises were made to certain individuals or nations. For instance, when God said that He would make Abraham's seed to multiply as the stars of heaven, that promise is not for you or me. Some promises were made to the Jews and do not apply to the Gentiles.

Then there are promises without conditions. When He promised Adam and Eve that the world should have a Saviour, no power in earth or perdition could keep Christ from coming at the appointed time.

When Christ left the world, He said He would send us the Holy Ghost. In ten days the Holy Ghost came.

Right through the Scriptures we find that some of the promises are with and some without conditions; and if we don't comply with the conditions, we cannot expect them to be fulfilled.

I believe everyone will be obliged to testify in the evening of life that, when he complied with the condition, the Lord fulfilled His Word to the letter.

The old Hebrew hero Joshua was an illustration. After having tested God forty years in the Egyptian brickkilns, forty years in the desert and thirty years in the Promised Land, his dying testimony was: "Not one thing hath failed of all the good things which the Lord promised."

You could heave the ocean easier than break one of God's promises. So when we come to a promise like the one we have before us now, bear in mind that there is no discount upon it. "Come unto me, all ye that labour and are heavy laden, and I will give you rest."

Perhaps you are hoping that Mr. Moody is not going to preach on this old text. But I am. When I take up an album, it does not interest me if all the photographs are new; but if I know any of the faces, I stop at once. So with these old, well-known texts. They have quenched our thirst before, but the water is still bubbling up—we cannot drink it dry.

Probe the human heart and you find a want, and that want is rest. The cry of the world today is, "Where can rest be found?" Why are theaters and places of amusement crowded at night? What is the secret of Sunday driving, of the saloons and brothels? Some think they are going to get it in pleasure; others think they are going to get it in wealth; others, in literature. They are seeking but finding no rest.

Where Can Rest Be Found?

If I wanted to find a person who had rest, I would not go among the very wealthy. The man we read about in the 12th chapter of Luke thought he was going to get rest by multiplying his goods, but he was disappointed. "Soul, take thine ease." I venture to say that there is not a person in this wide world who has tried to find rest in that way and found it.

Money cannot buy it. Many a millionaire would gladly give millions if he could purchase it as he does his stocks and shares. God has made the soul a little too large for this world. Roll the whole world in, and still there is room. There is care in getting wealth, and more care in keeping it.

Nor would I go among the pleasure-seekers. They have a few hours' enjoyment, but the next day there is enough sorrow to counterbalance it. They may drink the cup of pleasure today, but the cup of pain comes on tomorrow.

To find rest I would never go among the politicians or among the so-called great. Congress is the last place on earth I would go. In the Lower House they want to go to the Senate; in the Senate they want to go to the Cabinet; and then they want to go to the White House; and rest has never been found there.

Nor would I go among the halls of learning. "Much study is a weariness to the flesh." I would not go among the upper ten, the "bon-ton," for they are constantly chasing after fashion.

Have you noticed their troubled faces on our streets? And the face is index to the soul. They have no hopeful look. Their worship of pleasure is slavery. Solomon tried pleasure and found bitter disappointment. And down the ages has come the bitter cry, "All is vanity."

Now there is no rest in sin. The wicked know nothing about it. The Scriptures tell us the wicked "are like the troubled sea that cannot rest." You have, perhaps, been on the sea when there is a calm, when the water is as clear as crystal; and it seemed as if the sea were at rest. But looking further, you see that the waves come in and that the calm is only on the surface.

Man, like the sea, has no rest, nor has he had since Adam fell; and there will be none for him until he returns to God again and the light of Christ shines into his heart.

Rest cannot be found in the world; and, thank God, the world cannot take it from the believing heart! Sin is the cause of all this unrest. It brought toil and labor and misery into the world.

Now for something positive. I would go successfully to someone who has heard the sweet voice of Jesus and has laid his burden down at the cross. There is rest, sweet rest. Thousands could certify to this blessed fact. They could say, and truthfully so:

I heard the voice of Jesus say,
  "Come unto Me and rest.
Lay down, thou weary one, lay down,
  Thy head upon My breast."
I came to Jesus as I was,
  Weary and worn and sad.
I found in Him a resting-place,
  And He hath made me glad.

For four thousand years no prophet or priest or patriarch ever stood up and uttered a text like this. It would be blasphemy for Moses to have done so. Do you think he had rest when he was pleading for the Lord to let him go into the Promised Land? Do you think Elijah could have uttered such a text as this when, under the juniper tree, he prayed that he might die? And this is one of the strongest proofs that Jesus Christ was not only man, but God—God-Man. And this is Heaven's proclamation, "Come unto me . . . and I will give you rest." He brought it down from Heaven with Him.

Now, if this text were not true, wouldn't it have been found out by this time? I believe it as much as I believe in my existence. Why? Because I not only find it in the Book, but in my own experience. The "I wills" of Christ have never been broken, and never can be.

Thank God for the word "give" in that passage! He doesn't sell it. Some of us are so poor that we could not buy it if it were for sale. Thank God, we can get it for nothing!

I like to have a text like this because it takes us all in. "Come unto me, ALL ye that labour." That doesn't mean a select few—refined ladies and cultured men. It doesn't mean good people only. It applies to saint and sinner. Hospitals are for the sick, not for healthy people. Do you think that Christ would shut the door in anyone's face and say, "I did not mean *all*; I only meant certain ones"? If you cannot come as a saint, come as a sinner. Only come!

A lady told me once that she was so hardhearted she couldn't come.

"Well," I said, "my good woman, it doesn't say all ye softhearted people come. Black hearts, vile hearts, hard hearts, soft hearts—all hearts come. Who can soften your hard heart but Himself?"

The harder the heart, the more need you have to come. If my watch stops, I don't take it to a drug store or to a blacksmith's shop but to the watchmaker's, to have it repaired. So if the heart gets out of order, take it to its Keeper to have it set right. If you can prove that you are a sinner, you are entitled to the promise. Get all the benefit you can out of it.

Now, a good many believers think this text applies only to sinners. But it is just the thing for them, too. What do we see today? The church, Christian people, all loaded down with cares and troubles. "Come unto me, all ye that labour." All! That includes the Christian whose heart is burdened with some great sorrow.

Christ the Burden-Bearer

In another place we read, "Casting all your care upon him, for he careth for you." We would have a victorious church if we could get Christians to realize that. But they have never made the discovery. They agree that Christ is the Sin-bearer, but they do not realize that He is also the Burden-bearer. "Surely he hath borne our griefs, and carried our sorrows." It is the privilege of every child of God to walk in unclouded sunlight.

Some go back into the past and rake up all the troubles they ever had; then they look into the future and anticipate that they will have still more trouble; then they go reeling and staggering all through life. They give you the cold chills every time they meet you. They put on a whining voice and tell you what a hard time they have had. I believe they embalm them and bring out the mummy on every opportunity. The Lord says, "Cast all your care on Me. I want to carry your burdens and your troubles." We want a joyful church, and we are not going to impress the world until we have it. We want to get long-faced Christianity off the face of the earth.

Take these people who have some great burden and let them come into a meeting. If you can get their attention upon the singing or preaching, they will say, "Oh, wasn't it grand! I forgot all my cares." They dropped their bundle at the end of the pew. But the moment the benediction is pronounced, they grab the bundle again. You laugh, but you do it yourself.

Sometimes they go into the closet, close the door and get so carried away and lifted up that they forget their trouble. But they take it up again the moment they get off their knees.

Leave your sorrow now; cast all your care upon Him. If you cannot come to Christ as a saint, come as a sinner. But if you are a saint with some trouble or care, bring it to Him. Saint and sinner, come! He wants

all. Don't let Satan deceive you into believing that you cannot come
if you will. Christ says, "Ye will not come unto me." With the command comes the power.

A man in one of our meetings in Europe said he would like to come,
but he was chained and couldn't.

A Scotchman said to him, "Ay, man, why don't you come, chain
and all?"

"I never thought of that," he answered.

Are you cross and peevish, and do you make things unpleasant at
home? My friend, come to Christ and ask Him to help you. Whatever
the sin is, bring it to Him.

What Does It Mean to *Come*?

Perhaps you say, "Mr. Moody, I wish you would tell us what it is
to **come**." I have given up trying to explain it. I always feel like the
colored minister who said he was going to confound (instead of expound)
the chapter.

The best definition is just—**come.** The more you try to explain it,
the more you are mystified.

About the first thing a mother teaches her child is to look. She takes
the baby to the window and says, "Look, baby, papa is coming!" Then
she teaches the child to come. She props it up against a chair and says,
"Come!" When by and by the little thing pushes the chair along towards
mama, that's coming.

You don't need to go to college to learn how. You don't need a
minister to tell you what it is.

Now will you come to Christ? "Him that cometh unto me, I will in
no wise cast out," He promises.

When we have such a promise as this, let us cling to it and never
give it up. Christ is not mocking us. He wants us to come with all our
sins and backslidings and throw ourselves upon His bosom. It is our
sins God wants, not just our tears. They alone do no good. And we
cannot come through resolutions. Action is necessary. How many times
at church have we said, "I will turn over a new leaf," but the Monday
leaf is worse than the Saturday leaf.

The way to Heaven is straight as a rule, but it is the way of the cross.
Don't try to get around it.

Shall I tell you what the "yoke" referred to in the text is? It is the cross which Christians must bear. The only way by which you can find rest in this dark world is by taking up the yoke of Christ. I do not know what it may include in your case, beyond taking up your Christian duties, acknowledging Christ and acting as becomes one of His disciples. Perhaps it may be to erect a family altar; or to tell a godless husband that you have made up your mind to serve God; or to tell your parents that you want to be a Christian. Follow the will of God; then happiness and peace and rest will come. The way of obedience is always the way of blessing.

I was preaching in Chicago to a hall full of women one Sunday afternoon. After the meeting a lady came and said she wanted to talk to me. After we had talked she said she would accept Christ. After more conversation she went home. I looked for her in the audience a whole week, but didn't see her until the following Sunday afternoon. She came and sat down right in front of me. Her face had such a sad expression. She seemed to have entered into the misery, instead of the joy, of the Lord.

After the meeting I went to her and asked her what the trouble was.

"O Mr. Moody, this has been the most miserable week of my life!"

I asked her if there was anyone with whom she had trouble and whom she could not forgive.

"No, not that I know of."

"Well, did you tell your friends about having found the Saviour?"

"Indeed I didn't. I have been all the week trying to keep it from them."

"Well," I said, "that is the reason why you have no peace."

She wanted to take the crown but not the cross. My friends, you must go by the way of Calvary. If you ever get rest, you must get it at the foot of the cross.

"Why," she said, "if I should go home and tell my infidel husband that I have found Christ, I don't know what he will do. I think he would turn me out."

"Well," I said, "go out."

She went away, promising that she would tell him; for she did not want another wretched week. She was bound to have peace.

The next night I gave a lecture to men only. In the hall were eight thousand men and one solitary woman! When I got through and went into the inquiry meeting, I found this lady with her husband. She introduced him to me (he was a doctor and a very influential man) and said, "He wants to become a Christian."

I took my Bible and told him about Christ, and he accepted Him.

I said to her after it was all over, "It turned out quite different from what you expected, didn't it?"

"Yes," she replied, "I was never so scared in my life. I expected he would do something dreadful, but it has turned out so well."

She took God's way and got rest.

I want to say to young ladies: perhaps you have a godless father or mother, a skeptical brother who is going down through drink; and perhaps there is no one who can reach them but you. How many times a godly, pure young lady has taken the light into some darkened home! Many a home might be lit up with the Gospel if the mothers and daughters would only speak the word.

The last time Mr. Sankey and I were in Edinburgh, a father, two sisters and a brother used every morning to take the morning paper and pick my sermon to pieces. They were indignant to think that the Edinburgh people should be carried away with such preaching.

One day one of the sisters, while going by the hall, thought she would drop in and see what class of people went there. She happened to take a seat by a godly lady who said to her, "I hope you are interested in this work."

She tossed her head and said, "Indeed I am not! I am disgusted with everything I have seen and heard."

"Well," said the lady, "perhaps you came prejudiced."

"Yes, and the meeting has not removed any of it, but has rather increased it."

"I have received a great deal of good from them."

"There is nothing here for me. I don't see how an intellectual person can be interested."

To make a long story short, she got the lady to promise to come back. When the meeting broke up, just a little of the prejudice had worn away. She promised to come back again the next day; then after attending three or four more meetings, she became quite interested.

She said nothing to her family. Finally when the burden became too heavy, she told them. They laughed and made her the butt of their ridicule.

One day the two sisters were together, and the other one asked, "Now what have you got at those meetings that you didn't have in the first place?"

"I have a peace that I never knew before. I am at peace with God, myself and the world." And she said, "I have self-control. You know, sister, if you had said half the mean things before I was converted that you have said since, I would have been angry and answered back. But if you can recall, I haven't answered back once since I have been converted."

The sister said, "You certainly have something that I have not." The other told her it was for her too, and she brought the sister to the meetings, where she found peace.

Like Martha and Mary, they had a brother, but he was a member of the University of Edinburgh. He be converted? He go to these meetings? It might do for women, but not for him.

One night they came home and told him that a chum of his own, a member of the University, had stood up and confessed Christ; and when he sat down his brother got up and confessed; and so with the third one.

When the young man heard it, he said, "Do you mean to tell me that he has been converted?"

"Yes."

"Well then, there must be something in it."

He put on his hat and coat and went to see his friend Black. Black got him down to the meetings, and he was converted.

We went to Glasgow. We had not been there six weeks when news came that that young man had been stricken down and died. When he was dying he called his father to his bedside and said, "Wasn't it a good thing that my sisters went to those meetings? Won't you meet me in Heaven, father?"

"Yes, my son, I am so glad you are a Christian; that is the only comfort I have in losing you. I will become a Christian and will meet you again."

I tell this to encourage some sister to go home and carry the message of salvation. It may be that your brother may be taken away in a few months. My dear friends, are we not living in solemn days? Isn't it time for us to get our friends into the kingdom of God? Come, wife, won't you tell your husband? Come, sister, won't you tell your brother? Won't you take up your cross now? The blessing of God will rest on your soul if you will.

While in Wales a lady told me this little story. An English friend of hers, a mother, had a sick child. At first they considered there was no danger, until one day the doctor came in and said that the symptoms were very unfavorable. Taking the mother out of the room, he told her that the child could not live. This came like a thunderbolt.

After the doctor had gone, the mother went into the room where the sick child lay and began to talk to the little one, to try to divert his mind.

"Darling, do you know you will soon hear the music of Heaven? You will hear a sweeter song than you have ever heard on earth. You will hear them sing the song of Moses and the Lamb. You are very fond of music. Won't it be sweet, darling?"

Turning his head away, the little, tired, sick child said, "O mama, I am so tired, so sick that I think it would make me worse to hear all that music."

"Well," the mother said, "you will soon see Jesus. You will see the seraphim and cherubim and the streets all paved with gold." She went on picturing Heaven as described in Revelation.

The little tired child again turned his head away and said, "O mama, I am so tired that I think it would make me worse to see all those beautiful things!"

At last the mother took the child up in her arms and pressed him to her loving heart. Now the little sick one whispered, "O mama, that is what I want! If Jesus will only take me in His arms and let me rest!"

Dear friend, are you not tired and weary of sin? Are you not weary of the turmoil of life? You can find rest on the bosom of the Son of God.

(From the book, *The Overcoming Life,* published by Moody Press, Chicago)

AMZI CLARENCE DIXON
1854-1925

ABOUT THE MAN:

Born on a plantation near Shelby, North Carolina, on July 6, 1854, Amzi Clarence Dixon was a microcosm of an era of Fundamentalism. His father, a Baptist preacher, was a godly man, so young Clarence consistently received the highest caliber of Christian example and training.

Destined to become a great Bible expositor and elegant pulpiteer, A. C. Dixon knew early in life that he must preach the Gospel.

After graduating from Wake Forest College, Dixon served two country churches in North Carolina. Leaving both congregations in a state of revival, he then went to study under John A. Broadus at Southern Baptist Theological Seminary.

Dixon is most often remember for his big-city churches in the North, though he always considered himself a Southerner. He enjoyed powerful and fruitful pastorates at many places, but particularly at the well-known Chicago's Moody Church and London's Metropolital Tabernacle.

During his 10-year ministry at Hanson Place Baptist Church in Brooklyn (1890-1900) Dixon often rented the Brooklyn Opera House for Sunday afternoon evangelistic services.

In 1901, he became pastor of Ruggles Street Baptist Church, Roxbury, Massachusetts, a Boston suburb. Here Dixon taught at the Gordon Bible and Missionary Training School and wrote his famous *Evangelism Old and New*, an attack on the Social Gospel movement.

In 1906 he accepted the pulpit of the Chicago Avenue Church (Moody Memorial Church), and he spent the war years ministering at Spurgeon's Tabernacle in London.

During these years he was conspicuous at Fundamentalist gatherings; he spoke at great Bible conferences.

A. C. Dixon suffered a heart attack and died on June 14, 1925, just one month before the Scopes Trial. Dixon, like many other Fundamentalists, fought the good fight almost to the midnight hour of his life.

VI.

Comfort for the Weak

A. C. DIXON

*"And he said unto me, My grace is sufficient for thee: for my strength
is made perfect in weakness. Most gladly therefore will I rather glory
in my infirmities, that the power of Christ may rest upon me. Therefore
I take pleasure in infirmities, in reproaches, in necessities, in persecutions, in distresses for Christ's sake: for when I am weak, then am I
strong."*—II Cor. 12:9,10.

When a Roman emperor returned from conquest and was given a
triumphant entrance into the Eternal City, it was customary to put a
slave in the chariot with him, whose duty it was to remind him now
and then that he, too, was human. As he looked upon the trophies
of victory and listened to the huzzahs of the people, he must not forget
that he was made of common stuff.

Such was something like the experience of the Apostle Paul. He won
many a victory and was worthy of many a triumphal procession. In the
midst of it all, he was in danger of being exalted above measure. So
God put with him in the chariot of life what he calls a "thorn in the
flesh," a messenger of Satan to buffet him and thus remind him that
he was weak and human.

The word translated "thorn" may be more accurately rendered "stake,"
which was the kind of instrument on which prisoners were impaled when
thrown from a precipice or crucified. It does not mean a splinter under
the fingernail, but an experience like being impaled upon a stake—
unutterable anguish of body or mind.

Just what this thorn in the flesh was, I am not certain. After having
investigated it as thoroughly as possible, I feel a little like the old country preacher who made a sermon on the subject with seven divisions,
each one of which was the opinion of a different commentator, and

closed his sermon with a rousing exhortation in which he insisted that nobody knew what it meant. It is probable, however, that it was a physical weakness which caused Paul intense pain—perhaps soreness of eyes, the result of the blinding on the way to Damascus. Whatever it was, he was very anxious to get rid of it and prayed to the Lord three times that He would remove it. The text is God's answer, in which we have: A Comforting Fact; A Comforting Promise; A Comforting Conclusion; A Comforting Privilege.

I. A Comforting Fact

Every fact to the eye of faith may be comforting because "all things work together for good to them that love God." But the most comforting fact of which I know is in the words, "My strength is made perfect in weakness."

A mother's strength is made perfect in weakness. Should the house be on fire, she could carry out three or four children, whereas, in a quiet time, it would give her pain to lift one. The strength of the United States might be brought out by a war with Russia, but her strength is made more perfect by the weakness of Russia's starving millions. It is better to show our strength by helping the weak than by shaking our fists at little governments like Chile.

A student in the Union Theological Seminary, New York, tells of a sick young man who was brought from the hospital to one of the rooms in the seminary that he might be nursed by some friends among the students. No professor in that seminary did as much good for two or three months as this invalid young man. His weakness called out the strength of the students who were glad to sit up with him all through the night and minister to him; and, as they saw his sweet, submissive and joyful Christian character, they were developed in grace.

We cannot establish a professorship of sympathy in our seminaries; but if such a thing were possible, it would go further than anything else toward making perfect the strength of the rising ministry. Comforting beyond measure is the thought that God's strength is manifested in proportion to my weakness.

II. A Comforting Promise

Paul desired a display of power which should put him beyond the need of grace. God restrained His power that He might make His grace flow forth. We often pray God to use His power when what we most need is His grace; and when He refuses to display His power, we may always claim the promise: "My grace is sufficient for thee." Only sufficient, not superfluous.

Yesterday I sat by the side of a young lady whom the doctor had given up to die. She was almost ashamed to meet God but with a smile declared that she was willing to go, if it was His will. "A year ago, however," she said, "I could not have said that." My reply was, "It was not needful a year ago that you should say it. God's grace is sufficient. He gave you grace then for what you needed; He will give you grace now in the more trying hour."

May God heal her, if it be His will; but whether she is healed or not, she has grace sufficient, and that is better than healing without the grace. It is better to be in need and have God supply the need than to be without need and without His supply.

Robert Hall preached better because he knew what physical suffering meant.

Richard Baxter wrote better because of his bodily infirmity.

Charles Spurgeon did the best work of his life while an invalid.

The sufficiency of His grace appears clear when we think that it comes to us through Jesus Christ. "He was touched with the feeling of our infirmities. Himself took our infirmities and bore our sicknesses." Christ knew what it was to be weary, weak and sick. He put Himself in man's condition that we might know how He could sympathize with us.

Suspecting that the bakers were cheating the poor, starving people, the Grand Duke Sergius, the Governor of Moscow, ordered the police to make an investigation; and they reported in favor of the bakers. Suspecting that something was wrong, the Grand Duke put on the garb of a peasant, went among them, lived as they lived for awhile, and learned for himself the suffering of his poor people. How close it brought the Grand Duke to the starving peasantry, when they learned that, in order to ascertain their wants, he had become as one of them!

And how close it should bring us to Jesus when we reflect that, in order to make plain the sufficiency of His grace, He took upon Himself our very weakness and put Himself in the place of need! For prosperity and adversity, for sickness and health, for riches and poverty, for failure and success, the promise is always good, "My grace is sufficient for thee."

III. A Comforting Conclusion

All conclusions drawn by faith are comforting. Reason is a servant, not a master. It is the most abject slave in the world. It does the bidding of ignorance, of sin, of virtue, of vice, of knowledge, of faith or of unbelief. It has little or no moral sense. It works for those who assert their mastery over it.

I am sick. Unbelief says, "Therefore God does not treat me kindly; life is a failure." Faith says, "God has in this sickness a message of love for me. He may be laying me aside for repairs; He is making a need that He delights to supply."

I have lost by death my dearest friend. Unbelief says, "Therefore God made a mistake." Faith says, "Heaven is now more attractive: I have a treasure there. My friend has been saved from the evil to come. Out of this death may come more good than out of life."

Calamity sweeps away my property. Unbelief says, "Therefore God has forsaken me." Faith says, "God is trying me in the furnace. He wants to get rid of the dross and make the gold in me pure."

Paul draws the conclusion of faith: "Most gladly therefore will I rather glory in my infirmities, that the power of Christ may rest upon me."

The word *rest* means "to abide, as a tent or a house," a protection upon me. The polar bear is in some respects stronger than man. He carries his house about with him. He does not need a covering: the cutting wind and freezing cold do not affect him. He can lie down on a snowbank, with the thermometer below zero, and sleep soundly. But I would rather be a man needing a house and clothing than the polar bear independent of surroundings. I glory in the weakness which calls for protection.

A man in Cuba was brought out to be shot; and just as the soldiers were getting ready to fire, an American standing by took the Stars and Stripes and covered the prisoner with them, saying, "Fire if you dare! To shoot this man is to fire upon the United States government." His life was saved. The power of the United States rested upon him. I think, if I had been in his place, I should have worn that flag on the streets and slept in it at night.

So the power of Christ rests upon us. That prisoner could have declared himself independent of the United States and met the soldiers in his own strength; but foolish would he have been to do so. He let his weakness bring forth the strength of this government. What we need is thus to link our weakness with the power of Christ.

Two kinds of forces are not apt to work well together. Not many years ago the horse was the motive power in this country. Steam soon displaced it, and now it seems that electricity may displace steam. It is difficult to harness the horse and steam together. How would it do to hitch six horses to a steam engine on the way to Chicago? They would be an obstacle on the track.

Yet much of our time is spent in trying to hitch our little strength to the omnipotence of God. Instead of using what we have in supplying the engine with coal and water, submitting to the conditions that make speed and power, we want to put our strength in the front, and thus we become more of a hindrance than a help.

When an electric car stopped in Boston some time ago, one of the passengers asked, "What is the matter?" "Oh!" said the conductor, "Nothing but dirt on the track." The dirt broke the current of power.

Our strength is often but dirt on the track, hindering the work of God. What we need above all things is to realize that we are weak and that God's strength waits to be made perfect in our weakness, for He prefers faith in Him to any sort of reliance upon ourselves.

Therefore we may gladly glory in infirmities. It is natural for some people, however, to look for things about which they may complain. They are like little Tommy, who was crying as if his heart would break, when he suddenly looked up to his mother through his tears, saying, "Mama, what was I crying about?"

"I think, Tommy," she replied, "it was because I would not let you have the bronze statue on the mantelpiece."

"No, that was not it," continued Tommy, still crying: "it was because you would not let me go out in the cold; but I am going to cry some more about that statue," and he promptly raised his boo-hoo.

Tommy was looking for something to cry about. He was not anxious to be happy, but miserable. He wanted to draw a conclusion of pain rather than joy; and if we have that desire, of course we may be gratified.

I am glad that I have not microscopic eyes. My eyes are just good enough to see the light, without seeing the motes in it; the flowers, without beholding the worms; the food and water, without seeing the millions of animalculae that squirm in them.

May we have eyes of faith to see the good and to draw from all the facts of life and the promises of the Word, conclusions that comfort our souls!

IV. A Comforting Privilege

"On which account I take pleasure in infirmities, in reproaches, in necessities, in persecutions, in distresses for Christ's sake." There was a time when Paul did not take pleasure in infirmities. He tells us that he was anxious to get rid of the infirmity that clouded his life. But when he saw that God supplied the grace, he began to love the supply better than freedom from infirmity. He saw that it was better to have darkness with stars brought out by it, than all sunshine and no stars; that the cold winds of winter are as necessary for the world's development as the cheerful warmth of spring and summer; that the mantle of snow is as good for earth as its mantle of grass and flowers. But for the snow mantle, the mantle of flowers might not be.

When a man learns that God's strength is perfected through his infirmity, necessities, persecutions and distresses, he will by and by begin to welcome them as an angel sent from Heaven to minister to him.

Necessity makes most men. If it is necessary that you should go from the $50,000 house on Splendid Street to the $5,000 one on Humble Street, rejoice in the necessity. God has in that necessity some purpose of love deeper and better than if it had never existed.

A French shoemaker was taken prisoner by a Turkish sultan. The sultan, desiring his new palace frescoed, ordered the shoemaker into his presence and commanded him to do the work because, as he said, all Frenchmen were artists.

The shoemaker, however, was artist only with his awl and waxend, in fitting leather to feet, and so remonstrated with the sultan and begged to be excused.

But the sultan said, "Frenchmen are liars as well as artists, and unless you do the work, I will cut off your head."

Thus ended the interview.

The shoemaker, seeing the necessity of painting or dying, decided to learn to paint; and with what help he could gather, toiling night and day, he soon completed the work to the satisfaction of the sultan, who praised him for his skill and gave him his liberty.

This necessity turned the shoemaker into an artist; and but for such a necessity, he would have died with his awl in hand.

The necessities of life make merchants, physicians, statesmen, preachers, mechanics; indeed, are the molding forces transmuting men and women into their better selves.

The things we do not want are often the things we need. What we shrink from—as a child from medicine—may be for our healing.

Here's a story for the children, illustrating this fact.

A little girl was sent to a neighbor's house in a mountain district, to bring home two geese which had been purchased. She had to drive them through a dark wood in the evening twilight. She did not fear the shadows, but beyond the forest was a house with a fierce dog in the yard. This dog she feared, and as she approached the house her little heart was throbbing in her throat.

Suddenly she heard a rattling in the leaves, and a wildcat sprang out upon one of the geese. Not realizing her danger, she rushed to the help of her charge; and the wildcat, leaving the goose, attacked her and was tearing her clothes and flesh, when out from the gate the fierce dog bounded, rushed upon the scene and, seizing the wildcat with his sharp teeth, soon made an end of him. The dog the little girl dreaded was just what she needed. She thought little of the dangers of the woods; the danger that she feared was really her safety.

As we pass through life, amid the shadows that gather about us, we dread the dogs of adversity, of great distress, more than we do the little wildcats of selfishness and sin that waylay us. But our need is sometimes that these very dogs with sharp teeth should have access to us and destroy the things that would destroy us. God knows it, and He turns them loose upon us.

Believe me, Christian, the weights of life may be its wings; the sorrows, its joys; the adversity, its true prosperity; the darkness, its most radiant light. The burdens upon us may be the lever that lifts us up. Take courage, then, under any burden.

> The camel at the close of day
>   Kneels down upon the sandy plain
> To have his burden lifted off,
>   And rest again.
> My soul, thou too shouldst to thy knees
>   When twilight draweth to a close,
> And let thy Master lift the load,
>   And grant repose.
> The camel kneels at break of day
>   To have his guide replace his load,
> Then rises up anew to take
>   The desert road.
> So thou shouldst kneel at morning's dawn,
>   That God may give thee daily care,
> Assured that He no load too great
>   Will make thee bear.

BASCOM RAY LAKIN
1901-1984

ABOUT THE MAN:

On June 5, 1901, a baby boy was born to Mr. and Mr. Richard Lakin in a farmhouse on Big Hurricane Creek in the hill country of Wayne County, West Virginia. Mrs. Lakin had prayed for a "preacher man" and had dedicated this baby to the Lord even before he was born.

Lakin was converted in a revival meeting at age 18. Following his conversion, he became a Baptist preacher. With a mule for transportation, he preached in small country churches in the mountains and hills of West Virginia and Kentucky. The transportation changed as well as the size of his congregations.

In 1939, he became associate pastor of Cadle Tabernacle, Indianapolis, and upon the death of Founder Cadle, became pastor of that once great edifice of evangelism that seated 10,000, and had a choir loft of 1,400. Lakin preached to over 5,000 on Sunday mornings and half that many on Sunday nights.

Cadle Tabernacle had no memberships. It was a radio-preaching center broadcasting from coast to coast. In those fourteen years there, Ray Lakin became a household word across America.

In 1952, he entered full-time evangelism. His ministry carried him around the world, resulting in an estimated 100,000 conversions, and legion the number entering the ministry.

He was the preacher's friend, the church's helper, the common man's leader, and for sixty-five years, God's mighty messenger.

He was one of the most sought-after gospel preachers in America. On March 15, 1984, the last of the old-time evangelists took off for Glory. He would soon have been 83.

VII.

Why Good People Have Trouble

B. R. LAKIN

Satan has always harassed Christians with this question, "Why do good people have trouble?" If the enemy of the souls of men can inject a doubt as to the wisdom of God by asking "Why?" "How?" or "When?" he will have raised a question as to His omniscience.

I wish to point out, by the use of the Scripture, that there are reasons why the righteous suffer and that they all are a part of the beautiful scheme of God's dealing with mankind. Just as in all things that God orders or permits there is design, there is a divine reason for the suffering of God's children.

First of all:

SUFFERING MAY BE "CHASTENING"

"For whom the Lord loveth he chasteneth, and scourgeth every son whom he receiveth."—Heb. 12:6.

Because we as God's children are often disobedient, we need and receive the chastening of our heavenly Father. Chastening may not always be in the form of physical suffering, but often it is.

Not only is chastening of God, but it proves our sonship.

"If ye endure chastening, God dealeth with you as with sons; for what son is he whom the father chasteneth not? But if ye be without chastisement, whereof all are partakers, then are ye bastards, and not sons."—Heb. 12:7,8.

Not only is it God's design that we be chastened, but it is His desire that we 'endure this chastening' as sons.

Many Christians chafe under the chastening hand of God. Satan causes them to ask, "Why?" This "why" reveals a lack of knowledge of our own guilt and unworthiness. For if we would look into the black depths of our hearts and see all of the fleshly selfishness there, we would not wonder that God, through affliction, is trying to purge out the dross of our lives in the "furnace of suffering."

If we could see the end from the beginning, as God does, we would laugh through our tears to see the wonderful improvement which our heavenly Father's chastisement works in our lives.

Children never appreciate correction when they are enduring it; but in later years, when they have children of their own, they gain an appreciation of their father's chastisement and reverence for his discipline which made for better and stronger character.

"Furthermore we have had fathers of our flesh which corrected us, and we gave them reverence: shall we not much rather be in subjection unto the Father of spirits, and live?"—Heb. 12:9.

We would do well to recognize affliction as often being the chastisement of the Lord and make the days of quiet suffering a time for spiritual introspection and inventory.

There is a story of a highland shepherd who grew weary of the "bell sheep" leading the flock into dangerous and precipitous slopes. One day, in desperation, he deliberately broke the sheep's leg; and after it healed, it had learned its lesson. It never walked in forbidden paths again.

Sickness and affliction have often been the processes whereby the Good Shepherd has made His sheep better. As the musician tightens the strings on his violin almost to the breaking point that he might attune them to the harmonies of the infinite, so God, through affliction, tunes His children to Himself that they might sing to the praise of His glory.

Remember that God's chastening is in love and for your profit—"for our profit, that we might be partakers of his holiness" (Heb. 12:10).

David said, "Thy rod and thy staff, they comfort me." It is generally known that the "staff" was used by the shepherd to keep the sheep from getting in "forbidden paths," but the "rod" was used to whip the sheep when he wandered away.

David wisely found comfort in both the staff and the rod. Chastisement in the life of a growing child is just as essential to the development of his character as precept. It is the way we learn that it "does not pay to do wrong."

So chastisement, whether in the form of affliction or anguish in another form, is all in the divine process and is intended for our profit and good. Just as the husbandman cuts back the vines that they might produce better, the Good Husbandman of the skies often lets the knife of affliction fall upon us that we might bear more abundant fruits of righteousness.

SOMETIMES SUFFERING COMES AS A MINISTRY

"But the God of all grace, who hath called us unto his eternal glory by Christ Jesus, after that ye have suffered a while, make you perfect, stablish, strengthen, settle you."—I Pet. 5:10.

Job was called to a ministry of suffering, and his patience in affliction made him an example that has survived the centuries. The world, with its material philosophy, reasons that Christians serve God with an ulterior motive. Job's accuser, Satan, said in effect, "Sure, you serve God! Look at your broad acres of rich soil, your fat herds of cattle and your stout houses and barns. Doth Job serve God for naught?"

But God had called Job to a ministry of suffering, and He permitted Satan to take everything away from him except his life. "And the Lord said unto Satan, Behold, all that he hath is in thy power; only upon himself [his life] put not forth thine hand" (Job 1:12).

Satan took Job's cattle, his herds of sheep, his servants, his children and his houses; but Job arose and said, "The Lord gave, and the Lord hath taken away; blessed be the name of the Lord."

Satan approached the Lord again and said, "All that a man hath will he give for his life. But put forth thine hand now, and touch his bone and his flesh, and he will curse thee to thy face" (Job 2:4,5).

Satan then afflicted Job with boils from the crown of his head to the sole of his feet. He took a potsherd to scrape himself withal, and he sat down among the ashes, but the record says, "In all this did not Job sin with his lips."

Job was a minister of suffering, and his patience in affliction was a greater sermon to the gainsayers of his day than the eloquence of the ancient prophets.

A broken vial of perfume produces more fragrance than a whole one. Sometimes our lives, like the alabaster box, must be shattered by affliction so the beauty of Jesus may be seen in us.

Fanny Crosby lost her eyesight at an early age. Instead of being cynical about her seeming misfortune, she lifted her heart like a nightingale in the gloom of her darkness and sang the hymns that have made her name immortal. She was called to a ministry of suffering and responded to the divine call and became a minister of joyfulness to untold millions.

There was found in an African mine the most magnificent diamond in the history of the world. It was presented to the King of England to shine in the crown of state. It was sent to Amsterdam, the diamond center of the world, to be cut. The greatest lapidary of them all was called in to cut the gem, and what do you suppose he did with it? He cut a notch in it; then, taking a chisel, he struck it a mighty blow, and it fell into two pieces.

"What carelessness!" you say; but not so. For weeks this particular blow had been studied and planned. Charts had been made of the diamond, and experts had discussed how best to cut it to advantage. It was not a mistake; it was a crowning achievement of the diamond-cutting art, for the two gems which were cut from the rough diamond are to-day the pride of the Queen of England and the marvel of the world of jewels.

Perhaps God has allowed a crushing blow to fall upon your life. It may seem, for the moment, to be an appalling mistake. But it isn't. You are "in his hand," and no man can take you out. In His infinite wisdom and love He may allow you to suffer for a season, but He will bring you out as gold "tried by the fire."

More eloquent than the ministry of preaching, singing or teaching is the ministry of suffering. If you are in the "furnace of affliction," then rejoice that He considered you strong enough to endure such a difficult ministry and serve Him faithfully.

SUFFERING IS SOMETIMES TESTING

"And he said unto me, My grace is sufficient for thee: for my strength is made perfect in weakness. Most gladly therefore will I rather glory in my infirmities, that the power of Christ may rest upon me."—II Cor. 12:9.

Affliction is a moral gymnasium where God's children are conditioned for the "race of life." The wise Apostle Paul gloried in his infirmities, for by them His strength was made perfect.

Jeremiah wrote of this great truth:

"Then I went down to the potter's house, and, behold, he wrought

a work on the wheels. And the vessel that he made of clay was marred in the hand of the potter: so he made it again another vessel, as seemed good to the potter to make it."—Jer. 18:3,4.

God ofttimes through affliction molds, shapes and breaks our lives; and from the shapeless mass the worthless clay is fashioned into a thing of usefulness and beauty.

Most of the great men of the centuries were refined and tested in the furnace of affliction.

Paul and Silas, with their backs bleeding and their feet and hands in stocks, might have let that experience in Philippi discourage them; but they dared to "sing at midnight," and the greatest victory of their lives emerged from what seemed to be the greatest defeat.

When "your back is against the wall," you are in an ideal position to fight back at life; and the winner is the one who can take the testings of affliction gracefully, believing implicitly that "all things work together for good to them that love God."

Pearls are beautiful jewels and possess a soft, delicate beauty unsurpassed by any other gems. They are the only costly jewels that have an animal origin. The lowly oyster is the ingenius creator of this gem. A foreign particle (perhaps a sharp piece of sand) finds its way inside the oyster shell. The oyster secretes a solution which covers the foreign particle, and eventually the pearl is formed. It is the child of suffering.

Our heavenly Father permits the foreign particle of affliction to enter our lives. His grace, being sufficient, is lavished upon us; and we are actually made to "glory in our infirmities," for we know that we shall come through the experience with a new radiance to reflect His beauty.

SUFFERING IS A TESTIMONY

The disciples, at the sight of the sightless young man, said, "Who did sin, this man, or his parents?" Jesus answered, "Neither . . . but, that the works of God should be made manifest."

Affliction gives the Christian the opportunity to make the works of God manifest. God either gives healing grace or grace to endure. In the case of the man born blind, it was the works of God manifest in the miracle of healing, and God's name was glorified. But with Paul, who suffered from a bodily infirmity, God gave him the grace of endurance, thus comprising a miracle as great as that of healing.

I believe in divine healing, but I believe God often permits His children to suffer so the world may see the sweetness with which His children are able to endure their infirmities.

To an inexperienced eye, a synthetic diamond is as brilliant as the genuine. But when these two stones are placed under water, the synthetic stone loses its brilliance while the genuine gains in luster.

God sometimes leads His children through the "waters of affliction" that the world may behold our brilliance in the hour of trouble.

> **Some through the water,**
> **Some through the flood;**
> **Some through the fire,**
> **But all through the blood.**
> **Some through great sorrow,**
> **But God gives a song**
> **In the night season and**
> **All the day long.**

Yes, the Architect of our destinies allows nothing to come to our lives except that which is for our ultimate good and blessing.

We can never realize that we have fully seen the Lord until we behold Him in the valley of the shadow of death. It is then that we can trustfully say, "I will fear no evil: for thou art with me."

It is in the midst of life's storms that we hear His blessed words, "Peace be still!" Not until we pass through some bereavement, suffering or persecution, do we fully appreciate the divine presence which sustains, comforts and gives peace in the tempest.

Christ comes so much nearer the soul in the valley than He does on the mountaintop. His presence is more keenly felt in the Desert of Suffering than it is in the Garden of Prosperity. It was in the Desert of Affliction that God spoke to Moses from the burning bush and caused him to make that great decision of "choosing rather to suffer affliction with the people of God, than to enjoy the pleasures of sin for a season" (Heb. 11:25).

The night seasons of suffering increase our spiritual vision and help us to see life in its true perspective. You may think you can see farther in the daytime than you can at night, but you can't. At night you can see the stars, and the nearest star is millions of miles away. God, in His infinite wisdom, knows when to draw the curtains of night over the soul, that in the gloom of affliction our spiritual vision may be increased and the beauty of our lives enhanced.

SUFFERING IS PARTICIPATION WITH CHRIST

"And if children, then heirs; heirs of God, and joint-heirs with Christ; if so be that we suffer with him, that we may be also glorified together."—Rom. 8:17.

Suffering with Christ! What a blessed privilege! The disciples rejoiced that their sufferings for Christ's sake identified them with the Lord. "And they departed from the presence of the council, rejoicing that they were counted worthy to suffer shame for his name" (Acts 5:41).

Christ was a man of sorrows and acquainted with grief. If we are to be identified with Him, we must be resigned to suffer for and with Him.

On a journey we are not so much concerned with the comforts en route as we are the joys upon the arrival at our destination. This world is not our home. We are as aliens in a strange land on our journey Home. Because "we are not of the world," the world hates us. It conspires to tear down our good name and thus rob Him, who saved us, of glory. We should be tolerant with a world which does not and cannot understand the mysteries of the things of God. We should remember Jesus' words, "Blessed are ye, when men shall revile you, and persecute you, and shall say all manner of evil against you falsely, for my sake" (Matt. 5:11).

They rejoice in our afflictions and begrudge what little prosperity we enjoy, but thank God, Jesus said, "Rejoice, and be exceeding glad: for great is your reward in heaven."

In these experiences, which may be inclined to make us cynical, we become participants with Christ. Christ was hated; we are hated. Christ was smitten; we are smitten. Christ was crucified; He said, "If any man will come after me, let him deny himself, and take up his cross, and follow me." Christ was afflicted; we are afflicted. He was wounded, bruised and chastised; but as a sheep led to the slaughter, "he opened not his mouth." His retort to their mockings and railings was, "Father, forgive them, for they know not what they do."

If we are to participate with Christ and be identified with Him, our reaction to persecution, suffering and affliction will be one of complete resignation to the will of God.

"For we which live are alway delivered unto death for Jesus' sake, that the life also of Jesus might be made manifest in our mortal flesh."—II Cor. 4:11.

Life is made more effulgent by suffering, pain and death. The singer with a broken heart sings with greater feeling and pathos than the one who has never tasted suffering.

The rose bush is "cut" in order that it may blossom more beautifully. We are persecuted, maligned and afflicted that we may be recreated in the image of Christ. Disappointment is often His appointment; and "All things work together for good to them that love God."

Why do the righteous suffer? Ah, the reasons are legion. But rest assured that no heartache, disappointment or affliction ever comes to the heart of one of God's children without His order and permission.

I watched some stone workers hewing an odd-shaped stone as it lay on the ground. "What are you going to do with that?" I asked. "We are cutting it here, so it will fit in up there," the worker answered, pointing to an opening high on the tower of the great building.

In our affliction down here, the Master is shaping and fashioning us according to His omniscient design, so we will fit in up There.

(From *50 Years of Plowing, Planting, and Watering*—Life Story of B. R. Lakin by Wm. K. McComas)

BRUCE D. CUMMONS
1924-

ABOUT THE MAN:

Dr. Bruce D. Cummons is founder and pastor of the Massillon Baptist Temple of Massillon, Ohio, and is currently in his fortieth year in that ministry. He is also president of Massillon Baptist College and administrator of Massillon Christian School.

Pastor Cummons was born in Parkersburg, West Virginia, July 25, 1924, and grew up there.

After three years of service in the Navy during World War II, he enrolled in and graduated from McKim Technical Institute of Akron, Ohio. Mr. Cummons then felt the call of God upon his life to preach the Gospel, and graduated from Bible Baptist Seminary of Fort Worth, Texas, under the leadership and training of Dr. J. Frank Norris and Dr. Louis Entzminger. Pastor Cummons also holds an honorary degree of Doctor of Divinity from BBS.

Dr. Cummons is also a graduate of Christian Writer's Institute of Chicago, Illinois, and is the author of over 35 books and booklets; several of these have been translated into other languages.

He is the Editor of the *Baptist Reporter,* and sermons from the *Reporter* have been reprinted in a number of periodicals, circulation numbering in the hundreds of thousands. In addition to the pastorate, he has conducted over 250 revival meetings, Bible conferences, and Faith-Promise mission conferences during his years of ministry.

For some twenty years of his ministry the "Grace and Peace" radio broadcast was aired over 40 to 50 stations, including overseas stations, all of which covered 80% of the land area of the world.

Today, the Massillon Baptist Temple has over 4,000 members, and averages 1200 per Sunday in Sunday School.

Pastor Cummons and his wife, Wanda, have been married for 43 years and have three daughters and nine grandchildren.

One of Pastor Cummons' favorite statements is: "God has been mighty good to this preacher! To God be the glory; great things He hath done!"

VIII.

An Answer to All of
Life's Problems

BRUCE CUMMONS

"As soon as Jesus heard the word that was spoken, he saith unto the ruler of the synagogue, Be not afraid, only believe."—Mark 5:36.

Life is filled with problems. Problems of ill health and ill-tempered people. Problems of financial adversity and the mad pace of endeavoring to keep up with the mounting bills caused by a growing family. Problems of strong temptations that threaten to overwhelm us. Problems of a broken home. A problem that all must face in its appointed time is man's last great enemy, Death. Problems aplenty, from the cradle to the grave.

If I were to tell you that there is one chapter in the Bible that covers EVERY PROBLEM YOU WILL EVER HAVE TO FACE from the cradle to the grave, would it not be worthwhile to study that particular chapter to find the answer to life's problems? This chapter not only deals with every problem man faces in life, but shows man how to face these problems and to emerge victorious in every circumstance!

It is chapter 5 of the Gospel according to Mark.

Of course, the Bible in its entirety has much to say about man and the multitude of difficulties and problems he faces along life's way. Yet it seems that the Holy Spirit summed them all up in this one brief chapter so that the poor sojourner of life, not well acquainted with the Bible, could turn to this one simple passage and find the answer to his particular problem.

The chapter, though short, is too long to reproduce here; so let us take a look at each of these problems in the order in which they appear in Mark 5, and then see how each was dealt with.

The first problem is the greatest and leads to the Bible solution of all others. This is the major problem man faces in life; and if he is not willing to face this difficulty and settle it in the right way, then there is no further answer to any of the heartaches of life.

The first major problem is

SIN!

The first seventeen verses of Mark 5 relate the story of a demon-possessed man. He lived among the tombs. This is where all sinners are considered to live; by the Word of God they are considered to be "dead in trespasses and sins."

Strong chains couldn't bind him. And certainly the powers of sin and Satan and demon-possession cannot be bound by the puny efforts of man.

He was "naked and undone," as are all sinners before God; and he was constantly torturing himself by the ravages of sin.

Here is the perfect picture of the sinner—lost, helpless to help himself and hopeless until he meets Jesus!

Sinner friend, this is the biggest problem you will ever have to face in life; and unless you are willing to settle this sin problem, you will go through life wasting all your years trying to cope with the burdens, heartaches and the difficulties, yet never finding a solution. You will die a disillusioned, disappointed, disheartened sinner and plunge into eternal Hell to suffer the pangs of the frustrated damned forever!

You may be just as bound by the sin of gambling or of drink as this demoniac was bound by the powers of Satan. Multitudes are bound today by lust, jealousy, hatred, "dope," dishonesty or the "nicer" sins of pride, self-righteousness, self-esteem, selfishness or unbelief; but they are all of Satan and lead a sinner to eternal Hell!

Psychiatry is a thriving practice. They tell us that one out of every ten will spend some time in a mental institute during his lifetime. Multitudes are resorting to the psychiatrist's couch and paying a high price for someone to listen to their problems and burdens. My friend, the world needs to learn the simple truths of Mark 5.

Confessing sins to man does not rid a person of the guilt of sin and, as has been proven again and again, it does not relieve the conscience of its guilt complex! There is only One who can forgive us our sins, cleanse us of our sins and take away all the "guilt complex," and that

One is Jesus! Christ is the One who paid our sin debt, and He is the One who cancels that debt as we place a personal faith in Him.

The demoniac was quick to learn this. He found the answer to the problem of sin and of demon-possession when he came to Jesus!

We read in verse 6, "But when he saw Jesus afar off, he ran and worshipped him." In the following passage he acknowledged Christ to be God and the Son of God. That's it! That's the answer!

He knew his own need and that he was unable personally to change his circumstances. He recognized Christ as the Son of God, the Saviour who could help him. He believed on the Lord and brought his burden of sin to Him and found the answer in Christ!

O sinner friend, believe me, but better yet, believe the Bible: you will never be able to settle your problems of sin nor to get rid of the weight of sin and the overwhelming control of Satan, until you acknowledge Christ to be your personal Saviour and settle things with Him! When you do this, you will find all you need to meet every sin and temptation.

The next great problem Mark 5 deals with is the problem of

THE HOME.

How much time is used by busy pastors in dealing with difficulties in the homes of the people unto whom he ministers!

The demoniac, now saved, sane and sober, wanted to go along with Jesus. That's a really good sign of genuine conversion! He "prayed him that he might be with him [Jesus] . . ." (vs. 18).

But rather than take him along with Him in His earthly ministry, Jesus said, "Go home . . ." (vs. 19). Until now this man couldn't "go home." One in his condition would tear up a home. Furniture smashed, lamps broken, windows kicked out, the wife crying and screaming in terror, and the children hiding under the bed when the power of the demons was upon him.

As a pastor, I've tried to help homes after the husband would come in drunk and begin his rampage. The children and wife would run off to the neighbors. It isn't a pleasant sight to go into a home where the new couch has been burned with cigarettes, the picture window has been broken, the furniture is in shambles and where dirty, hungry, white-faced children stand in a corner and tremble for fear!

If it isn't drink, an unruly temper breaks out in vile cursing and tantrum, and the home becomes an insane asylum for the duration. When the Devil gets into a person and sets out to break up a home, he will accomplish it about every time, unless people invite Jesus into their hearts and into their homes!

Other times it may be unfaithfulness to the marriage vows on the part of the husband or the wife. But in the final analysis, the home problem comes right back to the sin problem, a problem that can only be fixed by settling it with the Saviour. I firmly believe that every home problem can be solved with Christ in the hearts of mother and dad.

God gives a perfect plan for the home, and His plan cannot fail.

By God's good grace and through the power of the Word and the Gospel, I have seen many homes that were nearly broken, and others that were broken, brought back together and changed from a literal "hell on earth" to a little "heaven on earth." It has not been by my ability as a "marriage counselor"; it has been by Christ and His Gospel saving and changing people and uniting hearts in love. That has salvaged many a home from the "rocks."

In our mind's eye we can see this man, now made whole by Jesus, returning home to his friends and loved ones. The wife looks out the window and says, "Children, here comes your father!" The children run to the bedroom and crawl under the bed or hide in the closets. But mother says, "Don't run, little ones; come and look! Daddy's all dressed up. His hair is combed, he's clean shaven, and he's smiling! Come, look! Something sure has happened to your father!"

He enters the home and begins to bubble out the story. "Honey, it's wonderful! I met the Lord, and He changed my life and made me whole. He gave me a new life and made me sane and sober. I'm no longer a wild man! Sweetheart, you've got a new husband! Kiddies, you've got a new daddy! Things will be different now!"

With his arms around his wife and the children hugging their father's knees, a home is brought back together, because Jesus has entered a heart and life.

This is what could well have happened when Jesus said to this man, "Go home. . . ." I've been blessed by the Lord to see this happen again and again in homes down through the years of my ministry!

Dear friend, there is an answer to your home problem, and that is in CHRIST! Believe it, will you?

The third great problem that people face along the way of life is the problem of

POVERTY.

As Jesus went on His way to help a man by the name of Jairus, He was delayed by another who also was in great need.

A woman, who had been ill for twelve long years with "an issue of blood," came to Jesus as He passed by. This woman was poverty stricken. Verse 26 tells us that she "had spent all that she had," yet her need was not supplied.

How many today have spent every penny they can lay their hand to, yet haven't enough to buy bread and meat for their hungry children!

You may say, "Now, preacher, surely you aren't going to say that Jesus is able to put bread and meat on my table, give me a job and supply all my material needs!" Yes, my friend, that is exactly what I am going to say!

There is not a faithful member of the church that I pastor who today does not live in a better home, wear better clothes, drive a better car and make more money than he did before he got saved!

You see, the sinner wastes his money on booze, cigarettes and other foolish things of the world. He loses work because of his dissipation. But after he gets saved, he can dress his whole family in better clothes because the liquor traffic doesn't get it. The average smoking family burns up from five to seven dollars a week in tobacco. When the family gets saved, that money may go into bread and milk.

Then when you become a faithful partner with God and begin to give joyfully at least a tithe of what God gives you, you can be sure He always pays it back bountifully! Some Christians do not believe this, so they go on spending God's money on themselves and wondering why He doesn't bless them more.

If you will trust Christ to save your soul and tell Him your financial and material needs, you will find that He will take care of you and provide even miraculously when He needs to, so that your need will be supplied.

Massillon is a steel town. A few years ago a great number of men were out of work. Some of our good folk of the church were getting into desperate straits. Some were fearful of losing their homes. Some felt they would have to move to another area to find work. It was a trying, testing time.

I called for noonday prayer meetings just to pray for this one particular burden—the need of jobs for the men of our church. This proved to be a wonderful testimony to the truth I had been preaching to our people down through the years.

To the best of my knowledge, every man who attended those noon-day prayer meetings soon went back to work or found other occupations, whether in the steel industry or in other industries.

One young couple who were about to lose their home didn't lose it. Today they are active in the Sunday school work of the church and working steadily.

Another couple, who had been "up and down" financially for years, came to these special prayer meetings; just recently they told me that he hadn't missed a day of work since then!

I couldn't name the number of times men have reminded me of those prayer meetings and the result in steady employment because God still lives and hears and answers prayer.

Circumstances may vary according to the area of the land in which we live, but I am confident that the God who fed Elijah during the days of drought can still provide for His own. It may not be "venison from the forest"; it may be bologna from the supermarket, but He will supply all your needs according to His riches in glory. The bank of Heaven isn't broke yet!

This has been proven in my very life. During Bible school days, it was often a question as to where the next meal was coming from, yet it always arrived in time.

During the days of organizing the work of the Baptist Temple, there were trying and testing times, many days with little or no income. But I've walked with the Lord for many years; and since He has never yet failed to supply my needs, I'm certain that I can trust Him the rest of the way.

The fourth problem we see in this marvelous passage is the problem of

SICKNESS.

I have stated many times in private and from my pulpit that I believe many people suffer physical sickness in one form or another who do not need to be sick!

Certainly some are sick, as Jesus said of the man born blind, "for the glory of God." When the mighty Apostle Paul suffered a physical infirmity, God said, "My grace is sufficient for thee." Trophimus and Timothy both suffered times of sickness, as did others of Bible days.

So it would be foolish to say that every illness in a Christian is because of sin or of disobedience.

Let us not be too quick to judge a brother when he becomes ill and begin to probe to see if we can discern some "sin" in his life for which God is punishing him. Not all sickness is chastisement. Some is for God's own purpose and glory. Some may be chosen, as was Paul, to be a special vessel of God for suffering (Acts 9:16).

However, I believe many could enjoy good health if again they would bring it to Jesus and learn to trust Him.

This woman had suffered a physical disease for twelve years and had spent everything she had on physicians, but she was still sick.

When she, by faith, pushed through the crowd and touched His garment, immediately she was made whole. Jesus said to her, "Daughter, thy faith hath made thee whole. . . ." This was a touch of faith!

My friend, never mind what the crowd says, nor how much they stand in the way. Make sure you know Jesus first of all in the salvation of your soul and in the pardon of your sins, then learn to bring every need to Him and trust Him to supply your need!

During my ministry I have seen many who were restored to health and to service for Christ. Some were restored gradually and over a period of time. Others were restored immediately and were never bothered with that problem again.

This certainly is not to discredit good doctors and the many who work so faithfully in hospitals and in other places relieving the suffering and helping them on their way to recovery. In my busy rounds of visiting the sick and the shut-ins, in homes, rest homes and hospitals, I have come to know many very fine doctors. Three I know are professing Christians, and I am sure they are doing the work the Lord would have them do.

The other day my little girl fell on the way home from school, running her teeth through her lip. I took her to a doctor whom we have known for many years. He put three stitches in her lip. The stitches will keep the lip from being scarred and ill-shapen. Certainly we should all appreciate what medical science can do. But it was the Lord who caused it to knit and heal.

However, this woman in Mark 5 had been to many physicians, and was still ill. Not medical science; only the Lord could meet her need.

A number of years ago I sustained a back injury while working at the church (when I was the janitor as well as the pastor). It was a very painful injury and caused me much discomfort for some years. In the doctor's language, the X-ray showed "a minimal thinning of an injured disc," and I was informed that it might necessitate surgery in the future.

Then began to develop, as is often the case, arthritis of the feet, hands and back. During the process of a few years I went to five different doctors, trying to get some relief. "Rheumatoid arthritis" was the verdict. I realized that I was on the way to becoming a cripple.

When I got up in the morning, my feet would pain. I had to stand on them for a little while before I could walk. While typing, my wrists hurt like boils. After completing a day of preaching, I was completely exhausted. My pain-wracked body felt like crying out, "I can't go on like this!"

My good men of the church listed the matter on their prayer lists, but the problem continued.

One morning about 4:00 a.m., unable to sleep, I went to my study, opened the Bible to the Gospel according to Mark, got down on my knees and began to read. God broke my heart that morning. My tears fell upon the pages of the Book. As I studied Mark 5, I prayed something like this: "O God, if You will me to preach in a wheelchair, I'm willing. If You will me to be a cripple, Lord, I want Thy will. Whatever is Your decree, I will be satisfied. But Lord, Thou didst save me and call me to preach, and I believe that I can be a better preacher with a strong, healthy body. I know that Thou art able to make me well. Wilt Thou do this for me in the name of my blessed Saviour, and for His sake? I promise to give Thee all the glory!"

It seemed that the Lord was speaking to my heart and saying, "Can you trust Me?" In those early hours it seemed that the Bible was written just for me and that Christ was dealing with me through His Word about this very problem that had plagued me for so long. I said, "Yes, Lord, I can trust Thee!"

I went back to bed. A week passed, then a month, then two months. Then my wife said, "You haven't been complaining lately about any pain. How are you feeling?" I answered, "Honey, I've been waiting for you to notice this. I haven't been complaining because I haven't any pain to complain about!" Then I told her about that early morning prayer meeting over the Gospel according to Mark.

Several years have gone by, God is my witness and to Him be the glory: I have no pain, there has been no need for surgery, and I preach as many times on Sunday as I get a chance to! I preach in revival meetings all over this land. I don't know what it is to have an arthritic pain or even a headache! I can run, hunt, climb, play ball, and I'm the one who leads the calisthenics at youth camp each summer!

I've kept my word to God and have given this word of testimony time and again. I do want people to know that my Lord is able to hear and answer prayer and to meet all of life's problems, if people will but learn to trust Him!

Then, in the fifth place, there is that problem of

DEATH.

Unless Jesus comes for us, we must all face that time of physical death.

Jesus finally comes to the home of Jairus and is greeted with the word that his twelve-year-old daughter is dead. The servants said, "Thy daughter is dead: why troublest thou the Master any further?" (vs. 35). But notice the next precious word from our Lord: "Be not afraid, only believe"! (vs. 36).

You see, death is no trouble to the Master, for He conquered Death, Hell and the grave for us! He is the Victor over Death, and so are all who have received Him as Saviour.

A twelve-year-old Christian girl and a member of the church I pastor, was injured in an accident a few years ago. It didn't seem to be too serious. I went to the hospital late in the evening to see her and said, "Martha, how are you feeling now?" She answered, "Not very good, Brother Cummons. Oh, but with Jesus I'm all right; other than that, I'm not very good." Yes, thank God, with Jesus it's always all right for the child of God!

I had prayer with the little girl and went home. The next morning I was surprised to hear that she had passed away during the night. The hospital said evidently a blood clot had suddenly formed and she was gone.

I used for the funeral service this text from Mark, about the little twelve-year-old girl who had died; how it was no trouble at all to Jesus. I told the parents that this death of their precious one was no problem to Jesus, either; that He had just reached down from Glory and said, "Come on home with Me, Martha. I need you up here in Heaven with Me now." I gave them the comforting thought that one blessed day He will again reach down from Glory and say, "Damsel, I say unto thee, arise" (vs. 41)!

Death is no problem to Christ, nor to the Christian. The body dies and goes back to the earth, and the soul and spirit of the child of God go to be with Jesus until the morning of the resurrection when He will raise from the grave a new, glorified, immortal body, fashioned after the likeness of His own! Should this present a problem to the child of God? No!

My friend, every problem you will ever face, from the cradle to the grave, falls under one of these five categories:

The problem of SIN.

The problem of the HOME.

The problem of POVERTY.

The problem of SICKNESS.

The problem of DEATH.

The only way you will ever be able to face these problems victoriously is by knowing Christ as your personal Saviour and by learning to trust Him in the midst of every trial.

I do urge you to believe that Christ died for your sins, was buried and was raised again the third day, and that He will save you right now, if you will believe on Him.

Then you will join the host of Christian folk who have learned to walk with Christ from earth to Glory, without fear of the problems of life.

JAMES HALL BROOKES
1830-1897

ABOUT THE MAN:

James Hall Brookes was born in 1830 in North Carolina.

He attended Miami University (Ohio) and Princeton Theological Seminary where he graduated in 1854. He was ordained as a Presbyterian minister and was pastor of Walnut Street Presbyterian Church in St. Louis, Missouri for 39 years.

He was the founder of *Truth or Testimony for Christ,* and was editor for 23 years.

He was the author of between 250 and 300 tracts and pamphlets.

He died in 1897 at the age of 67.

IX.

The Mystery of Bodily Suffering!

JAMES H. BROOKES

All who believe in the providence and Word of God recognize His hand in sickness or in other physical ailments and discomforts. The Lord Jesus did not exaggerate in the least when He said, *"Are not two sparrows sold for a farthing? and one of them shall not fall on the ground without your Father. But the very hairs of your head are all numbered"* (Matt. 10:29,30).

Nothing apparently is more casual than the tossing of pebbles into a cap or urn; yet even these are under divine direction. "The lot is cast into the lap; but the whole disposing thereof is of the Lord" (Prov. 16:33).

A soldier in the tumult of battle "drew a bow at a venture," but it sped to the accomplishment of Jehovah's predicted purpose (II Chron. 18:19-33).

Joseph's brethren threw him into a pit, from which he emerged to enter a dungeon; but God sent him before them to preserve life (Gen. 45:5).

The omnipresence, the omniscience, the omnipotence, the very existence of God, make it certain that He touches everything everywhere, whether with or without secondary causes; and any other view is as unphilosophical and unscientific as it is unscriptural. It is absurd, therefore, to suppose that sickness or any bodily suffering comes upon us by accident or by the iron rule of a natural law that knows no master and has no object.

I. GOD DISCIPLINES THROUGH SICKNESS!

Sometimes it is sent as a chastening. "The Lord struck the child that Uriah's wife bare unto David, and it was very sick" (II Sam. 12:15).

It was well with the child, for it was safely sheltered in the bosom of Him who struck it; but the blow was designed to reach the father's heart.

"For this cause many are weak and sickly among you, and many sleep. For if we would judge ourselves, we should not be judged. But when we are judged, we are chastened of the Lord, that we should not be condemned with the world."—I Cor. 11:30-32.

The intervention of natural law does not in the least obscure His hand, according to the plain testimony of the Holy Spirit of truth.

"It came to pass about ten days after, that the Lord smote Nabal, and he died."—I Sam. 25:38.

"David said furthermore, as the Lord liveth, the Lord shall smite him."—I Sam. 26:10.

"The Lord smote the king, so that he was a leper unto the day of his death."—II Kings 15:5.

"Neither did Jeroboam recover strength again in the days of Abijah: and the Lord struck him, and he died."—II Chron. 13:20.

"Thou hidest thy face, they are troubled: thou takest away their breath, they die, and return to their dust."—Ps. 104:29.

"Immediately the angel of the Lord smote him, because he gave not God the glory: and he was eaten of worms, and gave up the ghost."—Acts 12:23.

Thus it is all through the Bible; and he who reads the Book of God with an understanding heart must see His presence and power in every form of disease, whether commissioned to minister to the good of His people or sent to punish the proud and unbelieving.

Men are ready to accept a general providence while denying a particular—as if there could be any general without particulars, or as if little things were not essential to the production of great results. They admit that God brings about the revolution of kingdoms, which rise and fall like corks stuck with feathers in the game of shuttlecock; but they do not perceive that no event, connected with the end in view, can fly beyond the bounds of His providence.

He, however, is very explicit in asserting His control of all occurrences, either by His positive or permissive decrees.

"See now that I, even I, am he, and there is no god with me: I kill,

and I make alive; I wound, and I heal."—Deut. 32:39.

"The Lord killeth, and maketh alive: he bringeth down to the grave, and bringeth up. The Lord maketh poor, and maketh rich: he bringeth low, and lifteth up."—I Sam. 2:6,7.

"He doeth according to his will in the army of heaven, and among the inhabitants of the earth: and none can stay his hand, or say unto him, What doest thou?"—Dan. 4:35.

"Shall there be evil in a city, and the Lord hath not done it?"—Amos 3:6.

Nothing more perhaps need be said to those who bow before the authority of the sacred Scriptures to convince them that their bodily afflictions, no matter how sore they may be, are to be traced directly or indirectly to the will of God. Why He permits them is another question; and what Christians are to do when smarting under His stroke is a question of very great importance.

II. ERRORS IN THE "IT'S ALWAYS GOD'S WILL TO HEAL" TEACHING

Thousands of godly and sincere people insist that the prayer of faith, if followed by anointing with oil, will rebuke and remove disease—and hence that all medical or remedial agencies should be discarded because their use implies a lack of confidence in the power and willingness of God to heal. Many of them claim, and no doubt truthfully, that they have been cured of divers maladies in answer to prayer; and they do not see why the benefits they have received should not be extended to others and, indeed, to all sufferers.

1. The Success of the Cultists

But if we would calmly and intelligently consider this subject, which is of vital moment to the sick, it must not be forgotten that similar claims, substantiated by abundant evidence, are put forth by those with whom the Christian can have no fellowship.

Spiritualists, manifestly led by Satan, point with triumph to the numbers healed of deadly diseases by mediums.

Christian Science, so-called, that is not Christian but wholly devilish in its blasphemous assertions and teachings, can tell of thousands who have been restored to health by their mutterings.

Heaps of abandoned crutches and other memorials of conquered disease at Lourdes, France, attest the reality of the benefit received by the pilgrims who crowd together for healing from the Virgin Mary.

Scores of educated men and women bear witness to the healing power wielded by an utterly fanatical sect known as "Overcomers," and marvelous cures are constantly reported as emanating from similar sources.

Of course it is not intimated that these indisputable facts disprove the genuineness of the cures wrought by the instrumentality of brethren who stand on much higher and holier ground. But they show that the believer should not be moved from Scripture by mere success.

Long ago it was ordained that if a prophet give a sign or a wonder and "the sign or the wonder come to pass," his prophecy was to be despised and he himself put to death when he turned the people from the Lord (Deut. 13:1-5). He tells us that the time is coming when false Christs and false prophets "shall show great signs and wonders; insomuch that, if it were possible, they shall deceive the very elect" (Matt. 24:24); and under the Antichrist, the false prophet

"doeth great wonders, so that he maketh fire come down from heaven on the earth in sight of men, And deceiveth them that dwell on the earth by the means of those miracles which he had power to do in the sight of the beast."—Rev. 13:13,14.

2. Most "Cures" Are "Mental"

Most of the cures wrought by faith healing, as it is called, are of a nervous and hysterical character. Persons of morbid temperament can easily imagine that they have spinal disease or cancer or tumor or consumption or any other malady; and to them it is a horrible reality for a time. Anything that will take their minds away from themselves and lead them to believe that restoration is possible is usually an effective remedy.

But a true child of God would rather be sick than resort to methods that dishonor the Lord Jesus Christ and are contrary to His Word. Nor will he permit pious frauds, perpetrated in the interests of a theory, to go unrebuked. Thus when a person arose in a great faith healing meeting and declared that a diseased eye had been removed from his head but, as a result of his faith and anointing, God had put a new eye in the empty socket and healed the other eye, which was almost blind, every honest man, and particularly every Christian present, ought to have denounced the imposter.

3. A "Misrepresented" Commission

Our faith healing brethren as a general thing go too far or they do not go far enough. They lay great stress upon the power the Lord gave His apostles to heal the sick, but the commission extends much beyond this.

"Heal the sick, cleanse the lepers, raise the dead, cast out devils."— Matt. 10:8.

"In my name shall they cast out devils; they shall speak with new tongues; They shall take up serpents; and if they drink any deadly thing, it shall not hurt them; they shall lay hands on the sick, and they shall recover."—Mark 16:17,18.

Those who claim supernatural power in the exercise of faith do not pretend to cleanse the lepers, to raise the dead, to drink poison; yet surely they ought to be able to do these things as well as to heal, if they are acting under the apostolic commission.

4. Today's "Results" Are Different

The cures wrought by the Lord Jesus and the apostles were instantaneous and complete. There was no slow and imperfect recovery, as with nearly all modern faith healers, nor were there any failures except in one instance of unbelief, when a father brought his son, grievously tormented by a foul spirit, to the disciples "that they should cast him out; and they could not" (Mark 9:18).

But the failures in the faith healing of our day are vastly in excess of the number cured. The public knows only of those who have been restored to health, while perhaps every experienced pastor in the country is acquainted with some who have resorted in vain to this method of restoration. Probably not one in one hundred receive any permanent benefit from the professional faith healers, and the disappointed sufferers are tempted to despair, lest the failure is to be found in their lack of faith.

5. The "Gift" Is Not for All

The gift of healing is not bestowed upon all, as generally believed and taught. It is plainly written,

"To one is given by the Spirit the word of wisdom; to another the word of knowledge by the same Spirit; To another faith by the same Spirit; to another the gifts of healing by the same Spirit. . . . Are all apostles? are all prophets? are all teachers? are all workers of miracles? Have all the gifts of healing? do all speak with tongues? do all interpret?"—I Cor. 12:8,9,29,30.

If we were to admit, then, that the gift of healing was not confined to the times of the apostles, but that it might be bestowed now if there were faith to receive the power, it does not follow that everyone has the gift or that every sufferer can be relieved. Therefore, the assertions so often heard or read, that anybody who has faith can heal or be healed, are utterly unscriptural, as is the common disregard of the injunction, "Is any sick among you? let him call for the elders of the church; and let them pray over him, anointing him with oil in the name of the Lord" (James 5:14). A devout man or a pious woman, going about to call for the sick and to anoint them often unsolicited, can by no possible stretch of the imagination be converted into the elders of the church.

6. A Key Element in Prayer Is Missing

In praying for the sick it is easy to lose sight of an essential feature of prayer. The Son of God could pray when His sweat was as it were great drops of blood falling down to the ground and as if He would give a touching example to His suffering followers,

"Abba, Father, all things are possible unto thee; take away this cup from me: nevertheless not what I will, but what thou wilt."—Mark 14:36.

"This is the confidence that we have in him, that, if we ask any thing according to his will, he heareth us."—I John 5:14.

Without submission to the will of God as infinitely right and infinitely wise, prayer is not prayer; and one is often shocked by an exhibition among the faith healers of a rashness and irreverence of demand that would

Snatch from His hand the balance and the rod,
Re-judge His justice, be the god of God.

A pastor at an early period in his ministry was summoned to visit a young mother who was in unutterable grief and distress by the dangerous illness of her little boy. The servant of Christ tried to console her and at length kneeled beside her quivering form and beside the cradle to pray. He asked the Lord that, if it were possible, if at all according to His will, if it were best for the sufferer and best for the mother, He would spare the child.

She grasped him by the arm in the midst of the prayer, saying, "I did not send for you to pray in that manner. I care not what God's will is; my will is that he shall live. I will not, oh, I will not give up my child!"

Strange to say, the child recovered; and the same mother lived to learn that the same child was swung from the gallows for murder.

Let us understand, as a first and fundamental principle of truth, that the Lord's will is always best; and though we may not be able to hear His voice when distracted by pain nor to see His meaning when blinded by tears, He is still saying, "What I do thou knowest not now; but thou shalt know hereafter" (John 13:7).

7. Even the Apostles Experienced Failure

Even the apostles could not always heal, nor were they exempt from the law of bodily suffering. At one time Paul was so used to restoring health "that from his body were brought unto the sick handkerchiefs or aprons, and the diseases departed from them, and the evil spirits went out of them" (Acts 19:12).

At another time he writes, "Trophimus have I left at Miletum sick" (II Tim. 4:20).

At one time he shook a viper into the fire that had fastened on his hand and felt no harm (Acts 28:3-5).

At another time he writes:

"There was given to me a thorn in the flesh, the messenger of Satan to buffet me, lest I should be exalted above measure. For this thing I besought the Lord thrice, that it might depart from me. And he said unto me, My grace is sufficient for thee: for my strength is made perfect in weakness."—II Cor. 12:7-9.

III. GOD'S BLESSING OFTEN COMES THROUGH SICKNESS

It may be good to be strong, but it is better to have the power of Christ tenting over us and around us in our weakness. It may be good to be in health, but it is better to have the sweet promise fulfilled, "The Lord

will strengthen him upon the bed of languishing: thou wilt make all his
bed in his sickness" (Ps. 41:3).

A beloved brother, greatly known for his service and testimony, said
not long ago, after more than a year's absence:

> Since I last saw you, I have passed six weeks upon a bed of sickness.
> And I would not exchange them for any six weeks of my entire life.
> God brought me so near to Himself that, like Paul, I almost heard
> unspeakable words which it is not possible to utter. The revelations
> of His compassion and tenderness were such that I could readily
> believe He will not only turn our bed but, as the martyred Bishop
> Hooper tells us, "rather than it should be undone, He will wash the
> dishes and rock the cradle." I learned more of Him and more about
> Him in those six weeks than ever before.

Yes, sickness is a rough but thorough teacher of experimental
theology; and it almost compels the soul of the believer to stay itself
upon God.

During Dr. Payson's last illness, a friend said to him, "I am sorry to
see you lying upon your back."

"Do you know why God puts us on our backs?" asked the smiling
sufferer.

"No," was the answer.

"In order that we may look upward."

While, therefore, it is perfectly proper to pray about sickness and to
pray with a faith that is no faith unless it is in accordance with God's
will, let us remember that sickness is not the worst thing that can befall
a Christian. For nineteen hundred years all Christians have passed
through death, and multitudes of them through a death of violence.

We are doing no wrong when we pray for ourselves or for others,
"Lord, if it please Thee, show Thy healing power"; but we are certainly
doing right when we pray: "Father, glorify thy name" (John 12:28).

> **Yes, ask it for ourselves, if we need healing,**
> **Pleading those instances of olden cure;**
> **But if He then refuse, we still will trust Him,**
> **And He will make it happier to endure.**
> **Ay, happier to bear with Him the suffering,**
> **Or even death itself, with Him close by,**
> **For in His presence there is joy forever,**
> **And with Him near, it is not death to die.**

He has purposes of love to accomplish through disease and pain,
of which we may know nothing at present; and while still praying in

the simplicity of an unfaltering confidence, we are not to suppose that His omnipotence is as mere servant to obey our behests apart from His holier and wiser counsels.

If nothing else were gained by our sickness, it teaches us our need; for "they that be whole need not a physician, but they that are sick" (Matt. 9:12). It is when shut up in the sick chamber the Christian begins to sing with new meaning:

The great Physician now is near,
The sympathizing Jesus.

Whether, then, in active or passive service, let it be our aim to do or suffer the will of God.

We read of some

"who through faith subdued kingdoms, wrought righteousness, obtained promises, stopped the mouths of lions, Quenched the violence of fire, escaped the edge of the sword, out of weakness were made strong, waxed valiant in fight, turned to flight the armies of the aliens."—Heb. 11:33,34.

Of others we read that they

"were tortured, not accepting deliverance; that they might obtain a better resurrection: And others had trial of cruel mockings and scourgings, yea, moreover of bonds and imprisonment: They were stoned, they were sawn asunder, were tempted, were slain with the sword. . .they wandered in deserts, and in mountains, and in dens and caves of the earth."—Heb. 11:35-38.

Suppose ye that the sufferers of this second class were less acceptable to God or less dear to His heart than the doers of the first class with their magnificent achievements? Nay, if there was any difference, they were nearer to Him, as a loving parent always feels a special tenderness for his afflicted children. They obeyed His will and did their appointed work as truly and as well as their brethren in the field of battle.

The sorrowing and silent and submissive children of our Father shall soon find to their everlasting joy that "they also serve who only stand and wait."

I cannot say,
Beneath the pressure of life's care today,
  I joy in these:
  But I can say
That I had rather walk this rugged way,
  If Him it please.

I cannot feel
That all is well when dark'ning clouds conceal
  The shining sun:
  But then I know
God lives and loves; and say, since it is so,
  "Thy will be done."

I cannot speak
In happy tones; the teardrops on my cheek
  Show I am sad;
  But I can speak
Of grace to suffer with submission meek,
  Until made glad.

I do not see
Why God should e'en permit some things to be,
  When He is love;
  But I can see
Though often dimly through the mystery,
  His hand above.

I may not try
To keep the hot tears back; but hush that sigh,
  "It might have been":
  And try to still
Each rising murmur, and to God's sweet will
  Respond — AMEN.

TOM WALLACE
1925-

ABOUT THE MAN:

Dr. Tom Wallace has had a very busy and successful ministry.

After his conversion at General Motors Corporation in Wilmington, Delaware, he held noon services until he entered the ministry. And a busy, busy ministry it has been.

Dr. Wallace attended Tennessee Temple Schools and was on the staff of Highland Park Baptist Church, Chattanooga; pastored Baptist Bible Church, Elkton, Maryland, for 17 years. While there he founded Elkton Christian Schools; established a bus ministry with 18 routes; led the church in eight major building projects, increasing property values from $15,000 to $1,140,000; conducted two daily radio broadcasts; edited *The Visitor*, a monthly church newspaper.

Dr. Wallace served and is serving on many boards.

In 1971 he accepted the pastorate of Beth Haven Baptist Church, Louisville, Kentucky and remained there until 1986. Here many were saved. And in one year alone, he baptized more than 2,600 converts. While in Louisville, he founded Beth Haven Christian Schools and had six daily radio broadcasts.

In 1986 he went into full-time evangelism.

This warm-hearted evangelist and conference speaker is widely sought after as speaker at Bible conferences, banquets, workers' meetings, soul-winning seminars, youth events, etc.

X.

The Blessing of Trouble

TOM WALLACE

"For we would not, brethren, have you ignorant of our trouble which came to us in Asia, that we were pressed out of measure, above strength, insomuch that we despaired even of life: But we had the sentence of death in ourselves, that we should not trust in ourselves, but in God which raiseth the dead."—II Cor. 1:8,9.

"We are troubled on every side, yet not distressed; we are perplexed, but not in despair; Persecuted, but not forsaken; cast down, but not destroyed; Always bearing about in the body the dying of the Lord Jesus, that the life also of Jesus might be made manifest in our body."—II Cor. 4:8-10.

While attending a Bible conference several years ago, I heard Dr. Lee Roberson of Chattanooga, Tennessee, announce that he would speak the next evening on "The Secret of Greatness."

I arrived early the next evening with notebook in hand, ready to take down several points of instruction. I wanted to be sure to get the facts straight from the man who knew what he was talking about. Dr. Roberson, of course, is one of the greatest men alive today in the work of God.

After he was introduced to speak, he stood up, announced the text, and repeated his title: "I give you tonight the secret of greatness. It is found in one key word, and that word is 'TROUBLE.'"

I was so disappointed not to get a systematic formula of instruction from Dr. Roberson based upon his years of experience and success. But the more he preached, the more I realized that what he was saying surely was the true secret of greatness.

People react to trouble in several different ways. Some grumble, others gripe, many growl, a few groan; then there are those who grieve and thank the Lord; then some grow. Trouble will never leave one the same.

Someone has said that life is a bowl of cherries but some of the cherries are sour. I think it is necessary that we accept a problem as it is, adjust to it, then approach it with a determination to do something about it.

Trouble is nothing new to God's people. The Bible, of course, is filled with stories of those in trouble. The Hebrew children had their fiery furnace. Daniel had his lions' den. Joseph was cast into prison. Paul was shipwrecked and beaten with stripes. Peter was sent to prison. John was exiled at Patmos. James had his head cut off. David fled from Saul. Samson had his eyes put out. These are just a few.

Clyde Gordon, who is completely paralyzed from his neck down, edits a magazine called *The Triumph*. In it he said recently:

> **Christ is no security against storms,**
> **But He is perfect security *in* storms.**
> **He does not promise an easy passage,**
> **But He does guarantee a *safe* landing.**

Someone said recently, "The road to success is always under construction." It seems that those who have it hard always get more done.

I read in a magazine recently that great civilizations of history have been in the northern hemisphere. On the equator life is easy and comfortable; there have been no lasting achievements. Now let me point out some benefits of trouble.

I. TROUBLE UNIFIES

When someone dies in the family, loved ones gather from far and near for the funeral. People want to be together when in trouble. When someone is seriously ill, their friends and neighbors gather in to check on them and make sure things are all right.

During the serious tornado damage in Louisville, we began to get phone calls from out of state. One call came from our daughter Debbie in North Carolina, checking to make sure mom and dad were all right. Then a call came in from Pennsylvania from more loved ones. Then the phone rang again; a sister in Ohio was checking everything out in Louisville. These were basic family concerns.

Several years ago in Elkton, there was a serious accident. A car passing a truck ran into the back end of one of our school vans, killing two of our kindergarten children and injuring several others. During the ordeal of that tragedy, several families were drawn very close together, and our church was unified and harmonized in a new way. Trouble became a blessing in that it unified and harmonized our people around our church family and program for God.

Trouble not only draws people together, but it also draws them to the Lord. David said, "Before I was afflicted I went astray" (Ps. 119:67). Many a person has called for a preacher in time of trouble to make things right with God.

Then trouble also draws people to church. It is not uncommon to see a whole family show up at church after a funeral.

Sometimes when people get bad news from the doctor about their physical condition, they take a renewed interest in church. So trouble unifies.

II. TROUBLE IS COMMON

Paul said in I Corinthians 10:13, "There hath no temptation [trouble] taken you but such as is common to man: but God is faithful, who will not suffer you to be tempted above that ye are able; but will with the temptation [trouble] also make a way to escape."

One old preacher said that we ought to be good to everybody because everybody is having a tough time. God is no respecter of persons. He has no pets. In spite of this, we sometimes feel like victims. It seems that we suffer far more than others. But this is simply not the case. I think if all the truth were known, we would probably not trade places with anybody else in the whole world.

Just a few days ago a preacher came to see me who had more troubles than anyone I have seen for a long time. He told me a story of problems in the church, in the community, in his home and in his heart.

I had just talked a few moments before with a preacher's wife in a far-off state. There were serious problems in the life of her preacher-husband and in their church. She was asking for advice.

I talked just two days before that to a preacher who had come to the place where he felt he could no longer effectively serve the Lord in his setting. He wanted to resign and leave his pulpit and find a new place to start again.

And then our demand for counseling requests at the church has increased. It seems that pastors are spending more and more time counseling with people about their troubles and problems. Trouble is a very common thing.

III. TROUBLE DEEPENS SPIRITUALITY

David said,

"Thy righteousness also, O God, is very high, who hast done great things: O God, who is like unto thee! Thou, which hast shewed me great and sore troubles, shalt quicken me again, and shalt bring me up again from the depths of the earth. Thou shalt increase my greatness, and comfort me on every side."—Ps. 71:19-21.

Here we find the effect of trouble. It was a blessing in disguise, a benefit to the life of this good servant of God.

Paul emphasized that "all things work together for good to them that love God, to them who are the called according to his purpose" (Rom. 8:28). He also said, "Tribulation worketh patience" (Rom. 5:3). The graduate degree of spirituality comes from attending the *University of Hard Knocks.*

IV. TROUBLE PRODUCES REALITY

The world is filled with veneer, sham, hypocrisy and deceit. After a serious bout with trouble, we don't usually care as much about what people think. Pride is plowed under, the world loses its value, the appetites for sin lose their taste. God could have kept Daniel out of the lions' den, Paul and Silas out of jail, the Hebrew children from the fiery furnace; but it was good for all these to go through these experiences.

Dr. Jack Hudson made this statement in our church: "My soul demands reality." I thought it was interesting since Brother Jack has been through deep waters so many times with his own physical condition, with a serious arthritic condition and two or three hospital bouts for various other things. It doesn't seem strange, then, that Brother Hudson abounds with genuine sincerity.

Several times I have heard preachers remark, "He's for real." What a great attribute for a man of God!

V. TROUBLE FURTHERS THE CAUSE

In Philippians 1:12 Paul states, "That the things which have happened unto me have fallen out rather unto the furtherance of the gospel." The strength of a ship can only be demonstrated by hurricane. The power of God's grace can only be fully known when the Christian is subjected to some fiery trial. If God would make manifest the fact that He gives songs in the night, He must first make the night.

The weather bureau in the Caribbean island area uses planes to help keep check on the weather. These planes have learned how to take advantage of the cyclone winds in that area. When going north, they get out on the fringes of the cyclone winds and take advantage of the tremendous tailwinds. They actually ride the fringe of the storm and save time and gasoline. Then coming back south, they get on the other edge and take advantage of the same storm to go in the opposite direction.

Trouble should become a steppingstone to better understanding of the will of God and the teaching of the Bible, and also to mature and give us experience in our work for God.

VI. TROUBLE PRODUCES A CROWD

We read in James 1:12, "Blessed is the man that endureth temptation [trouble]: for when he is tried, he shall receive the crown of life." Someone has said:

> **For God has marked each sorrowing day**
> **And numbered every secret tear;**
> **And Heaven's long age of bliss shall pay**
> **For all His children suffer here.**

Those who go through fire and water should remember it is God's way of refining and cleansing you for your good and His glory.

Not only will victory and blessing be a result of this life, but a crown is going to be presented to those who endure suffering for His sake here. This, of course, will be presented at the judgment seat of Christ when all Christians will give an account of themselves according to the deeds done in the body. God is surely looking. His recording angels are keeping a good set of books. As in the case of Job, He will return all that we have lost and reward us with an abundant increase.

The purpose of the Lord is to present us faultless before His throne after the last days. Trouble is simply the factory God is using to produce the right type of product in our lives. Someone wrote:

> **He sat by a fire of sevenfold heat**
> **As He watched by the precious ore,**
> **And closer He bent with a searching gaze**
> **As He heated it more and more.**
>
> **He knew He had ore that could stand the test;**

He wanted the finest gold
To mold as a crown for the King to wear—
Set with gems with a price untold.

So He laid our gold in the burning fire,
Though we fain would have said Him nay,
And He watched the dross that we had not seen
As it melted and passed away.

And the gold grew brighter and yet more bright,
But our eyes were so dim with tears
We saw but the fire, not the Master's hand,
And questioned with anxious fears.

Yet our gold shone out with a richer glow
And it mirrored a form above
Of Him bent o'er the fire, unseen by us,
With a look of ineffable love.

Can we think that it pleases His loving heart
To cause us a moment's pain?
Ah, no, but He saw through the present cross
To bliss of eternal gain.

So, He waited there with a watchful eye,
With a love that is strong and sure;
And His gold did not suffer a bit more heat
Than was needed to make it pure.

VII. TROUBLE GLORIFIES GOD

Paul speaks of glory in trouble in Romans 5:3. When Adam and Eve were in trouble, God stepped in and met their need; and of course, we give glory to God for it. Noah's problems were solved by the God who cared. Again we want God to have glory. Joseph was delivered from prison; the children of Israel were delivered as they crossed the Red Sea; Elijah needed God's help in getting some rain; David's baby died; Paul and Silas were locked in the Philippian jail. There was great profit and benefit to these people in the times of their deliverance.

But all the glory goes to God. We are admonished in I Corinthians 6:20, "For ye are bought with a price: therefore glorify God in your body, and in your spirit, which are God's."

Now in summary let me say that trouble is good for a Christian. It may be hard to endure, but in the end it will bring forth the peaceful fruit of righteousness and a note of praise. Maybe we can understand now what James meant when he said, "Count it all joy when ye fall into divers temptations [trouble]."

GEORGE WASHINGTON TRUETT
1867 - 1944

ABOUT THE MAN:

North Carolina was George Washington Truett's birthplace. By the time he was 18, he was educated well enough to begin teaching in a one-room public school on Crooked Creek in nearby Towns County, Georgia. It was during that two-year apprenticeship that George was converted. Then he established an academy at Hiawassee, Georgia, in 1887. The student body eventually numbered over 300.

When the Truett family moved to Texas in 1889, George went to college—Baylor University—though not as a student. He was offered the position of financial secretary and was instrumental in saving Baylor from bankruptcy. Afterward he became a student, graduated, and unbelievably was elected to become Baylor's president!

But the same year of his graduation he was called to the First Baptist Church of Dallas, remaining there for 47 years, or until his death in 1944. Under his leadership the church grew into the largest church in the world at that time, with 18,124 additions and 5,337 baptisms.

But Dr. Truett had many pulpits besides the pulpit at First Baptist Church. He instituted the Palace Theatre services, held each noon the week before Easter, with nearly 2,000 attending. He preached out in the country churches all across the South, and the common folk heard him gladly. He preached from the steps of our nation's Capitol, and in world centers in London, Stockholm, Paris, Berlin, Jerusalem, etc. Everywhere Truett's preaching produced souls for Christ.

In 1927 he was elected president of the Southern Baptist Convention, which office he served for three terms.

By any standard, he ranks as one of the most popular and influential preachers in America in the first half of the 20th century. He was a world figure; was on close terms with presidents, senators and governors.

Dr. Truett was a great man, a great leader, and a great preacher of the Gospel. His biographers knew whereof they spoke when they explained the man and his ministry in two well-defined words: *"heart-power."*

XI.

What to Do With Life's Burdens

GEORGE W. TRUETT

(Preached in Fort Worth Revival, Noon Service, June 12, 1917)

"For every man shall bear his own burden.". . . "Bear ye one another's burdens, and so fulfill the law of Christ."—Gal. 6:5; 6:2.

"Cast thy burden upon the Lord, and he shall sustain thee."—Ps. 55:22.

In coming to speak at this first midday service, it has seemed to me that I could bring no more practical word than to talk to you about life's burdens. It is the lot of men and women everywhere to have burdens. There is an old Spanish proverb which points a familiar lesson: "No home is there anywhere that does not sooner or later have its hush." The proverb points its own lesson. You cannot mistake it. Sooner or later all have their burdens.

Many of our burdens may be seen. But the deepest and most poignant ones are not seen. If we knew what fierce battles some were fighting and what weighty burdens they were carrying, it would teach us lessons of restraint and charity and contentment beyond any that we have ever known. That very fact should give us pause and caution, even to a marked degree.

The Bible has three words to say about our burdens. Notice them:

"Every man shall bear his own burden."

"Bear ye one another's burdens, and so fulfill the law of Christ."

"Cast thy burden upon the Lord, and he shall sustain thee."

Those three sentences say all that is to be said.

"EVERY MAN SHALL BEAR HIS OWN BURDEN"

Let us glance at what the Bible says in its threefold message about our burdens.

First, our burdens are nontransferable: "Every man shall bear his own burden." Every life is isolated, separated and segregated from every other life. To a remarkable degree every life is lived alone. You were born into the world alone; and when you leave it, no matter where or how, you go into the valley of the shadow alone. And between your birth and death, the cradle and the grave, life is very largely lived alone. No man can perform your duty for you. "To every man *his* work," the Master teaches us. Not "to every man *a* work," nor "to every man *some* work," but "to every man *his* work."

There is a program for you to carry out, a niche for you to fill, a task for you to face. There is a life for you to live, separated from every other in all the world. Nobody can repent of sin for you, nor can anybody believe on Christ for you, nor can anyone make answer at the judgment bar of God for you. We must every one give an account of himself to God.

That means that nobody is to get lost in the crowd. There is to be no hiding behind others or behind organizations. Is there any danger more outstanding in these modern times than the danger that the individual shall get lost in the crowd? God sees the individual, and the individual must never get lost in the crowd. His eye is upon the one, and the one is to see to it, whatever others may or may not do, that he or she walks that path before the face of God that shall have the favor of God. Whether anybody else does right or not, you must. Whether anybody else is true or not, you must be.

If you have ever read the diary of Jonathan Edwards, you must have been greatly impressed with his words—I do not attempt to quote them verbatim—where he penned these two resolutions: "Resolved, first, that every man should do right, whatever it costs. Resolved, second, whether any other man does right or not, I will, so help me God." That is the supreme business of every human being, for "every one shall bear his own burden."

"BEAR YE ONE ANOTHER'S BURDENS"

Then the Bible points a second great word for us concerning our burdens: "Bear ye one another's burdens, and so fulfill the law of Christ."

This means that our burdens are ofttimes community burdens, social burdens, burdens to be shared with others. Others are to share their burdens with us. "Bear ye one another's burdens, and so fulfill the law of Christ."

It is always interesting and proper to note words of Scripture in their setting. Many of the fads and fancies and hurtful heresies in the world have come because the Scriptures have been wrested from their proper setting. We need always to let the Scriptures say what they meant to say and mean what they are designed to mean.

Immediately preceding where we are told to bear one another's burdens, a great verse stands out for our best consideration. "Brethren, if a man be overtaken in a fault, ye which are spiritual, restore such an one in the spirit of meekness; considering thyself, lest thou also be tempted." Bear ye, in this way, one another's burdens, the apostle is saying, and so fulfill the law of Christ.

The primary reference there to this great matter of mutual burden-bearing is that we should seek to help those about us who have gone astray. And just here is the most neglected task of all. Here are we plainly summoned to go out and give ourselves, without stint or reserve, to recover men and women who go wrong. "If any man be overtaken in a fault," help him. Criticize him? Denounce him? Throw stones at him? Talk about him? Nay, verily, "If a man be overtaken in a fault, ye which are spiritual, restore such an one in the spirit of meekness; considering thyself, lest thou also be tempted."

Even as I call your attention to this point of mutual burden-bearing, especially with regard to those who have gotten out of the right path and are going the wrong path, your minds are now alertly busy. You call to your remembrance certain ones who once began well but who have been bewitched away by some influence from the right path and are going the wrong path. Go after those to help them, our Scripture says.

Just there, my fellowmen, is the most neglected task of all. When men go astray and keep going astray, we are all too willing, too content, to allow them to go on, whereas we are summoned by this Scripture and by the whole message of the Gospel of grace to go out and seek to reclaim, to recover, to restore, all who are going wrong.

I am thinking now of a young fellow gloriously converted in my city some time ago who beforehand had had the miserable habit of

swearing—an inexcusable habit, without any defense at all for any
man—and yet that habit had such a hold upon him that it seemed second nature to him to swear. By and by he was graciously converted
under the call of Christ. Then he talked with the minister and said, "I
think I had better wait for six months or twelve, until I can prove to
myself clearly whether I can keep from swearing, before I shall join the
church."

But the minister said to him, "Not at all. The church is not an ag-
gregation of perfect people. No one is perfect. We are all sinners, saved
by grace. You come right on, if you have put your trust in Christ as
your personal Saviour, and take your place in the army of God, with
the rest of the soldiers, and help them and let them help you."

He did, and for months there was a devotion about him to Christ's
cause that, to the last degree, cheered all our hearts.

But after some months when the minister missed him from the mid-
week prayer meeting, and even from the Sunday services, he said to
his men, "Where is Charles?"

They said, "Haven't you heard?"

The minister said, "Not at all. What has happened?"

"Charles was provoked a little while ago to anger in a controversy
with one of our citizens. The hot words came and the blasphemous
sentences fell from his lips. Now he is all filled with shame and humilia-
tion, and he has not come to church since."

"Now," said the minister to the men, "find him. He must be recovered,
nor must you cease until he is recovered."

But the weeks went by and he was not recovered. One day, as the
minister went down a certain street, right there before him he saw Charles
coming. When Charles saw the minister, he turned quickly down an
alley. But the minister said, "Wait a minute, Charles; wait a minute!"
He waited, quite hesitatingly. The minister said, "Why are you dodg-
ing me, Charles?"

And with face averted and by this time covered with tears, he said,
"You know. They have told you. Nor is that all. I told you I had better
wait a few months before I joined the church. I told you of my frailty,
of my weakness. But now I am in the church, and the other day the
old anger came back, and I used hot, blasphemous words. I did not
sleep at all that night. My pillow was wet with my tears. All through
the night I talked with God. God spoke forgiveness to me, and I went

back the next morning and asked the man to forgive me. He cried with me, though he is not a church man, and forgave me."

"Now," I said, "Charles, would you come down to the prayer meeting and say about that much to us?"

He said, "If you think I ought, I will."

He was at the prayer meeting Wednesday night. When the place was made for him, he was on his feet and timidly told about what I have just described.

You should have seen the men and women gather around him. You should have seen them as they greeted him and as they sobbed with him and as they said, "Charles, we will help you. We will forgive you, and you will help us."

He was on the right road again! That is what this Scripture talks about. Whenever anybody goes astray, 'you who are spiritual restore such an one in the spirit of meekness, considering thyself, lest thou also be tempted. In this way bear ye one another's burdens, and so fulfill the law of Christ.'

But this Scripture has a broader meaning than that. We are not only to make it a point to do our best to recover people who have gone wrong and are going wrong, but we are to share burdens with those all about us, whatever their burdens are.

There are the burdens of the sorrowing. Even as I speak, your mind is busy. You call up some family wrapped about this very midday with great sorrow, or you call up some man or woman about whom the shadows hang with fearful weight this very hour. Go and share such one's sorrow, without delay.

Nor is that all. All about us are people with their weighty burdens, burdens terrific, heavy burdens. Go to them and share with them these weighty burdens. There is the teacher. There is the preacher. There is the ruler in the affairs of civil government. Weighty burdens are on their heads and hearts. Do not make it hard for those in places of public trust and responsibility to serve and to lead. Make it easy, with the right sort of cooperation and the right sort of burden-bearing.

How may we all help people? "Bear ye one another's burdens, and so fulfill the law of Christ." The most beautiful portrait we have of Jesus is given here in the Gospels, in five little words, "He went about doing good."

How may we all help people all about us? First, we may help them by living the right kind of lives. The highest contribution you will ever offer this community and this world is to offer to it the right kind of a life.

Gladstone never tired of saying, "One example is worth a thousand arguments." One Savonarola turned the tides of wicked Florence. One Aristides, the just man, perceptibly lifted Athens higher. Ten righteous men would have saved Sodom. The people of Constantinople said about John Chrysostom, the golden-mouthed, "It were better for the sun to cease his shining than for John Chrysostom to cease his preaching."

The best contribution that you can ever offer to this weary, needy world is to offer it the right kind of a life.

How may we all help people? We are to make it a point constantly—to believe in people. Every one of us needs the enthusiasm of Jesus for humanity.

He came to a man hated by his own race, Matthew, the tax-gatherer, sitting there at the poll tax booth; and He said to him, "Matthew, follow Me, and I will make a good man out of you." And from that hour Matthew followed Him.

He came to another hated tax-gatherer, Zacchaeus, the little man who climbed up in the tree. Pausing under that tree, the Master said, "Come down out of the tree. I will go home with you today." And from that hour Zacchaeus followed Jesus, a faithful friend of that great Master.

Like Jesus, we are to believe in people. I think nothing of that system of espionage which is forever spying out people, to catch up with their weaknesses and faults. We are to have, like Jesus, great passion and compassion and brotherliness and sympathy for a needy world. And we are to believe in people.

A little girl who waited upon her semi-invalid mother, day by day going across the street to get a pail of milk, was crossing the street one day when a passing car frightened her. She tripped and fell, and the milk was gone. A big man laughed cruelly—oh, how could he have done it!—then he said to the little child, in her dismay, "What a great beating mother will give you when you get home!" That brought the little girl to self-control, and she said, "Nothing of the sort, sir! My mamma always believes in giving me another chance."

So our Master believes in giving men another chance, and we are to have His temper and walk in His footsteps, always.

Nor is that all. We are to make it a point constantly to encourage people. Oh, it is a sin for any man on the earth to be a miserable discourager! Discouragement is a sin. When men and women are fighting a big battle, they do not need weights put on them by discouragement. They need wings, that they may rise and fly, as they grapple with the big tasks that daily confront them.

Bobbie Burns, in the heyday of his great power as a writer, saw a little boy following him around in a certain community. Turning to the little boy, Bobbie Burns said, "Walter, what do you wish?"

Little Walter timidly said, "Oh, I wish that someday I might be a great writer like you and have people talking about me like they talk about you."

And Bobbie Burns, that great-hearted man, stopped and put his hand on the head of little Walter and, speaking words of inspiration and cheer, said, "You can be a great writer someday, Walter, and you will be."

That little boy was Sir Walter Scott. And to the day of Sir Walter's death, he could never speak of Bobbie Burns except with a sob of gratitude; for Burns had spoken the word in season to the weary heart of a little boy.

Yonder was a fire in the big city. The firemen flung their ladders together and went up in their brave fashion to the topmost story to rescue the people in such peril. One after another was rescued by the brave fire laddies, until all had been rescued, it seemed. No! Yonder is a white face at that upper window. They wrapped something about one of the fire laddies and, breasting the fierce flames, he went again to that window, put the robe around the little woman and started down. But they saw him tremble as the fire raged around him. It seemed that he would fall with his precious burden. But the fire chief cried to his men, "Cheer him, boys! Cheer him, boys!" They cheered him, cheer after cheer. Heart came back, and he came down with the precious life saved.

Oh, you and I are to give our lives to cheering a needy world! Ponder this beautiful sentence from Isaiah: "They helped every one his neighbour; and every one said to his brother, Be of good courage."

"CAST THY BURDEN UPON THE LORD"

Now there is one more word to say, and it is the best of all: "Cast thy burden upon the Lord, and he shall sustain thee." If you will read this 55th Psalm, from which that great promise is taken, you will find that the utterer of such a promise wanted to flee away. "Oh, that I had wings like a dove," he cried, "for then would I fly away, and be at rest."

The burdens were so weighty, the awful conflict was so fiery: "I will just leave it all. I will just throw this thing down and get away. I will flee. I will run. I will give it up. I will not stay with it."

Who has not felt that? Who has not felt—"I have had as much of this as I can bear. I will get out of it. I will run. I will fly. I will get away"? But that will not win; for when you get away out there in the wilderness, you will have your burden yet, for you have your memory, you have your personality, and you have yourself.

You cannot thus get away from life's burdens. There is the burden of perplexity for you, no matter where you go; and there is the burden of the consciousness of neglected duty, no matter where you go; and there is the burden of some sin athwart your conscience, like some ghastly cancer, no matter where you go.

What are you to do with these burdens of perplexity and neglected duty and sins? What are you to do? Where are you to go? There is only one place: "Cast thy burden upon the Lord, and he shall sustain thee."

How will He sustain you? He will do it in one of two ways. He may take the burden away. Sometimes He does, blessed be His name! You have come sometimes, as have I, into that deep Garden of Gethsemane, when that black Friday broke all our plans; and in our dire desperation we have prayed with the Master, "If it be possible, let this cup pass from me. If it be possible, forbid that I should drink this bitter cup that is being put to my lips." The cup was taken away, and we did not have to drink it at all.

Time and again as you faced a certain great burden you have prayed that God would remove it. He heard and the burden was taken away.

But suppose it is not. Sometimes it is not. Ofttimes it is not. We pray, but there is the burden yet. Now, what if God shall not take the burden away?

Then He has promised to come in with divine reinforcement and help us bear that burden and be victor, no matter how weighty it is nor how fiery in its biting power in our life.

Paul had reinforcement. He had a thorn in the flesh. I do not know what it was, nor do you; but it was something very trying. If ever there was a genuine man in the world, it was the Apostle Paul. He was the highest product that Christianity has ever produced. This same man said, "There was given to me a thorn in the flesh." He called it the "messenger of Satan," sent to buffet him. And he said, "I went like the Master in the garden, and thrice did I beseech the Lord that He would take that thorn away, but He did not take it away. He left it to goad me and harass me and burn me and pain me. But He said to me, 'Paul, Paul, my grace is sufficient for you' "—not "shall be," but "is." "My grace is sufficient for you," here and now, ever present and never failing. No matter where you go nor what shall come, "my grace is sufficient for you."

And from that time on we have no more record of Paul's praying that that thorn might be taken away. From that time Paul said: 'Most gladly, therefore, will I rather glory in my thorn, glory in my infirmities, that the power of Christ may rest upon me.' Said Paul: "I had rather have my thorn in the flesh, which is ever present with me, and have God's added grace, than to be without that thorn and miss that added grace and light and love from God."

Now, doesn't that explain much? He will give you increased grace, grace upon grace, if He does not take the burden away when you call to Him to take such a burden away.

Oh, my men and women with your burdens, whatever they are, here is the way out: "Cast thy burden upon the Lord, and he shall sustain thee." Seek not to bear it alone. Seek not to fight out your battle alone. Seek not to solve that perplexity alone. Seek not to stem that flood alone. Seek not to go through that long and bitter night alone. Take the Master into your counsels, into your plans. Turn yourself over to Him with your burden, whatever it is, and He shall sustain you.

One of the great words in the Bible is that fine word *sustain*. He shall sustain you. No matter what your burden is—I dare to say it—no matter what your burden is, you shall get sustaining strength from God, and your heart shall surely know it, if you will only cast yourself honestly upon Him.

In a world of burden and battle and perplexity and clouds and shadows and night and death, have you learned the secret of peace? You will never know it until you learn how to cast your burden upon the Lord.

I am thinking now of a strong man yonder in the city, whose beautiful wife was taken from him after an illness of just a few hours. The man was left with a little flaxen-haired girl of some four or five summers. The body was carried out to the cemetery for a simple committal service. Every heart was broken. The grief was so appalling.

Then when the service was over, neighbors gathered around the big man and said to him, "You, with this little baby girl, must come and stay with us for several days. You must not go back to that home now."

But the brokenhearted man said, "Yes, I must go right back to the same place where she was, to the room from which she went away, and I must fight it out with this baby right there." And back they went.

He told about it all the next day. The baby was late and long going to sleep. Oh, was there ever anything more pathetic than the cry of a bairn for the little mother that will never come back again! Long and late the little one, in the crib there by the bed, sobbed, because she could not go to sleep. The big man reached his hand over to the crib, petted and mothered her as best he could. After awhile the little girl stopped her crying—just out of sorrow for him. And in the darkness of that quiet time the big man looked through the darkness to God and said, "I trust You, but, oh, it is as dark as midnight!"

Then when the little one started up her sobbing again, the father said, "Papa thought you were asleep, baby."

She said, "Papa, I did try. I was sorry for you. I did try, but I can't go to sleep, papa." Then she said, "Papa, did you ever know it to be so dark? Papa, I cannot even see you, it is so dark." Then, still sobbing, the little thing said, "But, papa, you love me if it is dark, don't you? You love me if I don't see you, don't you, papa?"

He reached across with those big hands, took the little girl out of her crib, brought her over on his big heart and mothered her until at last the little thing fell to sleep. Then when she was asleep, he took his baby's cry to him and passed it up to God, saying, "Father, it is as dark as midnight. I cannot see at all. But You love me if it is dark, don't You? I will trust You, though You slay me. With my baby and my grief and my utter desolation, I will turn my case over to You." Then the darkness was like unto the morning!

God always comes to people who trust Him.

Have you learned the secret of peace? Henry Van Dyke points the secret in his poem on "Peace." Mark the words:

> **With eager heart and will on fire,**
> **I sought to win my great desire.**
> **"Peace shall be mine," I said. But life**
> **Grew bitter in the endless strife.**
> **My soul was weary, and my pride**
> **Was wounded deep. To Heaven I cried:**

"God give me peace, or I must die."
The dumb stars glittered no reply.
Broken at last, I bowed my head,
Forgetting all myself, and said:
"Whatever comes, His will be done."
And in that moment, peace was won.

Whatever your burdens—of sin or grief or doubt or disappointment or regret or remorse or conscious fear and failure—dare to cast your burden, yourself, your all, today and forever upon the Lord. Do it now while we pray.

(Reprinted from *A Quest for Souls*)

T. DE WITT TALMAGE
1832-1902

ABOUT THE MAN:

If Charles Spurgeon was the "Prince of Preachers," then T. DeWitt Talmage must be considered as one of the princes of the American pulpit. In fact, Spurgeon stated of Talmage's ministry: "His sermons take hold of my inmost soul. The Lord is with the mighty man. I am astonished when God blesses me but not surprised when He blesses him." He was probably the most spectacular pulpit orator of his time—and one of the most widely read.

Like Spurgeon, Talmage's ministry was multiplied not only from the pulpit to immense congregations, but in the printed pages of newspapers and in the making of many books. His sermons appeared in 3,000 newspapers and magazines a week, and he is said to have had 25 million readers.

And for 25 years, Talmage—a Presbyterian—filled the 4,000 to 5,000-seat auditorium of his Brooklyn church, as well as auditoriums across America and the British Isles. He counted converts to Christ in the thousands annually.

He was the founding editor of *Christian Herald,* and continued as editor of this widely circulated Protestant religious journal from 1877 until his death in 1902.

He had the face of a frontiersman and the voice of a golden bell; sonorous, dramatic, fluent, he was, first of all, an orator for God; few other evangelists had his speech. He poured forth torrents, deluges of words, flinging glory and singing phrases like a spendthrift; there was glow and warmth and color in every syllable. He played upon the heartstrings like an artist. One writer described him as the cultured Billy Sunday of his time. Many of his critics found fault with his methods; but they could not deny his mastery, nor could they successfully cloud his dynamic loyalty to his Saviour and Lord, Jesus Christ.

XII.

God's Tear Bottle

T. DE WITT TALMAGE

"Put thou my tears into thy bottle."—Ps. 56:8.

This prayer was pressed out of David's soul by innumerable calamities, but it is just as appropriate for the distressed of all ages.

Within the past century, travelers and antiquarians have explored the ruins of many of the ancient cities; and from the very heart of those buried splendors of other days have been brought up evidences of customs that long ago vanished from the world.

From among tombs of those ages have been brought up lachrymatories, or lachrymals, which are phials made of earthenware. It was the custom of the ancients to catch the tears that they wept over their dead in a bottle, and to place that bottle in the graves of the departed; and we have many specimen of the ancient lachrymatories, or tear bottles, in our museums.

The text intimates that God has an intimate acquaintance and perpetual remembrance of all our griefs and a phial or lachrymatory or bottle, in which He catches and saves our tears; and I bring to you the condolence of this Christian sentiment.

But why talk of human griefs when we have but to look out and behold the largest prosperity—a great harvest soon to be gathered in all the land. Multitudes of men with no cares save how they may safely invest their large accumulations. Joy in the city mansion and mountain cabin. Joy among the lumbermen of Maine as they shove their rafts into the water. Joy among the emigrants, far out upon the vast prairie. Joy, joy!

Why talk about grief? Alas! the world has its pangs. Now, while I speak, there are before me thick darknesses of soul that need to be lifted. I stand in the presence of some who are about to break under the assault of temptation, and perchance, if no words appropriate to their case be uttered today, they perish forever.

I come on no fool's errand. I put upon your wounds no salve compounded by human quackery; but pressing straight to the mark, I hail you as a vessel midsea cries to a passing craft, "Ship ahoy!" and invite you on board a vessel which has Faith for a rudder, Prayer for sails, Christ for Captain and Heaven for an eternal harbor.

Catharine Rheinfeldt, a Prussian, keeps a boat with which she rescues the drowning. When a storm comes on the coast and other people go to their beds to rest, she puts out in her boat for the relief of the distressed. Hundreds of the drowning has she brought safely to the beach.

In this lifeboat of the Gospel I put out today, I hope, by God's help, to bring ashore at least one soul that may now be sinking in the billows of temptation and trouble. The tears that were once caught in the lachrymatories brought up from Herculaneum and Pompeii are all gone, and the bottle is as dry as the scoria of the volcano that submerged them; but not so with the bottle in which God gathers all our tears.

I. GOD KEEPS PERPETUALLY THE *TEARS* *OF REPENTANCE*

Many a man has awakened in the morning so wretched from the night's debauch that he has sobbed and wept. Pains in the head, aching in the eyes, sick at heart and unfit to step into the light, he grieves, not about his misdoing, but only about its consequences.

God makes no record of such weeping. Of all the million tears that have gushed as the result of such misdemeanor, not one ever got into God's bottle. They dried on the fevered cheek or were dashed down by the bloated hand or fell into the red wine cup as it came again to the lips, foaming with still worse indication.

But when a man is sorry for his past and tries to do better—when he mourns his wasted advantages and bemoans his rejection of God's mercy and cries amidst the lacerations of an aroused conscience for help out of his terrible predicament, then God listens; then Heaven bows down; then sceptres of pardon are extended from the throne; then his crying rends the heart of heavenly compassion; then his tears are caught in God's bottle.

You know the story of Paradise and the Peri. I think it might be put to higher adaptation. An angel starts from the throne of God to find what thing it can on the earth worthy of being carried back to Heaven.

It goes down through the gold and silver mines of earth but finds nothing worthy of transportation to the Celestial City. It goes down through the depths of the sea where the pearls lie but finds nothing worthy of taking back to Heaven.

But coming to the foot of a mountain, it sees a wanderer weeping over his evil ways. The tears of the prodigal start but do not fall to the ground, for the angel's wing catches them and, with that treasure, speeds back to Heaven. God sees the angel coming and says, "Behold the brightest gem of earth and the brightest jewel of Heaven—the tear of a sinner's repentance!"

Oh, when I see the heavenly Shepherd bringing a lamb from the wilderness, when I hear the quick tread of the ragged prodigal hastening home to find his father, when I see a sailor boy coming on the wharf and hurrying away to beg his mother's pardon for long neglect and unkindnesses, when I see the houseless coming to God for shelter and the wretched and the vile and the sin-burned and the passion-blasted appealing for mercy to a compassionate God, I exclaim in ecstasy and triumph: *"More tears for God's bottle!"*

II. GOD KEEPS A TENDER REMEMBRANCE OF ALL YOUR *SICKNESSES*

How many of you are thoroughly sound in body? Not one out of ten! I do not exaggerate. The vast majority of the race are constant subjects of ailments. There is some one form of disease that you are peculiarly subject to. You have a weak side or back or are subject to headaches or faintnesses or lungs easily distressed. It would not take a very strong blow to shiver the golden bowl of life or break the pitcher at the fountain.

Many of you have kept on in life through sheer force of will. You think no one can understand your distresses. Perhaps you look strong, and it is supposed that you are a hypochondriac. They say you are nervous, as if that were nothing! God have mercy upon any man or woman who is nervous!

At times you sit alone in your room. Friends do not come. You feel an indescribable loneliness in your sufferings. But God knows; God feels; God compassionates. He counts sleepless nights; He regards the acuteness of the pain; He estimates the hardness of the breathing.

While you pour out the medicine from the bottle and count the drops,

God counts all your falling tears. As you look at the phials filled with nauseous draughts and at the bottles of distasteful tonic that stand on the shelf, remember that there is a larger bottle than these which is filled with no mixture by earthly apothecaries, but it is *God's bottle* in which He hath gathered all our tears.

Again, God remembers all the *sorrows of poverty*. There is much want that never comes to inspection. The deacons of the church never see it. The controllers of almshouses never report it. It comes not to church, for it has no appropriate apparel. It makes no appeal for help but chooses rather to suffer than expose its bitterness.

Fathers who fail to gain a livelihood so that they and their children submit to constant privation; sewing women who cannot ply the needle quickly enough to earn them shelter and bread. But whether reported or uncomplaining, whether in seemingly comfortable parlor or in damp cellar or in hot garret, God's angels of mercy are on the watch. This moment those griefs are being collected.

Down on the back streets, on all the alleys, amidst shanties and log cabins, the work goes on. Tears of want seething in summer's heat or freezing in winter's cold—they fall not unheeded. They are jewels for Heaven's casket. They are pledges of divine sympathy. They are *tears for God's bottle!*

III. THE LORD PRESERVES THE REMEMBRANCE OF ALL *PATERNAL ANXIETIES*

You see a man from the most infamous surroundings step out into the kingdom of God. He has heard no sermon; he has received no startling providential warning. What brought him to this new mind? This is the secret: God looked over the bottle in which He gathers the tears of His people, and He saw a parental tear in that bottle which had been for forty years unanswered. He said, "Go to now, and let Me answer that tear!" and forthwith the wanderer is brought home to God.

Oh, this work of training children for God is a tremendous work. Some people who think it easy have never tried it.

A child is placed in the arms of the young parent. She is a beautiful plaything. You look into the laughing eyes. You examine the dimples in the feet. You wonder at her exquisite organism. Beautiful plaything!

But on some nightfall as you sit rocking that little one, a voice seems to fall straight from the throne of God, saying, *"That child is immortal!*

The stars shall die, but that is an *immortal!* Sun shall grow old with age and perish, but that is an *immortal!*"

Now I know that with many of you this is the chief anxiety. You earnestly wish your children to grow up rightly, but you find it hard work to make them do as you wish. You check their temper, correct their waywardness. In the midnight your pillow is wet with weeping. You have wrestled with God in agony for the salvation of your children. You ask me if all that anxiety has been ineffectual.

I answer, *No.* God understands your heart. He understands how hard you have tried to make that daughter do right, though she is so very petulant and reckless. And what pains you have bestowed in teaching that son to walk in the paths of uprightness, though he has such strong proclivities for dissipation.

I speak a cheering word. God heard every counsel you ever offered him. God has known all the sleepless nights you have ever passed. God has seen every sinking of your distressed spirit. God remembers your prayers; He keeps eternal record of your anxieties; and in His lachrymatory—not such as stood in ancient tomb but in one that glows and glitters beside the throne of God—He holds all those exhausting tears.

The grass may be rank upon your grave and the letters upon your tombstone defaced by the elements before the divine response will come; but He who hath declared, "I will be a God to thee, and to thy seed after thee," will not forget; and someday in Heaven, while you are ranging the fields of light, the gates of pearl will swing back and, garlanded with glory, that long wayward one will rush into your outstretched arms of welcome and triumph.

The hills may depart, earth may burn, the stars fall and time perish; but God will break His oath and trample upon His promises—*never!* NEVER!

IV. GOD KEEPS A PERPETUAL REMEMBRANCE OF ALL *BEREAVEMENTS*

These are the trials that throw the red hearts of men to be crushed in the winepress. Troubles at the store, you leave at the store. Misrepresentation and abuse of the world, you may leave on the street where you found them. The lawsuit that would swallow your honest accumulations may be left in the courtroom. But bereavements are *home* troubles, and there is no escape from them.

You will see that vacant chair. Your eye will catch at the suggestive picture. You cannot fly the presence of such ills. You go to Switzerland to get clear of them; but more sure-footed than the mule that takes you up the Alps, your troubles climb to the tip-top and sit shivering on the glaciers. You may cross the seas, but they can outsail the clipper or merchantman. You may take caravan and put out across the Arabian desert, but they follow you like a simoom, armed with suffocation.

You plunge into the Mammoth Cave, but they hang like stalactites from the roof of the great cavern. They stand behind with skeleton fingers to push you ahead. They stand before you to throw you back. They run upon you like reckless horsemen. They charge upon you with gleaming spear. They seem to come haphazard—scattering shots from the gun of a careless sportsman.

But not so. It is good aim that sends them just right; for God is the Archer.

This summer many of you will especially feel your grief as you go to places where once you were accompanied by those who are gone now. Your troubles will follow you to the seashore and will keep up with the lightning express in which you speed away. Or tarrying at home, they will sit beside you by day and whisper over your pillow night after night.

I want to assure you that you are not left alone and that your weeping is heard in Heaven.

You will wander among the hills and say, "Up this hill last year our boy climbed with great glee and waved his cap from the top"; or, "This is the place where our little girl put flowers in her hair and looked up in her mother's face," until every drop of blood in the heart tingled with gladness and you thanked God with a thrill of rapture. And you look around, as much as to say, "Who dashed out that light? Who filled this cup with gall? What blast froze up these fountains of the heart?"

Some of you have lost your parents within the last twelve months. Their prayers for you are ended. You take up their picture and try to call back the kindness that once looked out from those old wrinkled faces and spoke in such a tremulous voice. You say it is a good picture, but all the while you feel that after all it does not do justice. And you would give almost anything—you would cross the sea, you would walk the earth over—to hear just one word from those lips that a few months ago used to call you by your first name, though so long you yourself have been a parent.

Now you have done your best to hide your grief. You smile when you do not feel like it. But though you may deceive the world, God knows. He looks down upon the empty cradle, upon the desolated nursery, upon the stricken home, upon the broken heart, and says, "This is the way I thresh the wheat; this is the way I scour My jewels! Cast thy burden on My arm, and I will sustain you. All those tears I have gathered in My bottle!"

But what is the use of having so many tears in God's lachrymatory? In that great casket or vase, why does God preserve all your troubles? Through all the ages of eternity, what use of a great collection of tears?

I do not know that they will be kept there forever. I do not know but that in some distant age of Heaven an angel of God may look into the bottle and find it as empty of tears as the lachrymals of earthenware dug up from the ancient city.

Where have the tears gone? What sprite of Hell hath been invading God's palace and hath robbed the lachrymatories?

None! These were sanctified sorrows, and those tears were changed into pearls that now are set in the crowns and robes of the ransomed.

I walk up to examine this heavenly coronet, gleaming brighter than the sun, and cry, "From what river depths of Heaven were these gems gathered?" And a thousand voices reply, "These are *transmuted tears from God's bottle!*"

I see sceptres of light stretched down from the throne of those who on earth were trod on of men; and in every sceptre point and inlaid in every ivory stair of golden throne I behold an indescribable richness and luster and cry, "From whence this streaming light—these flashing pearls?" And the voices of the elders before the throne and of the martyrs under the altar and of the hundred and forty and four thousand radiant on the glassy sea, exclaim, *"Transmuted tears from God's bottle!"*

Let the ages of Heaven roll on—the story of earth's pomp and pride long ago ended; the Koh-i-noor diamonds that made kings proud, the precious stones that adorned Persian tiara and flamed in the robes of Babylonian processions, forgotten; the Golconda mines charred in the last conflagration; but firm as the everlasting hills and pure as the light that streams from the throne and bright as the river that flows from the eternal rock, shall gleam, shall sparkle, shall flame forever *these transmuted tears of God's bottle.*

Meanwhile, let the empty lachrymatory of Heaven stand forever. Let no hand touch it. Let no wing strike it. Let no collision crack it. Purer than beryl or chrysoprasus, let it stand on the step of Jehovah's throne and under the arch of the unfading rainbow. Passing down the corridors of the palace, the redeemed of earth shall glance at it, think of all the earthly troubles from which they were delivered and say each to each, "That is what we heard of on earth." "That is what the psalmist spoke of." "There once were put our tears." *"That is God's bottle!"* And while standing there inspecting this richest inlaid vase of Heaven, the towers of the palace dome strike up this silvery chime: *"God hath wiped away all tears from all faces."*

Wherefore comfort one another with these words!

ROBERT GREENE LEE
1886-1978

ABOUT THE MAN:

R. G. Lee was born November 11, 1886, and died July 20, 1978.

The midwife attending his birth held baby Lee in her black arms while dancing a jig around the room, saying, "Praise Gawd! Glory be! The good Lawd done sont a preacher to dis here house. Yas, sah! Yes, ma'am. Dat's what He's done gone and done."

"God-sent preacher" well describes Dr. Lee. Few in number are the Baptists who have never heard his most famous sermon, "Payday Someday!" If you haven't heard it, or read it, surely you have heard some preacher make a favorable reference to it.

From his humble birth to sharecropper parents, Dr. Lee rose to pastor one of the largest churches in his denomination and head the mammoth Southern Baptist Convention as its president, serving three terms in that office. Dr. John R. Rice said:

"If you have not had the privilege of hearing Dr. Lee in person, I am sorry for you. The scholarly thoroughness, the wizardry of words, the lilt of poetic thought, the exalted idealism, the tender pathos, the practical application, the stern devotion to divine truth, the holy urgency in the preaching of a man called and anointed of God to preach and who must therefore preach, are never to be forgotten. The stately progression of his sermon to its logical end satisfies. The facile language, the alliterative statement, the powerful conviction mark Dr. Lee's sermons. The scholarly gleaning of incident and illustration from the treasures of scholarly memory and library make a rich feast for the hearer. The banquet table is spread with bread from many a grain field, honey distilled from the nectar of far-off exotic blossoms, sweetmeats from many a bake shop, strong meat from divers markets, and the whole board is garnished by posies from a thousand gardens.

"Often have I been blessed in hearing Dr. Lee preach, have delighted in his southern voice, and have been carried along with joy by his anointed eloquence."

XIII.

Christ's Comfort

R. G. LEE

(Preached on radio while at Evansville Rescue Mission, Evansville, Indiana, 1946)

The fourteenth chapter of John's Gospel comes to us drenched in the tears of multitudinous contritions, warm with the fingers of agony and death and fragrant with the faith of the young and the old. This book comes to us filled with echoes of those who have overcome the world, and their voices testify to His saving and keeping power.

This wonderful book with this wonderful chapter stands as a lighthouse for storm-tossed Christian mariners; stands as an undiminished reservoir of consolation; stands as a shadow of a great rock in a weary land; stands as a commissary of food to the spiritually hungry. It is a fountain of refreshing to those who thirst after righteousness; a chest of medicines for the wounded on life's battlefield; an army of weapons for those who would fight the good fight of faith. This wonderful chapter is the panacea for all heart trouble.

However, only those who have a genuine belief in Christ are warranted in claiming the comfort of this chapter.

We find that it is a comfort to those who are in trouble. "Man that is born of woman is of few days, and full of trouble," says Job. "Yet man is born unto trouble, as the sparks fly upward." No one is exempt from trouble. There is no back but has its burden, no soul but has its sorrow, no heart but has its ache and no life but has its troubles. *Trouble* is one word in every man's dictionary.

Dr. Rush used to say to young doctors, "You will need two pockets: one for your fees and a bigger one for your troubles."

Trouble is one reality that makes all the world akin. No bars or bolts or doors can keep trouble out or away.

But let us thank God for the balm He gives to troubled hearts; for the comfort and gladness He brings to those who are in grief.

Let us notice some of the ingredients found in this wonderful panacea in John 14.

The Comfort of Faith

Think of the comfort of faith. Jesus said,

"Let not your heart be troubled: ye believe in God, believe also in me."

We find in Hebrews 4:16, "Let us therefore come boldly unto the throne of grace, that we may obtain mercy, and find grace to help in time of need."

Where you find a flower, you know there must have been a seed. Where you find a river, you know there must have been a spring. Where you find a flame, you know there must have been fire. When you find a man beloved and blessed of God, you know there must have been faith, whether it is recorded or not, whether you see it or not. You cannot see faith; still it must be there. Faith is that which stands upon something which without faith would bear no weight. Faith is the germ of a victorious man's virtue. It is the fountainhead of his goodness. It is the living source of warmth and life through his life.

"But without faith it is impossible to please him: for he that cometh to God must believe that he is, and that he is a rewarder of them that diligently seek him" (Heb. 11:6). We might turn this around and say, "Without faith it is impossible to serve God."

Why do I say this? Because if a man is without faith, he will not try to serve God. If a man does not believe there is gold in the mountains, he will not try to dig the earth. If the farmer does not believe there is coming a harvest day, he will not till the soil. If he does not believe things can be made better, he will not try to make them better. If one does not believe there is goodness, he will not try to be good. If he does not believe there is truth, he will not try to be truthful. If he does not believe in the reality of purity, he will not try to be pure.

Jesus said, "Ye believe in God, believe also in me."

Believe in My power—"All power is given unto me in heaven and in earth."

Believe in My promises—"The promises of God are yea and amen."

Believe in prayer and in My prayer—"He ever liveth to make intercession for them."

Believe in My presence—"Lo, I am with you alway."

Believe in My preparation—"I go to prepare a place for you."

Believe in My purity—"Every man that hath this hope in him purifieth himself, even as he is pure."

Believe in My person—"I and my Father are one."

Think of the comfort of faith. "...but ye, beloved, building up yourselves in the most holy faith, praying in the Holy Ghost." The only kind of building that gives permanency and gives us men of might is this mighty thing we call faith.

> I never doubted when the snows were deep
> That underneath them the violets lay asleep.
> I never questioned when the winds were cold
> That maple leaves were waiting to unfold.
> And shall I now at touch of sorrow's hand
> Grow panic-stricken, fail to understand?
> I walked a dreary path of life in sleet,
> Yet looked ahead to grasses for my feet.
> I faced a silence when the woods were dumb,
> And always knew in time the birds would come.
> Will God let my winter be too long
> Who fills His world with sun and bloom and song?

Faith answers "no" to those questions.

"Believe in me." The presence of faith made the heart of Jesus happy. The absence of faith in others made the heart of Jesus ache. He knew that men live by faith, work by faith, endure by faith, get by faith, die by faith, and that by faith people are saved from their sins. "Believe on the Lord Jesus Christ, and thou shalt be saved" (Acts 16:31). Without faith life is like a dream that vanishes away, like a nightmare with a terrible ending, like a tragedy with no Shakespeare to write it. The presence of faith is a mighty power.

We know that faith is the evidence of things not seen, the substance of things hoped for. May God help us to know that without faith it is impossible to please God and help us to think upon the great victories which faith has and which it can and will have.

The Comfort of Hope

Comfort is just as definitely found in this chapter—from the first verse to the last—as you find salt in the waters of the sea, just as you find flowers in the springtime and just as you feel the cooling touch of the breeze when the summer breezes blow.

Jesus said:

*"In my Father's house are many mansions: if it were not so, I would
have told you. I go to prepare a place for you. And if I go and prepare
a place for you, I will come again, and receive you unto myself; that
where I am, there ye may be also. And whither I go ye know, and the
way ye know."*—Vss. 2-5.

Jesus taught His disciples that the temporary separation was to be
succeeded by an eternal reunion. The hope Jesus holds out is of an
everlasting Home when He should return and take His people Home
to be with Him.

Paul speaks of God as the God of hope: "Now the God of hope fill
you with all joy and peace in believing, that ye may abound in hope,
through the power of the Holy Ghost" (Rom. 15:13). And in I Thessalonians 4:13 we find these words: "But I would not have you to be ignorant, brethren, concerning them which are asleep, that ye sorrow
not, even as others which have no hope."

Back of all our troubles is God, back of all our sorrows, all our sins,
is God; God wanting to bring comfort in sorrow, God anxious to forgive
and deliver us out of all of our troubles and distresses. God is not feeding
His children on false hopes.

You remember that I said that so much of this chapter has no real
value for people who have never accepted Jesus Christ, because if you
reject God's Son, you cannot receive the things which come through
God's Son to people. God does not give ashes for beauty, but He gives
beauty for ashes, the oil of joy for mourning and the garment of praise
for the spirit of heaviness.

Mount Sinai may gleam with retributive fire, but the Gospel gleams
with hope. "In Adam all die," cries Genesis. "In Christ shall all be made
alive," says Hope. Christianity charges a man with hope, the hope that
he can come back, that he can recover, that he can be remade.

San Francisco was shaken to pieces by an earthquake, but San Francisco recovered—and so can man.

Chicago was burned to a pile of ashes by a terrible fire, but Chicago
recovered—and so can man.

Daniel was remade, and so can you be remade.

Jonah was a discredited man, but Jonah came back: "And the word
of the Lord came unto Jonah the second time." This shows that God
was putting hope into him and giving Jonah another chance.

Hope sees beyond the cloud, beyond the obstacle, beyond the hardship, beyond the weakness, beyond the failure, beyond the difficulty. Hope says to us, "Never accept the verdict of your defeat, the verdict of your melancholy, the verdict of your sickness, the verdict of your disaster, the verdict of your disappointment." The psalmist says, "Thou hast made me to hope." And Jesus said, "If it were not so [about there being mansions in His Father's House, many of them], I would have told you."

There is a plea for hope of future things because Christ shivered the last lance of materialism and called generations to their high hope of a Home in the Father's House. "For we know that if our earthly house of this tabernacle were dissolved, we have a building of God, an house not made with hands, eternal in the heavens" (II Cor. 5:1).

The Comfort of Love

Then I wish we might notice the comfort of love which we find in this chapter. Jesus said:

"He that hath my commandments, and keepeth them, he it is that loveth me: and he that loveth me shall be loved of my Father, and I will love him, and will manifest myself to him."

And you remember:

"Judas saith unto him, not Iscariot, Lord, how is it that thou wilt manifest thyself unto us, and not unto the world? Jesus answered and said unto him, If a man love me, he will keep my words: and my Father will love him, and we will come unto him, and make our abode with him. He that loveth me not keepeth not my sayings: and the word which ye hear is not mine, but the Father's which sent me. These things have I spoken unto you, being yet present with you."—Vss. 22-25.

Now when we come to think of this wonderful truth, we must not forget that God is talking. Jesus assures His disciples of His love, of His personal sympathy.

Perhaps you know what real sympathy is worth in the hour of sorrow. The comfort of divine love is wonderful. "As one whom his mother comforteth, so will I comfort you," is the promise of God. The comfort of divine love is a river where man's comfort is a rill. The comfort of divine love is a mountain where man's comfort is just a hill. The comfort of divine love is a sun where man's love can be no more than a candle.

God's love—God's love to us—God's love, longer than the longest day; God's love, longer than the longest hour; God's love, longer than the blackest night; God's love, deeper than the blackest sin! In view of the love of which Jesus has spoken, in view of the comfort which so many have experienced in His love, we can say with the hymn writer,

O Love, that wilt not let me go,
I rest my weary soul in Thee;
I give Thee back the life I owe,
That in Thine ocean depths its flow
May richer, fuller be.

O Light, that foll'west all my way,
I yield my flick'ring torch to Thee;
My heart restores its borrowed ray,
That in Thy sunshine's glow its day
May brighter, fairer be.

O Joy, that seekest me thro' pain,
I cannot close my heart to Thee;
I trace the rainbow thro' the rain,
And feel the promise is not vain
That morn shall tearless be.

O Cross, that liftest up my head,
I dare not ask to hide from Thee;
I lay in dust life's glory dead,
And from the ground there blossoms red
Life that shall endless be.

The Comfort of Prayer

Then we have in this beautiful chapter the comfort of prayer. Jesus said:

"And whatsoever ye shall ask in my name, that will I do, that the Father may be glorified in the Son. If ye shall ask any thing in my name, I will do it."—Vss. 13,14.

By this promise Christ puts a boundless check in the hands of all who keep His commandments and asks us to sign it.

Are you lonely?—pray; Livingstone did!

Are you in poverty?—pray; the widow did!

Are you in prison, in the penitentiary of fear?—pray; Peter and Paul did when cast into prison.

Are you facing death?—pray; Stephen prayed then.

Abraham's servant prays, and Rebekah appears.

Jacob wrestles and prays, and the angel is conquered and Esau's mind is wonderfully turned from the revengeful purpose he had harbored for twenty years.

Moses cries to God, and the sea is divided.

Moses prays, and Amalek is discomfited.

Joshua prays, and Achan is discovered.

Hannah prays, and Samuel is born.

David prays, and Ahithophel hangs himself.

Asa prays, and a victory is gained.

Daniel prays, and the lions are muzzled and the seventy weeks are revealed.

Mordecai bade Esther to fast, and Haman is hanged on his own gallows in three days.

Ezra prays at Ahava, and God answers.

Nehemiah prays, and the king's heart is softened in a minute.

Elijah prays, and rain descends apace.

Elisha prays, and the Jordan River is divided.

Elisha prays, and a child's soul comes back.

The church prays ardently, and Peter is delivered by an angel.

Paul and Silas prayed and sang praises, and the door of the prison house was opened, every man's band was loosed, and Paul came out of jail with a jail door under one arm and with a convert under the other.

That shows the mighty things that God does. Prayer has a thousand commands. Prayer has a thousand, and tens of thousands, of promises. Prayer has a thousand examples of rich success. We are told in God's Book that men ought always to pray. And there are more things wrought by prayer than ever the world dreamed of.

Dr. Dixon used to say:

> Whenever we depend upon organization, we get what organization can do. Whenever we depend upon man's works, we get what man's works can do. Whenever we depend upon money, we get just what money can do. Whenever we depend upon our preaching, we get just what our preaching can do. When we depend upon prayer, we get what God can do.
>
> And what you need and our homes need and our country needs and our churches need is what God can do! And that shall come through prayer.

I ran upon this little poem written by Rev. Robert D. Patterson of Ossining, New York. Listen to what he says:

> **Why run your race with shoestrings untied?**
>   **Slow is your pace, you trip in your stride.**
> **So is my stumbling life each day**
>   **Wherein I live and do not pray.**
>
> **Why sail your boat when the rudder is lost?**
>   **Unguided you float, by wind and wave tossed.**
> **So is my restless life each day**
>   **Wherein I live and do not pray.**
>
> **Why carry your lamp without any oil?**
>   **The dangers of night will add to your toil.**
> **So is my darkened life each day**
>   **Wherein I live and do not pray.**

We sometimes sing:

> **Sweet hour of prayer, sweet hour of prayer,**
> **That calls me from a world of care,**

But some, I fear, who sing that do not have the experience with God that they ought to have in the matter of prayer.

The Comfort of Peace

Then in this beautiful chapter we have the comfort of peace. While I shall talk just a minute on it, I hope that you shall have hours of peace through hearing these words on peace.

"Peace I leave with you, my peace I give unto you: not as the world giveth, give I unto you. Let not your heart be troubled, neither let it be afraid."—Vs. 27.

Peace is such a precious jewel that many people would give anything for it but truth. Somebody has said, "The peace of God will keep us from sinning under our troubles and from sinking under our troubles."

"For he is our peace." Christ is our peace with God. Christ reconciles us to God by His cross. The cross is the key to peace. There is no reason for war on God's side. We are not reconciled to God by the miracles of Christ. The men who saw His miracles were not won by them. Signs of power do not change the mind. Nicodemus was willing to accept Christ as a teacher come from God because of His miracles, but miracles did not regenerate Nicodemus, and without regeneration he will neither see nor enter the kingdom of Heaven. Rebellion and peace cannot exist at the same time between two parties. We must remember that Christ is our peace with ourselves.

David could have Uriah buried. David could compromise with conscience. David could then marry Bathsheba. David could repent and content Nathan. But David could not get rid of David. The searchlight of memory kept the grave of Uriah always in sight. His sin was always before him. He did not have to turn around to see it. He said, "My sin is ever before me." And he never got peace about it until with repentance he came and asked God to forgive him.

"Peace I leave with you"—sweet peace, the gift of God's love.

If you do not have peace in your heart about the present, about your sins and about the future, remember that Christ Jesus will give you peace. "My peace I give unto you: not as the world giveth, give I unto you."

JOHN SUMMERFIELD WIMBISH
1915-1982

ABOUT THE MAN:

Dr. John S. Wimbish was born in Macon, Georgia, on June 19, 1915. There he received his formal education and then trained with the National Cash Register Company in specialized selling.

Mr. Wimbish felt his call to the ministry in 1939 and immediately left the business world to begin preparation for the Lord's service. He was graduated from Moody Bible Institute in 1943 and returned to Macon to further his education at Mercer University. While there, he also pastored Avondale Baptist Church and conducted a daily radio program known as the OLD FAMILY BIBLE BROADCAST, which was carried on a network of fourteen stations, including short-wave outlets.

In 1946 he began his work as pastor of the historic First Baptist Church of Edgefield, South Carolina, a pulpit famous in history and achievement, having had, among other pastors, such outstanding men as Dr. R. G. Lee.

After a successful ministry of four and a half years in Edgefield, he resigned to accept the pastorate of Calvary Baptist Church, New York City, and on June 1, 1950, he began his ministry at New York's famed "Cathedral of Evangelism."

It was during Dr. Wimbish's pastorate in New York that the Calvary Radio Ministry (the world's oldest religious broadcast) achieved worldwide proportions through the short-wave facilities of HCJB in Quito, Ecuador, South America, and DZAS in Manila, The Philippines.

An ardent evangelist and supporter of missions, Dr. Wimbish, in 1954, made a 40,000-mile missionary tour through Asia, Africa and Europe. During his pastorate at Calvary, the missionary staff increased from eighteen to forty-four.

Dr. Wimbish served as pastor of the Seminole Heights Baptist Church from early 1958 through late 1968, during which time phenomenal growth was evidenced in both the spiritual and physical areas of the church. From October, 1968, through 1977, Dr. Wimbish held three different pastorates and then retired to Valrico, Florida. In his last years he served as Chaplain of the Hillsborough County Penal System and did interim pastoral work in many churches throughout the area. He died September 25, 1982 at age 67.

This message, "The Despair of Loneliness," was published February 1, 1957 in THE SWORD OF THE LORD.

XIV.

The Despair of Loneliness

JOHN SUMMERFIELD WIMBISH

"I am like a pelican of the wilderness: I am like an owl of the desert. I watch, and am as a sparrow alone upon the house top."—Ps. 102:6,7.

The psalm in which these verses are couched recites the glories of Immanuel, but as we scan these pathetic lines we also behold a picture of suffering and sorrow unequaled throughout the realm of secular literature. And as we lift verses 6 and 7 from the chapter and examine them with the eye of faith, we find that they pulsate with sadness and throb with solitude.

It is a prophetic utterance concerning the coming Messiah, Jesus of Nazareth. What do we find here?

"A pelican of the wilderness"—alone.

"An owl of the desert"—alone.

"A sparrow on the house top"—alone.

Consider with me now *"The Despair of Loneliness."*

Someone has well said:

> If our emotions were colors, rage would no doubt appear as flaming red, hate as chilly blue, love, the all-inclusive, would be represented by the full spectrum, and despair would show a drab gray.

Despair is indeed the last emotional resort—a kind of death in life. The despair of loneliness defies all description.

Chapter 5 of John depicts

I. THE LONELINESS OF SOCIETY

We see Jesus as He wends His way through the narrow streets of Jerusalem. Soon He reaches the sheep gate; and there, by the Pool of Bethesda, He observes the great multitude plagued with various infirmities, waiting for the moving of the water. Suddenly He notices a poor creature who seems more needy than all the rest; and tenderly He asks, "Wilt thou be made whole?"

The helpless paralytic looks up and answers, "Sir, I have no man, when the water is troubled, to put me into the pool."

Think of it! For thirty and eight years—long, weary, doleful years—this bundle of pain has been buffeted by the surging human tide of Jerusalem and, after all this time, he must needs say to Jesus, "Sir, I have no man." Absolutely friendless was he.

There is a loneliness of the ocean where there is never a sound save the booming of the surf along the rock-strewn shore; there is a loneliness of the prairie where there is never a voice save the weird howl of the coyote; there is a loneliness of the mountains where there is never a whisper save the sighing of the wind. But there is a loneliness which is far worse than these—the loneliness of society—the loneliness of a great and crowded city.

There lay the lonely sufferer by the Pool of Bethesda, and the thousands of the busy city were passing to and fro. The laughter of children could be heard, and the buzz and hum and roar of the marketplace fell upon his ear—but he had not one single friend to give him a helping hand. Oh, the loneliness of society!

In his fascinating book entitled *Alone,* Admiral Richard E. Byrd tells all about five months he spent in bewildering and soul-shattering darkness. He lived alone in a shack that was literally buried in the great glacial ice cap that covers the South Pole—an ice cap that holds nature's oldest secrets; an ice cap covering an unknown continent larger than the United States and Europe combined.

Admiral Byrd spent five months there alone. The days were as black as the nights. No living creature of any kind existed within a hundred miles. The cold was so intense that he could hear his breath freeze and crystallize as the wind blew it past his ears.

"At night," he says, "before blowing out the lantern, I formed the habit of planning the morrow's work." He had to in order to preserve his sanity. "It was wonderful," he continues, "to be able to dole out time in this way. It brought me an extraordinary sense of command over myself." And without constant activity the days would have been without purpose; and without purpose they would have ended, as such days always end, in disintegration.

You might think that, while in that frozen wasteland, Richard Byrd was of all people most lonely, and be inclined to pity him. Oh, beloved, save your pity, save your sympathy for the lonely man, the lonely woman here in this melting pot of the world—that poor creature living in the dingy tenement house chamber, who never receives a letter, who never hears one word of encouragement, who never experiences the handclasp of a friend.

If you could but read the hundreds and thousands of letters that come to my desk from our vast radio audience, you would know something of the lonely people who wander through the somber shadows of these canyons of steel and granite. Some of them would tear your heart out.

One dear, tested, tortured, troubled soul closed her letter in this way:

> I know little children are to be pitied sometimes, but not nearly as much as the old people. I am sending a small sum for your radio work and am asking you again to remember me in your prayer group. I have high blood pressure, and I get frightened, thinking I am going to die. My head is confused, and I say my prayers over and over, instead of leaving it in Jesus' hands. Nobody here to pray with me—I am all alone.

Isn't it significant that lonely hearts' clubs flourish in the great cities of the world. How incongruous, when riding on a Manhattan bus thronged with people, to look up and see a sign advertising some club where you can meet people!

We all agree that New York City can be the loneliest place in the world. The sense of loneliness is overwhelming to the stranger jostled by the tumultuous throng—where everyone is hurrying and no one seems to care for him.

Yes, spare your compassion for Richard Byrd and for the mountaineer in his lonely cabin in the Adirondacks and for the lighthouse-keeper passing his time on some desolate rock; for there is a loneliness more terrible than that of solitude—the loneliness felt by the friendless in the coldhearted metropolis.

If there were no lonely people in New York City, Broadway with all of its glitter, with all of its weird fascination, would go bankrupt. When you see the crowded theater or music hall, just know that lonely people are there paying their hard-earned money and saying to the clown or to the actor: "Help me surmount this growing sadness. Sing to me and drive from my life the weariness of my humdrum existence. Play on the harp string of my emotions and help me crush the stinging despair of loneliness."

One evening in 1808 a gaunt sad-faced man entered the offices of Dr. James Hamilton in Manchester, England. The doctor was struck by the melancholy appearance of his visitor. He inquired:

"Are you sick?"

"Yes, doctor, sick of a mortal malady."

"What malady?"

"I am frightened of the terror of the world around me. I am depressed by life. I can find no happiness anywhere. Nothing amuses me, and I have nothing to live for. If you can't help me, I shall kill myself."

"The malady is not mortal. You only need to get out of yourself. You need to laugh, to get some pleasure from life."

"What shall I do?"

"Go to the circus tonight to see Grimaldi, the clown. Grimaldi is the funniest man alive. He'll cure you."

A spasm of pain crossed the poor man's face as he said, "Doctor, don't jest with me: I am Grimaldi."

And in the twentieth chapter of John, verses 24 and 25, we find

II. THE LONELINESS OF SKEPTICISM

"But Thomas, one of the twelve, called Didymus, was not with them when Jesus came. The other disciples therefore said unto him, We have seen the Lord. But he said unto them, Except I shall see in his hands the print of the nails, and put my finger into the print of the nails, and thrust my hand into his side, I will not believe." —John 20:24, 25.

Here Thomas is set apart from the other disciples. His skepticism isolates him. I am sure when Thomas voiced his doubts as to Jesus' resurrection, the other disciples looked at him with dismay and disdain.

We see the doubter standing on the rim of the happy company—a solitary figure. Do you remember, it was Thomas who said, "Let us also go, that we may die with him"? One expositor reminds us that Thomas seems to have been "half in love with easeful death."

Oh, yes, beloved, Thomas was a lonely man that resurrection day. In fancy we see him wandering beneath the olive trees of Gethsemane, gripped by the despair of loneliness because of skepticism. With amazing rapidity the word spread, "Christ is risen!" but Thomas was wandering alone, groveling in the dust of despair. Skepticism is crushing indeed.

You remember when God promised Sarah that she would become the ancestress of the Lord Jesus Christ, Sarah laughed in the face of God because she did not believe it. And when the Lord denounced her skepticism, she denied it and said, "I did not laugh." And then, with firmness, God said, "But thou didst laugh." And the laugh of skepticism down through the centuries is only the echo of Sarah's laughter.

God condemns unbelief wherever He finds it. God says He will accomplish a thing, and men say it cannot be done. Some of you laugh at the miracles of the Word of God. You say they are contrary to the laws of nature. Let me ask you a question: What is a law of nature? IT IS GOD'S WAY OF DOING A THING!

Let us say that you ordinarily cross the Hudson River to get to New Jersey via the Washington Bridge. But next week you decide to go through the Lincoln Tunnel. Possibly the week after that you take the Holland Tunnel. You made a rule of using the Washington Bridge. Have you not the right to change it? I ordinarily come into the sanctuary through the door on the platform, but suppose sometime I should come in at the front door. Have I not the right to change my habit?

Beloved, the law of nature is nothing more than God's habit—His way of doing things—and if He makes a law, He has a right to change it any time He wants to change it.

Oh, how tragic is the laughter of skepticism! A loud, reverberating peal of skeptic laughter emerges from many of the universities of our city. They are very apt at manufacturing doubters. They turn them out by the thousands, and every last one of them will sooner or later be dreadfully lonely.

Late one Wednesday afternoon, the telephone in my study rang and an urgent voice said: "Oh, Pastor Wimbish, there's a girl here who badly needs your help. I met her a few moments ago on the street. You simply must see her."

A few minutes later, the woman who called was ushered into my study, and cringing by her side was one of the most pathetic looking creatures I have ever seen. There was a wild, frenzied look in her eyes and a nervous twitching on her face. Her tiny fists were clenched in fear.

As I spoke to her, she drew back as though fearful of being struck. I immediately knew that this young woman was the slave of many a beastly passion.

As I tried to quote John 3:16 to her, she said, "I don't want to hear that! Give me a cigarette!" Her benefactress explained that the pastor had none and then, twisting her hands in agony, she said, "Oh, so you're a preacher!"

Then she sprang to her feet, ran to the bookshelves, started knocking the books around and cried, "Do you have to read all these books to know that God loves you?" Then, like a panther, she wheeled about, flung herself toward my desk and fairly spit as she said, "Have you ever read Voltaire?" When I answered in the affirmative and asked, "Have YOU ever read Voltaire?" she answered, "Oh, yes, and I love him!"

And then I quietly asked, "Has he made you happy?"

With a wild cry, she said, "No, he hasn't made me happy. He has made me miserable. He has made me wish I were dead!"

Once again I begged her to be seated and told her I would like to have just a brief word of prayer. As I started to pray, never shall I forget how that poor, lonely skeptic reacted. She sprang from her chair, grasped my coat lapels and screamed, "Don't do that! That reminds me of when my sister died. They were scattering incense everywhere and praying." Then with a note of remorse in her voice, she said, "Oh, please forgive me. But since I attended [and she mentioned a leading university in this city], I have had no faith in God."

My dear friend, I beg you to remember that skepticism is a dark and doleful land. Some of you listening to me know what it is to have one hundred midnights pour their darkness into one hour! I declare unto you that there are men and women who would give all the wealth in the world, if they possessed it, to get back to the childlike faith of their fathers and mothers.

Let me say to every unbeliever that the charms of skepticism are false. In the end, rather than hearing sweet music of comfort, you will hear the pitiful dirge of despair.

I place upon the pulpit a copy of the Holy Scriptures. I consider it an inspired, infallible Book. But there are skeptics in this pagan city who want it torn to pieces.

One irreligious anthropologist shouts, "Take out all that about the creation and about Adam and Eve and their progeny." And the Book of Beginnings is torn from the Word of God.

And some unbelieving sociologist cries, "Take out all that about the miraculous guidance of the children of Israel in the wilderness." And the book of Exodus is ripped from the Divine Library.

Then a twentieth-century Pharisee, with flawless diction, proclaims, "There are things in Deuteronomy and Kings that are not fit to be read." And the pages of Deuteronomy and Kings are swept away by the wind of infidelity.

Next, some ungodly student of ancient languages speaks and says, "The book of Job is only a drama: it is utterly untrue. That ought to come out." And we tear out the book of Job.

Then some liberal theologian says, "Those passages in the New Testament which tell of the divinity of Jesus Christ ought to come out." And the evangelists leave us.

Finally some atheistic philosopher stands with perfect poise and calmly asserts, "The book of Revelation—how preposterous! It represents a man with the moon under his feet and a sharp sword in his hand." And that matchless Book is swept away.

Now we have just a few pages of the Bible left, and some foolish infidel stands and says, "I don't believe a word of the Bible from one end to the other." And the entire Book from Genesis to Revelation is swept away; and man, devoid of hope, turns his face toward the black of eternal darkness.

Let me say that this Bible is either true or it is false. If it be false, we Christians are as well off as any skeptic in the world; and if it be true, we are safer than every skeptic.

One of the most outspoken atheistic scientists of our day, in a book widely read and much quoted, said:

> Milton wrote of the fading of the pagan gods; and Milton's God too is joining them in limbo. God has become more remote and more incomprehensible and, most important of all, of less practical use to men and women who want guidance and consolation in living their lives. A faint trace of God, half metaphysical and half magic, still broods over our world, like the smile of a cosmic Cheshire Cat. But the growth of psychological knowledge will rub even that from the universe.

But the time will come for that blustering infidel to die, and then all his hypotheses and all his learned hypercriticisms will fade into insignificance.

As I reviewed his blasphemous writings, once again I remembered Theodore Parker, one of the most brilliant skeptics of a century ago. He made the Word of God seem ridiculous, and he sneered at Christianity until he came to die; then he said:

My life has been a failure. A failure domestically—I have no children; a failure socially—for I am treated in the streets like a pirate; a failure professionally—because I know but one minister who has adopted my sentiments.

For one quarter of a century Theodore Parker laughed at Christianity, and ever since Christianity has been laughing at Theodore Parker.

III. THE LONELINESS OF SIN

Turn to chapter 13 of John. Here we find the story of the Last Supper. In verse 21 Jesus prophesies the betrayal of Judas. In amazement, the innocent disciples look one to the other; and then the beloved John asked, "Lord, who is it?" And Jesus answered, "He it is, to whom I shall give a sop, when I have dipped it. And when he had dipped the sop, he gave it to Judas Iscariot, the son of Simon." And then we are told Satan entered into Judas. Immediately Jesus said, "That thou doest, do quickly." And verse 30 is pierced through and through with meaning: "He then having received the sop went immediately out: and it was night."

Why did Judas hurry away from that little company? As skepticism separated Thomas, so sin raised a barrier between Judas and his fellow disciples.

"And it was night." Yes, for those who travel the pathway of sin there is an engulfing pall of night that isolates them from all good and true fellowship. Sin always has been darkness. Sin always will be darkness. Sin is darkness now. Yes, Judas was lonely because of his sin.

You remember the tragic story of the demoniac of Gadara who had his dwellings among the tombs. Through the long hours of the night he roamed the mountains and visited the tombs—isolated from humanity because of sin.

You will recall that in the book of Leviticus we learn of the ancient laws concerning leprosy. In Old Testament times a man plagued with this hideous disease, which we all know is a type of sin, if approached by a fellow countryman was ordered by the law to cry out in a loud voice, "Unclean, unclean." And in Leviticus 13:46 we read, "All the days wherein the plague shall be in him he shall be defiled; he is unclean: he shall dwell alone; without the camp shall his habitation be."

Here we learn once again of the loneliness of sin.

In Hosea 4:17 God said, "Ephraim is joined to idols: let him alone."

Here again we find the loneliness of sin.

I confronted a lonely unbeliever last Sunday night. He had attended our service; and after greeting the people, I glimpsed him standing apart from the throng of joyful Christians here on 57th Street.

As I walked over to greet him, I saw the cynical sneer upon his face and the cigarette drooping foolishly from his lip. Almost at once I knew that I was meeting a lonely man. His poor heart had been pierced time and time again by sharp interrogation points.

In very plain language, he voiced his doubts to me, explaining that he had some sins he greatly enjoyed and he had no intention whatsoever of parting with them — a modern example of this verse: "Ephraim is joined to idols: let him alone."

One hour before his fatal duel with Alexander Hamilton, Aaron Burr, sitting in his library at Richmond Hill here in New York, wrote to his beloved daughter Theodosia, "Some very wise man has said, 'O fools, who think it solitude to be alone.'" Already, even before the fatal shot was fired and the bloody deed was done, he felt the loneliness of his sin. In a few hours he was a fugitive from the sudden and deep abhorrence of his fellow citizens, his political career was over forever, and his great ambitions wrecked.

There are lonely people in this city and thousands who carry heavy and difficult burdens of grief, anxiety, pain and disappointment. But I declare unto you that the loneliest soul of all is the man whose life is steeped in sin. Oh, my dear sir, my dear woman, every sin you deliberately cling to is a mighty power in you making for loneliness. There is a tragic loneliness in sin.

But think with me for a moment or two about

IV. THE LONELINESS OF SORROW

In chapter 11 of John we read of Mary and Martha. Lazarus, the brother of the Bethany home, was taken grievously ill; and his sisters sent word to Jesus saying, "Lord, behold, he whom thou lovest is sick." It will be remembered that Jesus tarried two days where He was; and when He arrived in Bethany, Martha said, "Lord, if thou hadst been here, my brother had not died." Surely both Mary and Martha wondered why Jesus did not come sooner to their help. They were sinking beneath the billows of great sorrow, and there was no helping hand.

I believe that, as Lazarus was ebbing away in delirium, he would ask, "Mary, is Jesus here yet?"

And with heartbreaking concern Mary would answer, "No, Lazarus, but He will come."

And then Lazarus would cry out again, "Martha, look out and see if Jesus is coming. Is He coming?"

With deep emotion Martha would say, "No, Lazarus, but He will come."

We know the victorious outcome of that story, but who can deny the loneliness of sorrow?

Some of you are overwhelmed by sorrow. You stand there in the sickroom and watch the one dearer than all the world to you fading like the petals of a withered rose.

The great Bible scholar, Dr. G. Campbell Morgan, once related this touching experience:

> I found my New York friend in his office, found him smitten, stricken, afflicted, because his wife had died not many days before. He was hot and angry. I so well remember something he said to me: "People are sending me books about the second coming and the resurrection. All may be true, but I don't want them; I want my wife!"

The man needed not a theological prescription but a living person. He craved fellowship. Only those who know Christ can travel down the narrow pathway of the cemetery and watch the flower-strewn casket lower into the new-made grave and come away with peace in the heart and victory in the life.

But consider with me in these closing moments,

V. THE LONELINESS OF THE SAVIOUR

What does our Scripture say?

"I am like a pelican of the wilderness: I am like an owl of the desert. I watch, and am as a sparrow alone upon the house top."—Ps. 102:6,7.

Verse 7 is very interesting because at the paschal season the streets of Jerusalem were packed with people. Multiplied thousands of human beings came from all over Judaea and swarmed into the city. There was great joy everywhere: all could hear the strum of the stringed instruments and the laughter of the gay populace.

If you had been in Jerusalem at that time, you would have thought it impossible to be alone; and yet here was our Lord Jesus watching the procession ". . . as a sparrow alone upon the house top," lamenting in sorrow and in solitude.

In chapter 53 of Isaiah, it was prophesied that Jesus would be despised, that Jesus would be rejected of men, that Jesus would be a man of sorrows and acquainted with grief, that the people would hide their faces from Him, that the people would loathe and hold Him in low esteem.

And in chapter 63 of Isaiah, it was prophesied that Jesus would tread the winepress alone.

Oh, who can contemplate the loneliness of the Saviour! "He came unto his own, and his own received him not" (John 1:11).

And at the last we hear Him crying out, "My God, my God, why hast thou forsaken me?"

Oh, my lonely friend, there is One who understands and cares. There is One who opens His heart to you. There is One who sticketh closer than a brother.

JOE HENRY HANKINS
1889-1967

ABOUT THE MAN:

"He was a weeping prophet" is the way Dr. Hankins was characterized by those who knew him best—one of the 20th century's great soul-winning preachers.

BUT—Hankins preached sharply, strongly against sin. Would to God we had more men of his mettle in a ministry today that has largely been given over to namby-pamby, mealy-mouthed silence when it comes to strong preaching against sin.

Dr. John R. Rice wrote of him: *"His method and manifest spiritual power would remind one of D. L. Moody. He has the keen, scholarly, analytical mind of an R. A. Torrey, and the love and compassion of souls of a Wilbur Chapman."*

Hankins was born in Arkansas and saved as a youth. He graduated from high school in Pine Bluff, then from Quachita Baptist College. He held pastorates in Pine Bluff, Arkansas; in Whitewright, Greenville and Childress, Texas. His last and most productive pastorate was the First Baptist Church, Little Rock, Arkansas. There, in less than five years, 1,799 additions by letter, 1,144 by baptism—an average of 227 baptisms a year—made a total of 2,943 members added to the church. Sunday school spiralled to nearly 1,400; membership mushroomed to 3,200 despite a deletion of 882 to revise the rolls.

In 1942, Hankins gave up the pastorate for full-time evangelism.

In 1967, Dr. Hankins passed on to the Heaven he loved to preach about. Be sure that he was greeted by a thronging host of redeemed souls—saved under his Spirit-filled ministry.

XV.

When Your Foot Is About to Slip

JOE HENRY HANKINS

(Preached at the First Baptist Church, Little Rock, Arkansas, 1941)

"But as for me, my feet were almost gone; my steps had well nigh slipped. For I was envious at the foolish, when I saw the prosperity of the wicked."—Ps. 73:2,3.

David is telling us of an experience through which he had passed, an experience through which every child of God has passed or will pass. David said, when he looked around and saw the prosperity of the wicked; when he saw how they seemed to get along in the world; when it seemed that everything their hands touched prospered and they didn't seem to have trouble like other people and it came very near tripping him up and causing him to lose faith in God: *"My steps had well nigh slipped."*

How many of you have had that same experience? How many times have I heard others say, "It doesn't pay to try to be honest; it doesn't pay to try to live right. Look at those people who leave God out of their lives, living in all sorts of sin and ungodliness, cheating and swindling in their business and living without any thought of God. Yet they get along better than those who live for God, those who live by the rules"? Did you ever hear it? They begin immediately to feel that God isn't fair, that it isn't right, that God isn't just. At such times we ask ourselves, *Does God really care? Is He concerned after all?*

After David got his feet back on the rock, regained his faith in God and was firmly and securely anchored, he said that, when he thought those things about God, he was as ignorant as a beast. Listen to his words: "So foolish was I, and ignorant: I was as a beast before thee."

The Devil uses things like that to upset the faith of a child of God. People all over the world who are trying to serve the Lord are asking, "Why doesn't God stop some of the things that are now going on? Why didn't God stop Hitler with all of his slaughter, suffering and devastation he caused in the world?" The Devil will try to use every misfortune that comes to upset our faith in God and cause us to accuse God foolishly.

Some people act as though they think that, because we are trying to serve God, He ought to deliver us from all trouble and never let us suffer anymore and give us an easy time the rest of our lives.

But if God did that, we would all be in the position of which the Devil accused Job when he said that he was serving God for pay. And instead of having people who serve God because He is God, people who honor God because He is God, people who worship God because of who He is and people who follow God because they love Him, love righteousness, right and holiness, the whole world would be running after God for pay.

That isn't the crowd God wants. If, when a person joined the church, he had no more sorrow, no more trouble or heartaches, we would have all the Devil's crowd in the church.

God isn't looking for hired servants. He is seeking children who will love Him because He is love, worship Him because He is God, adore Him for who He is; children with faith in Him, not for what He does but for who He is, those who would rather "suffer affliction with the people of God than to enjoy the pleasures of sin for a season." This is the type people God desires to have.

Every time some misfortune comes, the Devil will try to use it to upset our faith and cause us to doubt God. Sorrow comes, and you can't understand. Many times you ask, *Why?* Maybe the father has been taken away from the wife and children by the hand of death and you are left dazed and stunned by the blow. The Devil will come immediately and insinuate that God isn't fair, isn't just. And if you are not careful, you will listen to the Devil's lies, and your feet will be on slippery places.

When you are struggling to make ends meet and to keep the wolf away from the door, then look around and see the ungodly crowd have everything it wants, if you are not careful, you will allow the Devil to cause you to say God isn't fair, and you will find your feet on slippery ground and, like David, become envious. These things so upset him that he wondered if it pays to serve God.

Yesterday afternoon a member of this church, whose husband had lost his job, came to me and said, "He is asking if it pays to live right and be honest, when some crook comes along, gets your job and you are left without work."

Well, does it pay? Israel said:

"It is vain to serve God: and what profit is it that we have kept his ordinance, and that we have walked mournfully before the Lord of hosts? And now we call the proud happy; yea, they that work wickedness are set up; yea, they that tempt God are even delivered."—Mal. 3:14,15.

What profit is there after all?

I want us to notice where David found the answer to his question and the solution to his problem—how David regained his faith in God and got his feet out of the slippery places and on the rock again.

The reason I bring this message this morning is that I think, if there was ever a generation that needs this question settled; if there was ever a generation of Christians who need their feet planted firmly on the rock once for all, it is this generation. For beloved, it is going to take real faith in God for us to weather the storms we are having to face. The Devil is abroad in the world, and he is using everything he can to trip up God's people. Our boys are going away to camps to be trained for soldiers [preached at the beginning of World War II]. We don't know how soon they are going to be slaughtered by the thousands. And the Devil is using that very thing—our love and sympathy for them and our desire to help them—to try to lead us off into doing the wrong thing for them.

The appeal is going out to the ministers and churches of Little Rock to help recruit a thousand church women—young women, if you please—to dance with the soldiers! Now you talk about arousing my "Irish," my righteous indignation! When I read that, I boiled over! I was never so insulted in my life.

Of course, we love these boys out yonder in camp. Not many of them are our Arkansas boys, for they are in camp somewhere else; but we have some good boys over here. They come from homes just like ours. Their mothers are back home praying, just like we are praying for our boys away in camp. They love them, and their hearts are going out after them. Their heartstrings are being broken; their hearts are bleeding for their sons. We want to do everything we can for them. And the

Devil comes along and gets church women to go out and try to get a thousand of our young church women to be dance partners with them!

Yesterday a mother called me to thank me for what I had to say in our church paper about this. She said that this week five women in this town had called her daughter and insisted that she sign up for this thing. And all five of the women who called her were church women—middle-aged church women!

Do you know what we need in America today? More ma's and pa's with a little sense. There is nothing wrong with our young people; they have more conviction than the old folks. This girl said in reply to those who asked her to sign up, "I do not believe my pastor would go, and I don't think I shall go."

Thank God for young people with courage even under pressure to say, "No"!

One of these women who called the girl is teaching a Sunday school class (not in our church); and her hair is gray. When she called a young woman of our church to sign up and the girl refused, the older woman said, "It seems to me that, if our young men leave their homes and go into these training camps, the least we could do would be to entertain them."

I say that, when these soldier boys will probably be going into the very jaws of death in the next few months, we need to bring them closer to God, not farther away. But the Devil will use things like this to trip up the people of God.

How are you going to keep your feet on solid ground in a time like this? How did David keep his footing?

I. HE WENT INTO THE SANCTUARY

David said, "I went into the sanctuary of God; then I understood." Beloved, nothing in a Christian's life can take the place of worship at the house of God. That is one thing a Christian cannot get along without.

Some say, "I can worship God as well at home as at the house of God." No you can't! If you think you can, the Devil has deceived you and your feet are on slippery ground. Yes, you can meet God in other places, but God has always had an appointed time, an appointed day of worship and a medium of approach.

When Adam and Eve were cast out of the garden, God appointed a place at the east gate of the garden and set an angel there with a flaming sword, not to keep Adam and Eve away from the tree of life, but to keep the way to the tree of life open that they might have access to it through God's appointed means.

When Israel wandered in the wilderness, God told Moses to build a Tabernacle and set it up every time they stopped so that the people could bring their sacrifices and have access to God.

When Israel settled in the land, God said, "Build a Temple." Then God gave the outline, the specifications and plans for the most magnificent and most wonderful building man had ever erected, a place where God's people were to meet God in worship.

He has always had a time and place for worship. Yes, you can meet God anywhere. I meet God so many times in unexpected places. Sometimes out on the highway driving along alone, Jesus comes and takes a seat beside me, and we ride along together in wonderful fellowship. God has met with us so many times in our little family circle at home in the evenings when all is quiet and the family sits together to read out of God's Word and kneels to pray.

But there is no place on earth where God gets as close and is as real as in the house of God. Jesus said, "Where two or three are gathered together in my name, there am I in the midst of them." If I had to be without my church for six months, I do not believe, to save my life, I could keep from backsliding. And I don't think you can either.

God meets His people at the church. David said, "When I went into the sanctuary of God, then I understood; then I got a new revelation of God, a new grip on God. Then I got my feet on a rock again, in the house of God."

That is why it grieves my heart to see members of churches staying away from the services and churches closing on Sunday nights. This church will be open as long as I am pastor if I am the only one here. But thank God, I will not be here by myself! Some of you will always stand by me and be here with me. By the help of God, we will keep the light trimmed and burning when the darkness gets the deepest. My determination before God is that we will never close. Oh, in this day, how we need to realize that we cannot get along without the worship at the house of God!

II. WHAT DID DAVID FIND AT THE HOUSE OF GOD?

1. He realized that he had been overestimating the prosperity and

happiness of the wicked. They were not as happy as he thought they were. The grass always looks greenest away from you. And you think the other fellow is the happiest and getting along the best. But if you could look down in his heart, you wouldn't change places with him for the world. They seem happy, but they are seeking something that will satisfy but never finding it.

David said he had been overestimating the prosperity and happiness of the wicked crowd but that, after all, it was like a dream, and one day they would awake to the truth that they were deceived; one day they would be disillusioned. David realized that their prosperity was only in material things, when there is a deeper need in the human life than material things can possibly supply.

2. David came to know there is something better than material prosperity. O God, when will the human race learn that life consists "not in the abundance of the things which a man possesseth"! When will we learn that, if you could give man everything on earth; if you could pile at his feet all the money, all the honor, all the position and glory the world has to offer, in the end it would be like Alexander the Great who, at the age of thirty-two, wept because he had no more worlds to conquer.

3. David came to realize how greatly blessed he was. He realized that fellowship with God was better than anything the world had to offer. He said, "Nevertheless, I am continually with thee; thou hast holden me by my right hand. Thou shalt guide me with thy counsel and afterwards receive me to glory."

Oh, the hope that is an anchor to the soul—that fellowship with the Lord down through life—"joy unspeakable, and full of glory," and the guiding hand of God, and at the end received into glory!

4. David realized, also, that God was not One who took no interest in the struggles, sorrows and heartaches of His people, but One who was always present with them—not only always present with them but always present to help; that God will deliver His people.

It may be like it was with the infidel who said to the deacon, "I planted my wheat on Sunday, mowed it on Sunday, and I made a better crop than anybody else in the country." This deacon farmer answered back, "Yes, neighbor, I have watched you do that; but may I remind you, neighbor, that God doesn't pay off in full in the fall."

Truly Solomon was right when he said, "A little that a righteous man hath is better than the riches of many wicked."

5. David discovered that the prosperity of the wicked was fleeting. O child of God, the material things of life are only temporary! He said it was like a dream—you can have them for a little while; then they are gone. That is what influenced the choice of Moses when he chose to "suffer affliction with the people of God rather than enjoy the pleasures of sin for a season." The world's pleasure, wealth and glory is like a bubble the human race is chasing—like trying to find the "pot of gold" at the end of the rainbow. But the wealth we find in Jesus Christ is something that will last forever. "Lay not up for yourselves treasures upon earth, where moth nor rust doth corrupt, and where thieves break through and steal: But lay up for yourselves treasures in heaven, where neither moth nor rust doth corrupt, and where thieves do not break through nor steal." It isn't just for a season, but "when the battle's over we shall wear a crown in the New Jerusalem." We shall be received into glory with Him and share His glory, as Jesus prayed in John 17, 'The glory I had with the Father before the world was.'

6. David learned that there is something better than prosperity. He realized that spiritual things and the fellowship with God and the "joy unspeakable, and full of glory" that comes from God—the privilege of walking with God—are things the world not only cannot offer but cannot take away; that the God who walked with Daniel into the lions' den was his God and that in due time He would take care of the ungodly. "Then understood I their end."

7. He also understood that in due time God's saints shall come into their own. And in that realization David reached out his hand in the dark, took hold of the strong hand of a mighty God, and God placed his feet again on solid rock, established his goings, put a new song in his mouth and new strength in his life. 'He is the same yesterday, today and forever.'

Beloved, if you and I live to see the day when everything is gone—when the foundations have crumbled and everything is falling in—just remember that the thing that put David's feet on the rock was that he still had God, that he could always be assured of His guiding hand and, in the end, would be received into Glory. In that consolation and in the glorious hope and conquering faith he put his hand out in the dark and took hold of One from whom we cannot be separated and in whose strength we cannot fail.

Is it dark around you? Are you groping in uncertainty? Are your feet on slippery places? Reach out your hand in the dark, and you will feel the grip of His mighty hand.

While I was in a meeting in Sherman, Texas, I was staying in the home of the pastor. About two o'clock one morning a terrible storm arose. We were awakened by the crash of thunder, the flash of lightning and the fury of the storm. I heard the cry in the adjoining room of a little four-year-old, curly-headed girl, "Daddy! Daddy!"

After awhile I heard the father's voice say, "Sweetheart, what is it?"

Then I heard a little trembling voice say, "Daddy, reach me your hand. I'm afraid." In a moment I heard a quiet little voice say, "Daddy, it's all right now. Daddy, I'm not afraid of the storm now."

Friend, listen! As you walk through the Valley of the Shadows, reach out your hand in the dark and find that mighty Hand that takes the fear out of life. Stay with God. Stay with God in an hour like this, and your feet will be on solid rock.

Job found that Hand. We hear him say in the midst of the wreck of everything, "I know that my redeemer liveth, and that he shall stand at the latter day upon the earth: And though after my skin worms destroy this body, yet in my flesh shall I see God." Then as he holds that unseen but sure and certain Hand in the dark, we hear him saying, "Though he slay me, yet will I trust him."

Don't let the Devil lie to you about the God who will never, never fail.

> **The soul that on Jesus hath leaned for repose**
> **I will not, I will not desert to his foes:**
> **That soul, tho' all Hell should endeavor to shake,**
> **I'll never, no never, no never forsake.**

Paul and Silas found that unseen Hand in the Philippi jail and through its comforting and strengthening touch, were able, while their hands and feet were in stocks and their backs bleeding, to pray and sing praises to God till the foundations of the prison were shaken, the prison doors were opened and their bands were loosed.

Yes, child of God, "My God shall supply all your need according to his riches in glory by Christ Jesus."

XVI.

Never! Never! Never! Never! Never!

CHARLES H. SPURGEON

(Sermon delivered October 26, 1862, at Metropolitan Tabernacle, London)

"He hath said, I will never leave thee, nor forsake thee."—Heb. 13:5.

What power resides in "Thus saith the Lord"! The man who can grasp by faith, "He hath said," has an all-conquering weapon in his hand.

What doubt will not be slain by this two-edged sword? What fear is that which shall not fall smitten with a deadly wound before this arrow from the bow of God's covenant? Will not the distresses of life and the pangs of death; will not the corruptions within and the temptations without; will not the trials from above and the temptations from beneath—will not all seem but light afflictions when we can hide ourselves behind the bulwark of "He hath said"? Whether for delight in our quietude or for strength in our conflict, "He hath said" must be our daily resort.

"He Hath Said" Is a Promise of God

Hence, let us learn, my brethren, the extreme value of *searching the Scriptures.*

There may be a promise in the Word which would exactly fit your case, but you may not know of it, so therefore miss its comfort.

You are like prisoners in a dungeon, and there may be one key in the bunch which will unlock the door and set you free; but if you will not look for it, you may remain a prisoner still, though liberty is near at hand.

There may be a potent medicine in the great pharmacopia of Scripture, and you may still remain sick, though there is the precise remedy that would meet your disease, unless you will examine and search the Scriptures to discover what "He hath said."

Should we not, beside reading Scripture, *store our memories richly with the promises of God?*

We recollect the sayings of great men; we treasure up the verses of renowned poets; ought we not be profound in our knowledge of the words of God?

The Scriptures should be the classics of a Christian. As our orators quote Homer or Virgil or Horace when they would clinch a point, so we should be able to quote the promises of God when we would solve a difficulty or overthrow a doubt.

"He hath said" is the foundation of all riches and the fountain of all comfort; let it dwell in you richly as "a well of water, springing up unto everlasting life."

And, oh, my brethren, *how diligently should we test the Scriptures!* Besides searching them by reading and treasuring them by memory, we should test them by experience. So often as a promise is proven to be true, we should make a mark against it and note that we also can say, as did one of old, "This is my comfort in my affliction: for thy word hath quickened me." "Wait on the Lord," said Isaiah; then he added, "Wait, *I say,* on the Lord," as if his own experience led him to echo the voice of God to his hearers.

Test the promise. Take God's bank note to the counter and mark if it be cashed. Grasp the lever which He ordains to lift your trials, and try if it possesses real power. Cast this divine tree into the bitter waters of your Marah and learn how it will sweeten them. Take this salt and throw it into the turbid waters and witness if they be not made sweet, as were the waters of old by the Prophet Elisha. Taste and see that the Lord is good, for there is no want to them that fear Him.

The apostles, like their Master, were always very ready at quotations. Though they were inspired men and could have used fresh words, yet they preferred, as an example to us, to quote, "He hath said. . . ."

Let us do the same; for though the words of ministers may be sweet, the words of God are sweeter; though original thoughts may have the novelty of freshness, yet the ancient words of God have the ring, the weight, the value of old and precious coins, and they shall not be found wanting in the day when we shall use them.

It seems from our text that "He hath said" is not only useful to chase away doubts, fears, difficulties and devils, but that it also yieldeth nourishment to all our graces.

You perceive that, when the apostle would make us contented, he says, "Be content with such things as ye have, for *he hath said . . . .*"; and when he would make us bold and courageous, he puts it, *"He* hath said . . . therefore, *we* may boldly say, God is my helper, I will not fear what man can do unto me."

When the apostle would nourish faith, he does it by quoting from Scripture the examples of Abraham, of Isaac, of Jacob, of Moses, of Gideon, of Barak and of Jephthah. When he would nourish our patience, he says, "Ye remember the patience of Job." Or if it be our prayerfulness, he says, 'Elias was a man of like passions with us, and he prayed and prevailed.'

"He hath said" is food for every grace as well as death for every sin. Here you have nourishment for that which is good and poison for that which is evil. Search ye, then, the Scriptures; for so shall ye grow healthy, strong and vigorous in the divine life.

We turn at once, with great pleasure, to the wonderful words of our text, "He hath said, I will never leave thee, nor forsake thee." I have no doubt you are aware that our translation does not convey the whole force of the original and that it would hardly be possible in English to give the full weight of the Greek. We might render it, "He hath said, I will never, never leave thee; I will never, never, never forsake thee." Though that would be not a literal but rather a free rendering; yet as there are five negatives in the Greek, we do not know how to give their force in any other way. Two negatives nullify each other in our language; but here, in the Greek they intensify the meaning following one after another, as I suppose David's five stones out of the brook would have done if the first had not been enough to make the giant reel.

The verse we have sung just now is a very good rendering of the original—

> **The soul that on Jesus hath lean'd for repose,**
> **I will not, I will not desert to his foes;**
> **That soul, though all Hell should endeavor to shake,**
> **I'll never, no never, no never forsake.**

Here you have the five negatives very well placed and the force of the Greek, as nearly as possible, given.

In trying to expound this fivefold assurance, this quintessence of consolation, we shall have to draw your attention, first of all, to an awful condition, or what is negatived; second, to a gracious promise, or what is positively guaranteed; next, we shall observe notable occasions or times when this promise was uttered; a few words upon certain sweet confirmations which prove the text to be true; and then, in the fifth place, necessary conclusions which flow from the words of the promise.

I. LOST AND FORSAKEN—WHAT IT WOULD MEAN

Lost and forsaken—I am quite certain I shall fail in attempting to describe this state of mind. I have thought of it, dreamed of it, felt it in such feeble measure as a child of God can feel it; but how to describe it, I know not.

1. *Forsaking* implies *an utter loneliness.* Put a traveler in a vast howling wilderness, where for many a league there is no trace of man, no footstep of a traveler. The solitary wretch cries for help, but the hollow echo of the rocks is his only reply. No bird in the air; not even a prowling jackal in the waste; not an insect in the sunbeam to keep him company; not even a solitary blade of grass to remind him of God! Yet even there he is not alone: for yon bare rocks prove a God. The hot sand beneath his feet and the blazing sun above his head witness to a present Deity.

But what would be the loneliness of a man forsaken of God! No migration could be so awful as this; for he says, 'If I take the wings of the morning and fly to the uttermost parts of the sea, *thou art there.*' Such a state were worse than Hell; for David says, "If I make my bed in hell, behold, *thou art there."*

Loneliness is a feeling which none of us delight in. Solitude may have some charms, but they who are forced to be her captives have not discovered them. A transient solitude may give pleasure; to be alone, utterly alone, is terrible; to be alone, *without God,* is such an emphasis of loneliness that I defy the lip even of a damned spirit to express the horror and anguish that must be concentrated in it.

There is far more than you and I dream of in the language of our Lord Jesus when He says, "I have trodden the winepress *alone." Alone!* You remember He once said, "Ye shall leave me alone: and yet I am not alone, because the Father is with me." There is no agony in that sentence, but what must be His grief when He says—"I have trodden the winepress *alone!"*

"My God, why hast thou forsaken me?" is the cry of human nature in its uttermost dismay. Thank God, you and I by this promise are taught that we never shall know the desperate loneliness of being forsaken of God; yet this is what it would be if He should forsake us!

2. Mingling with this mournful solitude is a sense of *utter helplessness*. Power belongeth unto God; withdraw the Lord, and the strong men must utterly fail. The archangel without God passes away and is not; the everlasting hills do bow, and the solid pillars of the earth are dissolved. Without God our dust returneth to the earth; without God our spirit mourneth like David, "I am forgotten as a dead man out of mind; I am like a broken vessel."

Christ knew what this was when He said, "I am a worm, and no man." He was so utterly broken, so emptied of all power, that as He hung with dislocated limbs upon the cross, He cried, "My strength is dried up like a potsherd; thou hast brought me into the dust of death."

No broken reed or smoking flax can be so feeble as a soul forsaken of God. Our state would be as deplorably destitute as that of Ezekiel's infant, deserted and cast into the open field with none to swaddle and none to care for it, left utterly to perish and to die—such should we be if we could be forsaken of God! Glorious are those negatives which shut us in from all fear of this calamity.

3. To be forsaken of God implies *utter friendlessness*. A thousand times let Jehovah be blessed that very few of us have ever known what it is to be friendless! There have been times in the experience of some of us when we felt we stood without a friend in the particular spot which we then occupied, for we had a grief which we could not entrust to any other heart.

Every man who is eminently useful in the church will know seasons when as the champion of Israel he must go forth alone. This, however, is compensated by stronger faith and the moral grandeur of solitary heroism.

But what must it be to be some poor wretch whose parents have long since been buried; who has lost his most distant relatives; who, passing along the street, remembers the name of one who was once his father's friend, knocks at the door and is repulsed; recollects another—and this is his last hope—one he played with in his infancy—stands at that door asking for charity and is bidden to go his way? He paces the cold November streets while the rain is pouring down, feeling to his utter dismay that no friend breathes for him. Should he return to his own parish it would be like going to his own dungeon, and if he enters the workhouse, no eye there will flash sympathy upon him! He is utterly friendless and alone.

I believe that many a suicide has been produced by the want of a friend. As long as a man feels he has someone loving him, he has something worth living for. But when the last friend is gone and we feel that we are floating on a raft far out at sea, with not a sail in sight, we cry, "Welcome death!"

Our Lord and Master was brought to this state. He knew what it was to be forsaken, for He had no friends left. "He that eateth bread with me hath lifted up his heel against me." "All the disciples forsook him, and fled."

Brethren, many saints have lost all their friends but have bravely borne the trial; for turning their eye to Heaven, they have felt that, though without friends, they were still befriended. They have heard the voice of Jesus say, "I will not leave you orphans; I will come unto you"; and made strong by Divine friendship, they have felt that they were not utterly bereaved.

But to be forsaken *of God!* Oh, may you and I never know it! To be without a friend in Heaven; to look to that throne of Glory and to see the blackness of darkness there; to turn to mercy and receive a frown; to fly to love and receive a rebuke; to turn to God and find that His ear is heavy, that He will not hear and His hand restrained that He will not help—oh, this is terror, terror heaped on terror, to be thus forsaken!

4. Loneliness, helplessness, friendlessness—add these together, and then put the next—*hopelessness.*

A man forsaken of men may still entertain some hope. But let him be forsaken of God, and then hope hath failed; the last window is shut; not a ray of light now streams into the thick Egyptian darkness of his mind. Life is death; death is damnation—damnation in its lowest deeps. Let him look to men, and they are broken reeds; let him turn to angels, and they are avengers; let him look to death, and even the tomb affords no refuge. Look where he will—blank, black despair seizes hold upon him.

Our blessed Lord knew this when lover and friend had been put far from Him, and His acquaintance into darkness. It was only His transcendent faith which enabled Him after all to say, "Thou wilt not leave my soul in hell: neither wilt thou suffer thine Holy One to see corruption." The black shadow of this utter hopelessness went over Him when He said, "My soul is exceeding sorrowful, even unto death," and He "sweat as it were great drops of blood, falling down to the ground."

5. To make up this fivefold forsaking, against which we have the five negatives, let us add to all this loneliness, helplessness, friendlessness and hopelessness a sense of *unutterable agony*.

We speak of agony, but to feel it is a very different thing. Misery and despair—the *wrestling* of these with the spirit till the spirit is trodden down and crushed and broken and chooses strangling rather than life; a horrible sense of *every* evil having made one's heart its den; a consciousness that we are the target for all God's arrows; that *all* God's waves and billows have gone over us; that He hath forgotten to be gracious; that He will be merciful to us no more; that He hath in anger shut up the bowels of His compassion—this is a part of being forsaken of God which only lost spirits in Hell can know!

Our unbelief sometimes lets us get a glimpse of what this would be, but it is only a glimpse, only a glimpse. Let us thank God that we are delivered from all fear of this tremendous evil. By five wounds doth our Redeemer slay our unbelief.

Brethren, if God should leave us, mark the result. I picture to myself the very best state of one forsaken of God—it is uncertainty and chance. I would rather be an atom, which hath God with it, predestinating its track and forcing it onward according to His own will, than be an archangel left to my own choice to do as I would and to act as I please without the control of God. An archangel left without God would soon miss his way and fall to Hell, or he would melt away and drop and die; but the tiny atom, having God with it, would fulfill its predestinated course, be ever in a sure track and throughout eternity would have as much potence in it as at its first creation.

Dear friends, if the Lord should forsake us, to say the best of it, our course would be uncertain and, ere long, end in nothingness.

We know, further, that if God should forsake the best saint alive, that man would immediately fall into sin. He now stands securely on yonder lofty pinnacle, but his brain would reel and he would fall, if secret hands did not uphold him. He now picks his steps carefully; take away grace from him, and he would roll in the mire and wallow in it like other men.

When we thus describe being forsaken of God, is it not satisfactory to the highest degree to remember that we have God's Word for it five times over, 'I will never, never leave thee; I will never, never, never forsake thee'?

I know those who say we teach that, let a man live as he likes, yet if God be with him, he will be safe at the last.

We teach no such thing, and our adversaries know better. They know that our doctrines are invulnerable if they will state them correctly and that the only way in which they can attack us is to slander us and to misrepresent what we teach. Nay, verily, we say not so, but we say that where God begins the good work, the man will never live as he likes; or if he does, he will like to live as God would have him live; that where God begins a good work He carries it on; that man is never forsaken of God, but is kept even to the end.

II. A GRACIOUS PROMISE

We have before us now, in the second place, A GRACIOUS PROMISE, or what is positively guaranteed.

What is guaranteed in this promise? Beloved, herein doth God give to His people everything. *"I will never leave thee."*

Then no attribute of God can cease to be engaged for us. Is He mighty? He will show Himself strong on the behalf of them that trust Him. Is He love? Then with everlasting lovingkindness will He have mercy upon us. Whatever attributes may compose the character of Deity, every one of them to its fullest extent shall be engaged on our side.

Moreover, whatsoever God hath, whether it be in the lowest hades or in the highest Heaven, whatever can be contained in infinity or can be held within the circumference of eternity, whatever, in fine, can be in Him who filleth all things, and yet is greater than all things, shall be with His people forever, since "He hath said, *I* will never leave thee, nor forsake thee."

How one might enlarge here, but I forbear; ye yourselves know that to sum up "all things" is a task beyond all human might.

III. FIVE TIMES REPEATED!

More fully, however, to expound this promise, I would remind you of the five OCCASIONS in which it occurs in Scripture. The number five runs all through our subject. The sense and spirit of the text are to be found in innumerable places. Possibly there may be some other passages which approximate so very nearly to our text that you might say they also are repetitions. But I think there are five which clearly take the priority.

1. One of the first instances is to be found in Genesis 28:15:

"Behold, I am with thee, and will keep thee in all places whither thou goest, and will bring thee again into this land; for I will not leave thee, until I have done that which I have spoken to thee of."

Here we have this promise in the case of *a man of trials*. More than either Abraham or Isaac, Jacob was the son of tribulation. He was now flying away from his father's house, leaving the overfondness of a mother's attachment, abhorred by his elder brother who sought his blood. He lies down to sleep with a stone for his pillow, with the hedges for his curtains, with the earth for his bed, and the heavens for his canopy. As he sleeps, friendless, solitary and alone, God saith to him, 'I will never, never leave thee.'

Mark his after career. He is guided to Padan-aram. God, his Guide, leaves him not. At Padan-aram Laban wickedly and wrongfully cheats him in many ways; but God doth not leave him, and he is more than a match for the thievish Laban.

He flies at last with his wives and children. Laban, in hot haste, pursues him. But the Lord does not leave him. Mizpah's Mount bears witness that God can stop the pursuer and change the foe into a friend.

Esau comes against him. Let Jabbok testify to Jacob's wrestlings; and through the power of Him who never did forsake His servant, Esau kisses his brother, whom once he thought to slay.

Anon Jacob dwells in tents and booths at Succoth. He journeys up and down throughout the land. His sons treacherously slay the Shechemites. The nations round about seek to avenge their death, but the Lord again interposes, and Jacob is delivered.

Poor Jacob is bereaved of his sons. He cries, "Joseph is not, and Simeon is not, and now ye will take Benjamin away; all these things are against me."

But they are not against him. God has not left him, for He has not yet done everything that He had spoken to him of.

The old man goes into Egypt. His lips are refreshed while he kisses the cheeks of his favorite Joseph. And until the last, when he gathers up his feet in the bed and sings of that coming Shiloh and the sceptre that should not depart from Judah, good old Jacob proves that in six troubles God is with His people, and in seven He doth not forsake them; that even to hoar hairs He is the same, and until old age He doth carry them.

You Jacobs, full of affliction, you tried and troubled heirs of Heaven, He hath said to each one of you, 'I will never leave thee; I will never forsake thee.'

2. The next instance in which we find this same promise is in Deuteronomy 31:6. Here we find it spoken, not so much to individuals as to the whole body collectively. Moses said unto the people of Judah by the Word of God:

"Be strong and of a good courage, fear not, nor be afraid of them: for the Lord thy God, he it is that doth go with thee; he will not fail thee, nor forsake thee."

Beloved, we may take this promise as being spoken to God's church, *as a church.* These people were to fight the accursed nations of Canaan, to drive out the giants and the men who had chariots of iron. But the Lord said He would never leave them, nor did He, till from Dan to Beersheba the favored race possessed the promised land and the tribes went up to Jerusalem with the voice of joyful song.

Now, as the church of God, let us remember that the land lieth before us and we are called of God to go up and possess it. I would it were my lot yet more and more, like Joshua, to lead you from one place to another, smiting the enemies of the Lord and extending the kingdom of Messias! Let us undertake what we may; we shall never fail. Let us, by faith, dare great things, and we shall do great things. Let us venture upon notable exploits which shall seem fanatical to reason and absurd to men of prudence, for He hath said, 'I will never leave you nor forsake you.'

If the church of God would but know that her Lord cannot leave her, she might attempt greater things than she has ever done, and the success of her attempts would be most certain and sure. God never can forsake a praying people nor cast off a laboring church; He must bless us even to the end.

3. The third occasion upon which this promise was made is in Joshua 1:5 where the Lord says to Joshua:

"There shall not any man be able to stand before thee all the days of thy life: as I was with Moses, so I will be with thee: I will not fail thee, nor forsake thee."

Now this is *a minister's text.* If we be called to lead the people, to bear the brunt of the fight, the burden and heat of the day, let us treasure up this as our precious consolation, He will not fail us nor forsake us.

It needs not that I should tell you that it is not every man who can stand first in the ranks, and that, albeit there is no small share of honor given by God to such a man, yet there is a bitterness in his lot which no other men can know. There are times when, if it were not for faith, we would give up the ghost and, were not the Master with us, we would turn our back and fly, like Jonah, unto Tarshish.

But if any of you be called to occupy prominent positions in God's church, bind this about your arm, and it shall make you strong. He hath said to you, "I will never leave thee, nor forsake thee." Go, in this thy might; the Lord is with thee, thou mighty man of valor.

4. On the next occasion, this same promise was given by David in his last moments to his son Solomon (I Chron. 28:20). David was speaking of what he himself by experience had proved to be true, and he declares:

"Be strong and of good courage, and do it: fear not, nor be dismayed: for the Lord God, even my God, will be with thee; he will not fail thee, nor forsake thee, until thou hast finished all the work for the service of the house of the Lord."

Some Christians are placed where they need *much prudence, discretion and wisdom.* You may take this for your promise.

The Queen of Sheba came to see Solomon. She put to him many difficult questions, but God did not leave him nor forsake him; and he was able to answer them all.

As judge over Israel, many knotty points were brought before him. You remember the child and the harlots and how wisely he decided the case. The building of the Temple was a very mighty work—the like of which the earth had never seen. By wisdom given to him, the stones were fashioned and laid one upon another, till at last the top stone was brought out with shoutings.

You shall do the same, O man of business, though yours be a very responsible situation. You shall finish your course, O careful worker; though there are many eyes that watch for your halting, you shall do the same. Sister, though you need to have seven eyes rather than two, you shall hear the voice of God saying, "This is the way, walk ye in it." Thou shalt never be ashamed nor confounded, world without end.

5. Once more, and perhaps this fifth occasion may be the most

comforting to the most of you, Isaiah 41:17:

"When the poor and needy seek water, and there is none, and their
tongue faileth for thirst, I the Lord will hear them, I the God of Israel
will not forsake them."

You may be brought to this state today. Your soul may *need Christ,*
but you may not be able to find Him. You may feel that without the
mercy which comes from the atoning blood, you are lost. You may
have gone to works and ceremonies, to prayings and doings, to almsgiv-
ings and to experiences, and have found them all dried wells. Now you
can hardly pray, for your tongue cleaves to the roof of your mouth for
thirst. Now in your worst condition, brought to the lowest state into which
a creature ever can be cast, Christ will not forsake you. He will appear
for your help.

Surely one of these five occasions must suit you, and let me here
remind you that whatever God has said to any one saint, He has said
to all. When He opens a well for one man, it is that all may drink. When
the manna falls, it is not only for those in the wilderness, but we by
faith do eat the manna still. No promise is of private interpretation. When
God openeth a granary door to give out food, there may be some one
starving man who is the occasion of its being opened, but all the hungry
besides may come and feed, too. Whether He gave the word to
Abraham or to Moses matters not; He has given it to thee as one of
the covenanted seed.

There is not a high blessing too lofty for thee; nor a wide mercy too
extensive for thee. Lift up now thine eyes to the north and to the south,
to the east and to the west, for all this is thine. Climb to Pisgah's top
and view the utmost limit of the divine promise, for the land is all thine
own. There is not a brook of living water of which thou mayest not
drink. If the land floweth with milk and honey, eat the honey and drink
the milk. The fattest of the kine, yea, and the sweetest of the wines,
let all be thine, for there is no denial of any one of them to any saint.

Be thou bold to believe, for He hath said, "I will never leave *thee,*
nor forsake *thee."* To put everything in one, there is nothing you can
want, there is nothing you can ask for, there is nothing you can need
in time or in eternity, there is nothing living, nothing dying, there is
nothing in this world, nothing in the next world, there is nothing now,
nothing at the resurrection morning, nothing in Heaven that is not contained in this text—'I will never leave thee; I will never forsake thee.'

IV. THE SWEET CONFIRMATION

I shall give five blows to drive home the nail while I speak upon THE SWEET CONFIRMATIONS of this most precious promise.

1. Let me remind you that the Lord will not and cannot leave His people because of *His relationship to them*. He is your *Father;* will your Father leave you? Has He not said, "Can a woman forget her sucking child, that she should not have compassion on the son of her womb? yea, they may forget, yet will I not forget thee"?

Would you, being evil, leave your child to perish? Never, never! Remember, Christ is your *Husband*. Would you, a husband, neglect your wife? Is it not a shame to a man, unless he nourisheth and cherisheth her even as his own body, and will Christ become one of these ill husbands? Hath He not said, "I hate putting way," and will He ever put thee away? Remember, thou art *part of His body*.

No man yet ever hated his own flesh. Thou mayest be but as a little finger, but will He leave His finger to rot, to perish, to starve? Thou mayest be the least honorable of all the members, but is it not written that upon these He bestoweth abundant honor and so our uncomely parts have abundant comeliness?

If He be Father, if He be Husband, if He be Head, if He be All-in-all, how can He leave thee? Think not so hardly of thy God.

2. Then, next, *His honor* binds Him never to forsake thee.

When we see a house half-built and left in ruins, we say, "This man began to build and was not able to finish." Shall this be said of thy God, that He began to save thee and could not bring thee to perfection? Is it possible that He will break His Word and so stain His truth? Shall men be able to cast a slur upon His power, His wisdom, His love, His faithfulness?

No! thank God, no! "I give," saith He, 'unto my sheep eternal life, and they shall never perish, neither shall any man pluck them out of my hand.'

If thou shouldest perish, believer, Hell would ring with diabolical laughter against the character of God. And if ever one whom Jesus undertook to save should perish, then the demons of the pit would point the finger of scorn forever against a defeated Christ, against a God who undertook but went not through.

His honor is engaged to save
The meanest of His sheep;

All that His heavenly Father gave
His hands securely keep.

3. And if that be not enough, wilt thou remember besides this that *the past* all goes to prove that He will not forsake thee. Thou hast been in deep waters; hast thou been drowned? Thou hast walked through the fires; hast thou been burned? Thou hast had six troubles; hath He forsaken thee? Thou hast gone down to the roots of the mountains, and the weeds have been wrapped about thy head; hath He not brought thee up again? Thou hast borne great and sore troubles; but hath He not delivered thee?

Say, when did He leave thee? Testify against Him; if thou hast found Him forgetful, then doubt Him. If thou hast found Him unworthy of thy confidence, then disown Him, but not till then. The past is vocal with a thousand songs of gratitude, and every note therein proveth by an indisputable logic that He will not forsake His people.

4. And if that be not enough, ask thy father and *the saints that have gone before,* "Did ever any perish trusting in Christ?" I have heard that some whom Jehovah loved have fallen from grace and have been lost. I have heard lips of ministers thus prostitute themselves to falsehood, but I know that such never was the case. He keepeth all His saints; not one of them hath perished. They are in His hand and have hitherto been preserved.

David mourneth, "All thy waves and thy billows have gone over me"; yet he crieth, "Hope thou in God, for I shall yet praise him."

Jonah laments, "The earth with her bars was about me for ever"; yet ere long he says, "Salvation is of the Lord."

Ye glorified ones above, through much tribulation ye have inherited the kingdom; and wearing your white robes, ye smile from your thrones of Glory and say to us, "Doubt not the Lord, neither distrust Him. He hath not forsaken His people nor cast off His chosen."

5. Beloved friends, there is *no reason why He should* cast us off. Can you adduce any reason why He should cast you away?

Is it your poverty, your nakedness, your peril, the danger of your life? In all these things we are more than conquerors through Him that hath loved us. Do you say it is your sins? Then I answer: sin can never be a cause why God should cast away His people, for they were full of sin when He at first embraced their persons and espoused their cause. That would have been a cause why He never should have loved them;

but having loved them when they were dead in trespasses and sins, their sin can never be a reason for leaving them.

Besides, the apostle says, "I am persuaded, that neither death, nor life, nor angels, nor principalities, nor powers, nor things present, nor things to come"—and sin is one of the things present, and I fear it is one of the things to come—"Nor height, nor depth, nor any other creature, shall be able to separate us from the love of God, which is in Christ Jesus our Lord."

O child of God, there is no fear of your misusing this precious truth. The base-born professor of godliness may say, "I will sin, for God will not cast me away"; but you will not, ye heirs of Heaven; rather you will bind this about your heart and say, 'Now will I love Him who having loved His own, loves them even unto the end.' Glory be to God!

'Midst all my sin and care and woe,
His Spirit will not let me go.

Go, ye slaves who fear the curse of God and sweat and toil. We are His sons, and we know He cannot expel us from His heart. May God deliver us from the infamous bondage of the doctrine which makes men fear that God may be unfaithful, that Christ may divorce His own spouse, may let the members of His own body perish; that He may die for them and yet not save them.

If there be any truth taught us in Scripture, it is that the children of God cannot perish. If this Book teaches anything whatever, if it be not all a fiction from beginning to end, it teaches in a hundred places, "The righteous shall hold on his way, and he that hath clean hands shall wax stronger and stronger."

"The mountains shall depart, and the hills be removed; but the covenant of his love cannot depart from us, saith the Lord that hath mercy upon us."

V. WHAT WONDERFUL CONCLUSIONS
FROM THIS TRUTH!

And now, fifth, the SUITABLE CONCLUSIONS to be drawn from this doctrine.

1. One of the first is *contentment*. The apostle says, "Having food and raiment, let us be therewith content, for he hath said, I will never leave thee, nor forsake thee."

Ishmael, the son of Hagar, had his water in a bottle; he might have laughed at Isaac because Isaac had no bottle, but then here was the difference between them—Isaac lived by the well.

Now some of us have little enough in this world; we have no bottle of water, no stock in hand; but then we live by the well, and that is better still. To depend upon the daily providence of a faithful God is better than to be worth twenty thousand pounds a year.

2. *Courage* is the next lesson. Let us boldly say, "God is my helper, why should I fear what man can do unto me?" A child of God afraid! Why, there is nothing more contrary to His nature. If any would persecute you, look them in the face and bear it cheerfully. If they laugh at you, let them laugh; you can laugh when they shall howl. If any despise you, be content to be despised by fools and to be misunderstood by madmen. It were hard if the world loved us; it is an easy thing if the world hateth us. We are so used to be spoken of as altogether vile in our motives and selfish in our objects; so used to hear our adversaries misconstrue our best words and pull our sentences to pieces that, if they were to do anything else but howl, we should think ourselves unworthy.

"Who art thou, that thou shouldst be afraid of a man that shall die, and of the son of man which shall be made as grass; and forgettest the Lord thy maker, that hath stretched forth the heavens, and laid the foundations of the earth."

3. Then next, *we ought to cast off our despondency.* Some of you came here this morning as black as the weather. Just now we saw some gleams of sunshine peering through those side windows, until our friends hastened to draw the blinds, to shut out the dazzling brightness from their eyes. I hope, however, you will not shut out the rays of holy joy which break in upon you now. No, since He has said, "I will never leave nor forsake thee," leave your troubles in your pews and bear away a song.

4. And then, my brethren, here is argument for *the greatest possible delight.* How we ought to rejoice with joy unspeakable if He will never leave us! Mere songs are not enough; shout for joy all ye that are upright in heart.

5. And last, what ground there is here *for faith!* Let us lean upon our God with all our weight. Let us throw ourselves upon His faithfulness

as we do upon our beds, bringing all our weariness to His dear rest. Now right on our God let us cast the burdens of our bodies and our souls; for He hath said, 'I will never leave thee; I will never forsake thee.'

Oh, I wish this promise belonged to you all! But some of you must not touch it; it does not belong to some of you, for it is the exclusive property of the man who trusts in Christ.

"Oh!" saith one, "then I will trust in Christ." Do it, soul, do it; and if thou trustest in Him, He will never leave thee. Black as thou art, He will wash thee; He will never leave thee. Wicked as thou art, He will make thee holy; He will never leave thee. Though thou hast nought that should win His love, He will press thee to His bosom; He will never leave thee. Living or dying, in time or in eternity, He will never forsake thee but will surely bring thee to His right hand and say, "Here am I, and the children whom thou hast given me."

May God seal these five negatives upon our memories and hearts for Christ's sake. Amen.

XVII.

The Friend of the Sorrowing

D. L. MOODY

"He hath sent me to heal the brokenhearted."—Luke 4:18.

I want to take up this one thought—that Christ was sent into the world to heal the brokenhearted.

When the Prince of Wales came to this country a few years ago, the whole country was excited as to his purpose. What was his object in coming here? Had he come to look into our republican form of government or our institutions, or was it simply to see and be seen? He came and he went without telling us what he came for.

When the Prince of Peace came into this dark world, He did not come in any private way. He tells us that He came not to see and to be seen but to "seek and to save that which was lost," and "to heal the brokenhearted." In the face of this announcement it is a mystery why those who have broken hearts would rather carry them year in and year out than just bring them to the Great Physician.

How many men in Chicago are going down to their graves with a broken heart? They have carried their hearts weighted with trouble for years; yet when they open the Scriptures, they can see the passage telling us that He came here for the purpose of healing the brokenhearted. He left Heaven and all its glory to come to the world, sent by the Father, He tells us, for the purpose of healing the brokenhearted.

Broken Hearts Everywhere!

No class of people is exempt from broken hearts. The rich and the poor suffer alike. There was a time when I used to visit the poor, thinking that all the broken hearts were to be found among them. But within the last few years I have found there are as many broken hearts among the learned as the unlearned, the cultured as the uncultured, the rich as the poor. Could you but go up one of our avenues and down another, reach the hearts of the people and get them to tell you their whole story, you would be astonished at the wonderful history of every family.

A few years ago I had been out of the city for some weeks. When I returned I started out to make some calls. The first place I went to I found a mother, her eyes red with weeping. When I tried to find out what was troubling her, she reluctantly opened her heart and told me all. "Last night my only boy came home about midnight, drunk. I didn't know he was addicted to drunkenness, but this morning I found out that he has been drinking for weeks, and," she continued, "I would rather have seen him laid in the grave than have had him brought home in the condition I saw him in last night."

I tried to comfort her the best I could.

When I left that house I didn't want to go into any other house where there was family trouble. The very next house I went to, however— where some of the children lived who attended my Sunday school—I found that death had been there and laid his hand on one of them.

The mother spoke to me of her affliction. She brought to me the playthings and the little shoes of the child. The tears trickled down that mother's cheeks as she related to me her sorrow. I got out as soon as possible and hoped I would see no more family trouble that day.

The next visit I made was to a home where I found a wife with a bitter story. Her husband had been neglecting her for a long time. "Now," she said, "he has left me, and I don't know where he is. Winter is coming on, and I don't know what will become of my family."

I tried to comfort her, prayed with her and endeavored to get her to lay all her sorrows on Christ.

The next home I entered I found a woman crushed and broken-hearted. She told me her boy had forsaken her and she had no idea where he had gone.

That afternoon I made five calls, and in every home I found a broken heart. Everyone had a sad tale to tell.

If you visited any home in Chicago you would find the truth of the saying that "there is a skeleton in every house." I suppose while I am talking you are thinking of the great sorrow in your own bosom. I don't know anything about you; but if I came round to every one of you and you were to tell me the truth, I would hear a tale of sorrow.

The very last man I spoke to last night was a young mercantile man who told me his load of sorrow had been so great that many times during the last few weeks he had gone down to the lake and had been tempted to plunge in and end his life. His burden seemed too much for him.

Think of the broken hearts in Chicago tonight! They could be numbered by hundreds, yea, by thousands. All over this city are broken hearts. If all the sorrow represented in this great city were written in a book, this building couldn't hold that book and you couldn't read it in a long lifetime. This earth is not a stranger to tears; neither is the present the only time when they could be found in abundance. From Adam's day to ours, tears have been shed and a wail has been going up to Heaven from the brokenhearted.

I say it again: it is a mystery to me how all those broken hearts can keep away from Him who has come to heal them.

For six thousand years that cry of sorrow has been going up to God. We find the tears of Jacob put on record when he was told that his own son was no more. When his sons and daughters tried to give him comfort, he refused to be comforted.

We are also told of the tears of King David. I can hear him as the messenger brings the news to him of the death of his son, exclaiming in anguish, "O my son Absalom, my son, my son Absalom! would God I had died for thee."

When Christ came into the world, the first sound He heard was of woe—the wail of those mothers in Bethlehem. From the manger to the cross He was surrounded with sorrow. We are told that He often looked up to Heaven and sighed. Surely it was because there was so much suffering around Him. It was on His right hand and on His left— everywhere on earth; and the thought that He had come to relieve the people of the earth of their burdens and so few would accept Him, made Him sorrowful.

Let the hundreds of thousands just cast their burdens on Him. He has come to bear those burdens as well as our sins. He will bear our griefs and carry our sorrow. There is not in Chicago a burdened son of Adam who cannot be freed if he will only come to Him.

God Sent Jesus Expressly to Heal the Brokenhearted

Let me call your attention to this little word "sent"—"He hath sent me." If you will take your Bibles and read about those who have been sent by God, one thought will come to you: no man who has ever been sent by God to do His work has ever failed. No matter how great the work, how mighty the undertaking, how many difficulties had to be encountered, when they were sent by God, they were sure to succeed.

God sent Moses down to Egypt to bring three million people out of bondage. The idea would have seemed absurd to most people. Fancy a man with an impediment in his speech, without an army, without generals, with no records, bringing three million people from the power of a great nation like that of the Egyptians. But God sent him; and what was the result? Pharaoh said they should not go, and the great king and all his army were going to prevent them. But did he succeed? Since God sent Moses, he didn't fail.

God sent Joshua to the walls of Jericho. He marched around the walls, and at the proper time they came tumbling down, and the city fell into his hands.

When God sent Elijah to stand before Ahab, we read the result.

Samson and Gideon were sent by God, and we are told what they accomplished.

All through the Word we find that when God sent men they never failed.

Now, do you think for a moment that God's own Son, sent to us, is going to fail? If Moses, Elijah, Joshua, Gideon, Samson and all those mighty men He sent succeeded in doing their work, is the Son of Man going to fail? If He has come to heal broken hearts, is He going to fail? Is there a heart so bruised and broken that can't be healed by Him?

He can heal them all, but the great trouble is that men won't come. If there is a broken heart here tonight, just bring it to the Great Physician. If you break an arm or a leg, you run off and get the best physician. If you have a broken heart, you needn't go to a doctor or minister with it; the best physician is the Great Physician.

In the days of Christ there were no hospitals or physicians as we have now. When a man was sick, he was taken to the door and the passers-by prescribed for him. If a man came along who had had the same disease as the sufferer, he told him how he had been cured.

I had a certain disease for a few months, then recovered. When I met a man with the same disease, I had to tell him what cured me; I could not keep the prescription all to myself.

When He came there and found the sick at their cottage doors, the sufferers found more medicine in His words than there was in all the prescriptions of that country. He is a mighty Physician who has come to heal every wounded heart. The great difficulty is that people try to get some other physician. They go to this creed and that creed, to this doctor of divinity and that one, instead of coming directly to the Master. He has told us that His mission is to heal the broken hearts. Since He has said this, then let us take Him at His word and ask Him to heal.

Christians Have a Blessed Help in Trouble

I was thinking today of the difference between those who know Christ when trouble comes and those who know Him not. I know several members of families in this city who are stumbling into their graves over trouble. I know two widows in Chicago who are weeping and moaning over the death of their husbands. Instead of bringing their grief to Christ, they mourn day and night, with the result that in a few weeks or years at most, their sorrow will take them to their graves.

Three years ago a father took his wife and family on board that ill-fated French steamer, bound for Europe. When out on the ocean another vessel ran into her, and she went down.

When I was preaching in Chicago, that mother used to bring her two children to the meetings every night. It was a beautiful sight to see how those little children would sit and listen, with tears trickling down their cheeks when the Saviour was preached. It seemed as if nobody else in that meeting drank in the truth as eagerly as those little ones.

One night when an invitation had been extended to all to go into the inquiry room, one of these little children said, "Mamma, why can't I go in, too?" The mother allowed them to come into the room. Some friend spoke to them. To all appearances they seemed to understand the plan of salvation as well as their elders.

When that memorable night of shipwreck came, that mother went down and came up without her two children. Upon reading the news, I said, "It will kill her," and I quitted my post in Edinburgh—the only time I left my post on the other side—and went down to Liverpool to try to comfort her.

But when I got there I found that the Son of God had been there before me. Instead of my comforting her, she comforted me. She told me she could not think of those children as being in the sea. It seemed as if Christ had permitted her to take those children on that vessel only that they might be wafted to Him and that He had saved her life only that she might come back and work a little longer for Him.

If any of you have had some great affliction, if any of you have lost a loving father, mother, brother, husband or wife, come to Christ. God has sent Him to heal the brokenhearted.

Some of you, I can imagine, will say, "Ah, I could stand that affliction; I have something harder than that."

I remember a mother coming to me and saying, "It is easy enough for you to speak in that way; if you had the burden I've got, you couldn't cast it on the Lord."

"Why, is your burden so great that Christ can't carry it?" I asked.

"No, it isn't too great for Him to carry, but I can't put it on Him."

"That is your fault," I replied.

I find a great many people with burdens who, rather than just come to Him with them, strap them tighter on their backs and go away staggering under their load.

When I asked her the nature of her trouble, she told me, "I have an only boy, and he is a wanderer on the face of the earth. I don't know where he is. If I only knew, I would go round the world to find him. You don't know how I love that boy. This sorrow is killing me."

"Why can't you take him to Christ? You can reach him at the throne, even though he be at the uttermost part of the world. Go tell God all about your trouble. He can take away his sin. Not only that, if you never see him on earth, God can give you faith that you will see your boy in Heaven."

Then I told her of a mother who lived down in the southern part of Indiana. Some years ago her boy, a moralist, came up to this city. (A man has to have more than morality to lean upon in this great city.) He hadn't been here long before he was led astray. A neighbor happened to come up here and found him one night in the streets drunk. The neighbor at first thought he would not say anything about it to the boy's father, but afterward he felt it was his duty to tell. So from a crowd in the street of their little town, he took that father aside and told him what he had seen in Chicago.

It was a terrible blow. When the children had been put to bed that night, he said to his wife, "Wife, I have bad news. I have heard from Chicago today."

The mother dropped her work in an instant and said, "Tell me what it is."

"Well, our son has been seen on the streets of Chicago drunk."

Neither of them slept that night, but they took their burden to Christ. About daylight the mother said, "I don't know how, I don't know when or where, but God has given me faith to believe that our son will be saved and will never come to a drunkard's grave."

One week after, that boy left Chicago. He couldn't tell why, but an unseen power seemed to lead him to his mother's home. The first thing he said on coming over the threshold was, "Mother, I have come home to ask you to pray for me." And soon after, he came back to Chicago a bright and shining light.

If you have a burden like this, father, mother, bring it and cast it on Him, and the Great Physician will heal your broken heart.

Jesus More Tender Than President Lincoln

I can imagine some of you saying, "How am I to do it?" My friends, go to Him as a personal friend. He is not a myth. What we do is to treat Christ as we treat an earthly friend. If you have sins, just go and tell Him all about them. If you have some great burden, go bury thy sorrow, bury it in His bosom. When you go to people and tell them of your cares, your sorrows, they will tell you they haven't time to listen. But He will not only hear your story, however long it be, but will bind up your broken heart. Oh, if there be a broken heart here tonight, bring it to Jesus, and I tell you on authority that He will heal you. He has said He will bind your wounds up; not only that, He will heal them.

During the war a young man not yet twenty was court-martialed and sentenced to be shot. The story was this: The young fellow had enlisted. He was not obliged to, but he went off with another young man. They were what we would call chums.

One night when this companion was ordered out on picket duty, he asked the young man to go for him. The next night the young man was ordered out himself. Having been awake two nights and not being used to it, he fell asleep at his post. For the offense he was tried and sentenced to death.

It was right after the order issued by the President that no interference would be allowed in cases of this kind. This sort of thing had become too frequent, and it must be stopped.

When the news reached the father and mother in Vermont, it nearly broke their hearts. The thought that their son should be shot was too great for them. They had no hope that he would be saved by anything they could do.

But they had a little daughter who had read the life of Abraham Lincoln and knew how he loved his own children. She said, "If Abraham Lincoln knew how my father and mother loved my brother, he wouldn't let him be shot." That little girl thought this over and made up her mind to see the President.

She went to the White House. The sentinel, when he saw her imploring looks, passed her in. When she came up to the door and told the private secretary that she wanted to see the President, he could not refuse her.

She came into the chamber and found Abraham Lincoln surrounded by his generals and counselors. When he saw the little country girl, he asked her what she wanted. The little maid told her plain, simple story—how her brother, whom her mother and father loved very dearly, had been sentenced to be shot. They were mourning for him, and if he was to die in that way, it would break their hearts.

The President's heart, touched with compassion, immediately sent a dispatch canceling the sentence and giving the boy a parole so that he could go home and see that father and mother.

I tell you this to show you how Abraham Lincoln's heart was moved by compassion for the sorrow of that father and mother. And if the President showed so much, do you think the Son of God will not have compassion upon you, sinner? if you only take that crushed, bruised heart to Him, He will heal it.

Have you a drunken husband? Go tell Him. He can make him a blessing to the church and to the world. Have you a profligate son? Go take your story to Him. He will comfort you and bind up and heal your sorrow.

What a blessing it is to have such a Saviour who can heal the brokenhearted. May the text, if the sermon doesn't, reach everyone here tonight; and may every crushed, broken and bruised heart be brought to the Saviour and to hear His comforting words. He will comfort you as a mother comforts her child if you will only come in prayer and lay all your burdens before Him.

XVIII.

What to Do When Trouble Comes

TOM MALONE

"But not long after there arose against it a tempestuous wind, called Euroclydon."—Acts 27:14.

I had read the book of Acts through many times before this chapter really meant much to me. In fact, I had taught the book of Acts in the church and seminary several times and had often referred to it as a chapter which did not seem to have a great deal of pertinent teaching to a Christian.

My mind has changed drastically! This chapter has come to mean so much because it tells me what to do when trouble comes.

Trouble comes to one and all. The fact that we are saved and members of the family of God does not mean that no trouble will ever come our way.

In verse 13 of this wonderful chapter we read that "the south wind blew softly." It is always so refreshing when "the south wind blows softly." It is warm and gentle, and we welcome it. But there are other winds, too, some of which are most contrary, such as the "tempestuous wind" of verse 14.

There is no way to know when or whence trouble may come. It may come in the church or in the home or in your own individual life. It may come from a vicious enemy or from a trusted friend. It may come from the choir or the pulpit or from a church member. It may come in the form of death to someone dearly loved, or it may come when health is lost or dreams do not come true. Just be assured that it will come, so be prepared for it.

Job said, ". . .yet trouble came" (3:26).

Job said again, "Yet man is born unto trouble, as the sparks fly upward" (5:7).

Paul said, "We are troubled on every side, yet not distressed" (II Cor. 4:8).

The Scriptures clearly teach that every born-again child of God will be called upon to suffer for the cause of Christ. "For unto you it is given in the behalf of Christ, not only to believe on him, but also to suffer for his sake" (Phil. 1:29).

In this same letter, Paul expressed a deep longing to "know him...and the fellowship of his suffering" (3:10).

Peter also wrote of trouble and suffering:

"Beloved, think it not strange concerning the fiery trial which is to try you, as though some strange thing happened unto you: But rejoice, inasmuch as ye are partakers of Christ's sufferings; that, when his glory shall be revealed, ye may be glad also with exceeding joy."—I Pet. 4:12,13.

Now what shall we do when trouble comes? Shall we be defeated by it, or shall we overcome it by the power and grace of Christ and make it a stepping stone to loftier spiritual heights?

This glorious portion of God's wonderful Word teaches us that there are five practical things to do when trouble comes.

I. SPEND TIME ALONE WITH GOD

"But after long abstinence Paul stood forth in the midst of them, and said, Sirs, ye should have hearkened unto me, and not have loosed from Crete, and to have gained this harm and loss."—Acts 27:21.

Notice the expression, "after long abstinence Paul stood forth." Where had he been? There can be little doubt as to where Paul was during this terrific storm. He was down in the hold of the ship in holy prayer for divine deliverance. This was certainly the practice of great men and women of God in Bible times.

When Jacob faced the stormiest and most troublesome crisis of his life, namely the meeting with his brother Esau, he dared not face this crisis without first meeting God in the holy place of supplication.

"And Jacob was left alone; and there wrestled a man with him until the breaking of the day" (Gen. 32:24). He spent time "alone" with God.

"And he said, Let me go, for the day breaketh. And he said, I will not let thee go, except thou bless me" (vs. 26). He refused to let go, to give up, to quit praying until he knew he had been blessed and prepared by prayer.

"And he said, Thy name shall be called no more Jacob, but Israel: for as a prince hast thou power with God and with men, and hast prevailed" (vs. 28). His name, character and testimony were changed by this great experience.

Oh, that we would, in time of trouble, wait at the throne of grace until God's answer comes!

One of the greatest promises in God's Word is Isaiah 40:31, "But they that wait upon the Lord shall renew their strength; they shall mount up with wings as eagles; they shall run, and not be weary; and they shall walk, and not faint."

When trouble comes, we must wait upon the Lord or faint and fail.

Some of the Lord's saints I have known, who have gone to the secret place of prayer in times of life's tempestuous winds, have experienced great and miraculous events. Some Christians I have known have gone without food and water for hours, locked up in the secret closet of prayer. As a result, hardhearted sinners were converted, entangling problems were solved, sick bodies were healed, and great needs were abundantly supplied.

When the storm arose and the tempestuous winds blew, Paul sought the face of God in prayer and came out with an answer from Heaven. Many Christians today have surrendered to problems which could have been conquered by getting alone with God.

"There arose. . . a tempestuous wind."

II. RECKON UPON HIS PRESENCE

"For there stood by me this night the angel of God, whose I am, and whom I serve."—Acts 27:23.

How often in His Word does the Lord try to tell us that He will always be with us. How much it must have meant to Paul during this great storm to have the angel of the Lord appear to him in the night and tell him not to be afraid.

When trouble comes to the child of God, if he can only remember that the Lord will be with him and can reckon on His presence, he will be sustained.

Notice some great verses in the Bible which teach us that we can always depend on His presence.

"And he said, My presence shall go with thee, and I will give thee rest."—Exod. 33:14.

"Yea, though I walk through the valley of the shadow of death, I will fear no evil: for thou art with me; thy rod and thy staff they comfort me."—Ps. 23:4.

"Let your conversation be without covetousness; and be content with such things as ye have: for he hath said, I will never leave thee, nor forsake thee."—Heb. 13:5.

Some years ago I heard the exciting story of a very sick Christian whose faith was sorely tried in the dark hour of his illness and eventual death. This man had a devoted Christian doctor. One day the sick man said to him, "Doctor, I feel so alone. I am afraid. I fear facing the experience of death."

The fine Christian doctor pulled a chair up close to the side. Pointing to the chair, he said, "I want you to remember that Jesus is here with you all the time. He will never leave nor forsake you. Reckon upon the presence of the Lord so strongly that you can imagine Him sitting in this chair."

As the days and nights came and went, the dying Christian constantly kept a feeble hand on the arm of the chair, as if he were literally holding hands with Jesus.

One day he breathed his last and quietly slipped away to be with Jesus. When his family found him dead, his hand was on the arm of the empty chair. When the godly doctor was told of this, he said, "He was holding to the nail-scarred hand of Jesus and was conscious of His presence until he died."

Just as the "fourth man" walked into the fiery furnace with the three Hebrew children, so will Jesus walk with us when the "tempestuous winds" arise. The God who would be with Jeremiah in a miry pit and with Daniel in a lions' den and with Paul upon the angry bosom of a storm-tossed sea, will be with His children when trouble comes. Oh, it behooves you to learn the sweet lesson of reckoning upon His presence at all times!

III. BELIEVE THE PROMISES

Paul said, "I believe God, that it shall be even as it was told me" (Acts 27:25). Paul had learned to believe the promises of God even when all outward circumstances seemed to indicate that their fulfillment was impossible.

I have been so thrilled to learn in recent years that most of the great promises of the Word of God were given to the saints in times of great distress or while they were in the depths of sorrow or in the fires of hot persecution. So many of His promises are applicable to life's troubles and tempestuous winds. Notice what God has to say about His promises.

"God is not a man, that he should lie; neither the son of man, that he should repent: hath he said, and shall he not do it? or hath he spoken, and shall he not make it good?"—Num. 23:19.

"For all the promises of God in him are yea, and in him Amen, unto the glory of God by us."—II Cor. 1:20.

"In hope of eternal life, which God, that cannot lie, promised before the world began."—Titus 1:2.

When Adoniram Judson lay languishing in a filthy Burmese jail, his faith was sorely tried. He had gone to win the heathen to Christ but had been strung up by his thumbs and cruelly beaten; now he was suffering on a filthy straw bed in the vilest of prisons.

When in derision they taunted him by saying, "What do you think now of your plans to win the heathen to Christ?" his thrilling answer will live on to encourage the hearts of thousands of others: "The future is as bright as the promises of God." He believed God when trouble came!

Oh, the promises, the exceeding great and precious promises, are our unshakable rock amidst the crumbling sands of life. No "tempestuous wind" can ever change one divine promise. They are as certain and true and eternal as God Himself.

It was not easy for Abraham to believe the promise when he was nearly a century old and Sarah was ninety years of age and the promised heir had not yet been born. But what a thrill to read of his faith:

"He staggered not at the promise of God through unbelief; but was strong in faith, giving glory to God; And being fully persuaded that, what he had promised, he was able also to perform."—Rom. 4:20,21.

The Lord had told Paul that there would be no loss of life during this great storm and shipwreck. It turned out just exactly as God said.

This is always the case. God cannot and will not lie. I speak reverently when I say that His honor and holiness are at stake. He must keep His word, no matter how strong the tempestuous winds blow in the life of the child of God. How sweet and wonderful to rest in His promises and wait for their certain fulfillment!

IV. COUNT OUR BLESSINGS

Yes, Paul "gave thanks to God in the presence of them all." In fact, many of the great Christians mentioned on the pages of God's holy Word were able to find something to praise God for even in the hour of great trial or temptation.

This great spiritual attitude was always true of Paul. When distress and disappointment came, he counted his blessings. Notice his great optimism expressed in II Corinthians 2:14, "Now thanks be unto God, which always causeth us to triumph in Christ, and maketh manifest the savor of his knowledge by us in every place." Whether Paul was in jail or distress or persecution or disappointment, he always found cause for thankfulness.

This was true of the early Christians in the book of Acts. "And they departed from the presence of the council, rejoicing that they were counted worthy to suffer shame for his name" (Acts 5:41).

Even after they had been beaten and imprisoned and spitefully treated by the godless religious leaders, they rejoiced "that they were counted worthy to suffer shame for his name." These stalwart Christians refused to give in to the trouble, refused to succumb to melancholy or depression, refused to assume a persecution complex. Rather, they rejoiced and counted their blessings and were thankful. Persecution seemed as nothing to them.

I once heard of a man who only had one leg, and he said that he was tempted to complain until he saw a man who had no legs.

It was told that, during World War II, the home of a Christian family in England had been bombed to splinters. The family had been evacuated and were in another part of the country.

Word came of the tragedy that had struck his home. "You have lost everything. Your house and all your belongings have been bombed to splinters."

When the godly man heard that, he calmly replied, "No, I have not lost everything. The bombs of Hitler have not touched my faith. I still believe in the providential and sovereign watchcare of God. I still have my Christian wife and family. I have my hope of Heaven left. In fact, I have lost very little. I can thank God for that."

Yes, in the midst of the tempestuous winds of life, the well-grounded Christian can thank God for his blessings. When trouble comes, as it does to everyone, we must see the eternal, invisible realities.

V. GET RID OF EXCESS BAGGAGE

Acts 27:38 says, "And when they had eaten enough, they lightened the ship, and cast out the wheat into the sea." During this awful storm they lightened the load and cast the cargo into the sea. They got rid of all excess baggage.

It would not be correct to say that all trouble comes as a corrective measure from God, but it would be correct to say that in a time of testing we should search our hearts, as did David:

"Search me, O God, and know my heart: try me, and know my thoughts: And see if there be any wicked way in me, and lead me in the way everlasting."—Ps. 139:23,24.

When the tempestuous winds blow in the life of an obedient child of God or he finds himself in the midst of a stormy crisis, certainly he will want to search his heart. He must conclude with the help of the Holy Spirit as to whether this storm that has come, comes as a punitive measure or merely as a normal part of God's training or blessing in the life of His child. This conclusion can only be determined by a deep spiritual heart-searching and self-examination.

We are to examine ourselves. If one studies carefully the classic and wonderful passage in I Corinthians 11, which has to do with the proper observance of the Lord's table, he will see how important self-examination and heart-searching are. In verse 28 we read, "But let a man examine himself."

There is no better time for self-examination than in a time of crisis. Failure to examine one's self brings the certain chastisement of the Lord. This chastisement is set forth in at least three ways in the Bible: the punishment, the storm, the tempestuous wind itself may be God's punishment.

In verse 30 we read two other manifestations of the Lord's dealing with a disobedient child: "For this cause many are weak and sickly among you, and many sleep." So here we see that sometimes the loss of health is God's punishment and is the explanation of why the storm came.

Then the Bible says, "...and many sleep"—that is, some are taken prematurely to Heaven because they would not yield to the will of God.

So when the tempestuous wind blows, it is time to unload all the excess cargo and the baggage which is not according to the will of God.

I knew a good Christian some years ago who had no fruit in his life and was not a soul winner until the Lord deeply convicted him of the use of cigarettes. After the Lord had convicted this Christian of the unclean habit and he had given it up and had gotten the victory over it, he became one of the finest soul winners I have ever known.

I knew another Christian, a young mother with a beautiful baby. One day when the baby was taken to the hospital and the little one's life hung in jeopardy, she said to me, "Dr. Malone, never in all my life have I searched my heart as much as I have in recent hours. My baby's life hangs by a brittle thread of uncertainty, and I love my baby, and I want it to live. But as I pray, God has convicted me. And this time of sorrow in my life has been a time of great heart-searching. My life has become victorious, and if I ever wanted God to hear my prayers, I want Him to hear them now." God did hear her prayers, and the life of a little child was gloriously spared.

So it is that oftentimes the tempestuous wind comes to get us to search our hearts and to do the right thing.

May God help us to do it.

JACK HYLES
1926-

ABOUT THE MAN:

If we could say but one thing about Dr. Hyles, I guess we would call him MR. SOUL WINNING.

Born in Italy, Texas, he began preaching at age nineteen. He pastored several churches in that state, most notably the Miller Road Baptist Church in Garland that was no doubt the fastest growing church in the world for many years. In seven years it grew to the astounding number of 4,000 members.

Then on to the formal downtown First Baptist Church in the Calumet area of Hammond, Indiana. There, after fighting for separation in the church, he won victory after victory. Now that church is the largest Sunday school in the world. Attendance of over 25,000 is common on a Sunday.

Hammond Baptist Schools, Hyles-Anderson College, Hyles-Anderson Publications, and many other gospel projects have come forth from his fantastic ministry.

His best friend, the late Dr. John R. Rice, said about this giant: *"Jack Hyles is a tornado of zeal. He is pungent in speech, devastating in sarcasm. You will laugh and cry — and repent! Preachers who are not dead will preach differently after hearing him. Thousands point to a message from Jack Hyles as the time of a transformed life. He is simply beyond description, with a unique anointing from God."*

Dr. Hyles is the author of many books, including *Hyles Church Manual, Hyles Sunday School Manual, Kisses of Calvary,* and a great series of *How to. . .* books. He also has a large cassette ministry.

Place Dr. Jack Hyles among the giants of this generation!

XIX.

Compassion Makes a Difference

JACK HYLES

(Preached at Southwide Baptist Fellowship at Beth Haven Baptist Church, Louisville, Kentucky, 1978)

In battles and in great movements like this, we have to fight to keep our hearts. As we are attacked and as we face the enemy, if we don't watch, we will keep our heads right but lose our hearts.

"But ye, beloved, building up yourselves on your most holy faith, praying in the Holy Ghost, Keep yourselves in the love of God, looking for the mercy of our Lord Jesus Christ unto eternal life. And of some have compassion, making a difference: And others save with fear, pulling them out of the fire; hating even the garment spotted by the flesh."— Jude 20-23.

Creation Without Compassion

First came the light, then the firmament, then God lit the starry host in the sky, then He made the fishes of the sea and the animal kingdom. After that, everything was ready for man.

God made man in His own wonderful image. Every tree that grew was pleasant to the sight. Rivers flowed peaceably between verdant banks. Every sound was a melody; every scene, a delight.

There was no war to give unrest in the breast. There was no sickness to cause fear of death. The leaf never withered. The wind never chilled. No perspiration moistened the ground. There was no profanity. There was no heat, no cold. There was no sin. No blossoms were smitten by a tempest. Man had not yet learned how to sigh, nor learned how to weep. There was no withering frost to chill the rose and take its petal. No shadow of guilt was ever known for Adam. There was a choir of birds that always sang.

Yet something was missing. Here was the Garden of Eden. All that God had made was good, and God had made all that was good. And here was man, and here was a perfect garden of bliss.

But something was missing. Adam needed someone to share with him this wonder. He needed someone to laugh with him and rejoice with him and eat with him and enjoy it all with him. Adam yearned for companionship. He longed for communion with a kindred soul, one whose joys were like his own. The virgin world was cold and blank: something was missing.

Creation With Compassion

God looked down and from Adam took a rib. Here she comes dressed in all of her beauty. John Milton said she was adorned with all that Heaven and earth could bestow to make her amiable. Grace was in her step. Heaven was in her eye. Every gesture possessed dignity and love. Perfection was stamped on her.

The sons of God shouted for joy, and the morning stars sang together. Eden was transformed because now Adam has someone with whom he can fellowship. Someone to care. Someone to cheer. Someone to share. Someone to love. Now everything is complete.

Someone wrote:

> **The earth was sad,**
> **The Garden wild.**
> **The hermit sighed,**
> **Till woman smiled.**

Not a creature since Adam has escaped this need for someone to care. The weary housewife, busy with her day's activities, comes to the close of the day wishing that somebody could say, "I care, and I understand."

The trudging laborer, coming from the steel mill, comes home at night just wishing that someone could say, "I know you're tired and weary, and I care."

The lonely mother, the student's wife, the busy student, the harried boss and, I must confess, those of us who stand behind the pulpit are often encouraged by the realization that somebody cares.

Compassion's Contributions

Compassion. Compassion is the nurse given to mankind. Compassion cares for the helpless. Compassion mothers the orphan. Compassion feeds the hungry. Compassion clothes the cold. Compassion helps the helpless. Compassion raises the fallen. Compassion resides at the humble fireside, as those who love gather at the end of day. Compassion shines upon the coldness and warms it. Shines upon suffering and relieves it. Shines upon sorrow and shares it.

I would like to talk to you about something we had better work to keep. We can win all the victories we want to win, fight all the battles we want to fight, shed all the blood we want to shed, build all the great buildings we want to build; but if we lose the moist spot in our eyes, we have no need of all of our buildings. Compassion.

The College Student's Wife

Her name is Mrs. College Student's Wife. Her address is Upstairs Apartment, U.S.A. She fell in love when she was in the high school department in a fundamental church. Soon engagement came, and after awhile the man of God's choosing for her life married her.

They had to live in a little upstairs apartment at first because he had just gotten started at his business.

Then one day they got a car. It was a number of years old. How happy they were!

Then the day came when she found out she was expecting a baby. Another one came. The husband had gotten a promotion at work, and he now had enough money to buy a new car.

Then one day he said, "Sweetheart, I have gotten another promotion and a big raise in pay. Why don't we look for a new house?" So their dreams of many years were fulfilled as they began to search for just the right house that seemed to bear their image and mark.

One day they moved in. The little children were so pleased. They had their own room. The house was so lovely. And they got just the right furniture to match the carpet, just the right drapes to match the furniture, just the right everything to match everything else. Everything was so wonderful because the dreams of early childhood had been fulfilled. The lovely new home, the nice new car—everything was just right.

John taught a Sunday school class and was also an usher. She taught a Beginners class. She also sang in the choir.

One night the service was unusually sweet. Sitting in the choir, she noticed that John came down the aisle. She thought, *John hasn't done anything real bad. What could John be coming down the aisle for?*

John knelt at the altar and cried. She didn't understand it. When they got home John sat down and said, "Sweetheart, do you know why I went forward tonight? God has called me to preach. That means we have to go away to college."

"But, John . . . ."

"I know. I love it all, too. I dream with you."

"But, John, couldn't you just preach at the rescue mission here? After all, the hospitals need somebody to preach to them. John, we have dreamed . . . Our children . . . ."

You know the story.

The house was put up for sale. She prayed that the first folks who came by to look at it would drop dead on the spot! But they said, "It is just what we wanted!"

But she said, "But the faucets leak. There are not enough nails in the dry wall. And the floor is going to buckle when there comes a freeze." But they bought the house.

Then they sold the car. Then they said goodby to their church and went off to school. They could find only an upstairs apartment, much like the one they had had before. If they came to Hammond, it was snowing and below zero. If they came to Chattanooga, it was raining.

John said, "Now, honey, here is my schedule. I will get up at 6:00 a.m. and go to my first class at 7:00. School is over at 1:00. I go to work at 3:00 and work until midnight. It takes an hour to drive home. Then up again at 6:00 a.m. and off again to my first class."

Fundamentalism Needs Old-Fashioned Revival of Character and Compassion

Her name is Mama. Some folks in the South call her Grandma. Her address is Rest Home, U.S.A. She may bore you with her fellowship, as she has so very little of it. Sometimes she doesn't know exactly how to behave when someone comes to see her. You may have to shout to be heard. And food may be dripping from her mouth as she talks to you, for she does not realize exactly how she looks. She has no offering to give. Her hands may tremble, and you may notice a foul odor in the room.

You see, one day her youngest child stood at the altar. And as the recessional was being played, that daughter and her groom marched out the back. It seemed the whole bottom had fallen out of life. Oh, there was still the old man. She still loved him, and they still shared life together. Until one day, suddenly, he was taken.

She tried to keep her house because she didn't want to give up housekeeping. She was a feisty little rascal, and gritty to the end and full of spunk. But she began to fall a lot, especially in wintertime.

Then the children one day got together to try to decide what to do with mother. No one suggested she come and live with them. After all, you can't expect a son to take care of his aged mother just because she entered the jaws of death to give him life. You can't expect him to feed his aged mother and give a bed in his own house to her, just because she gave her life for him and did without and sacrificed and worked and prayed and hoped and dreamed and gave up and did without. You can't expect some son or daughter to be gracious or grateful enough, when mama can't take care of herself, to do what mama did when you couldn't take care of yourself.

If you want to see something that pictures the degradation and depravity of the United States of America, look at these rest homes dotting the horizon around this country. Fundamentalism needs an old-fashioned revival of integrity and character and decency and honor to take care of our own again.

So as they decided what to do with mother, she suggested, "I have an idea. There are some real nice rest homes around the country, and there are a lot of older people my age there, and I think I would enjoy being with them." She didn't mean what she said, but she thought that was the easy way out for you.

So the children took her there and left her. Her hands never open a letter today. Her ears never hear the ring of a phone. Her cheeks never feel the warmth of a kiss. Her feet never take her outside the home. Her eyes never see her loved ones. She never hears anybody say, "I love you." There she sits this morning.

Oh, by the way, you used to know her well because when you first started preaching you relished the opportunity of going to speak to her. But now you have carpets and buildings and chandeliers and padded pews. Now you have a big drive-in crowd of people, and you have sort of forgotten that that little gal prayed for you with power back yonder when you were a kid.

'The First Time...Anybody Prayed for Me'

I was in the hospital visiting one of our men. After I had prayed for him, I walked away, rushing to my morning broadcast. I heard an old voice say to me as I began to leave, "Hey, Reverend! Would you pray that prayer for me, too?"

I turned and saw a man who said he was 88 years of age. He said, "Reverend, nobody has ever prayed for me. Would you pray that prayer for me, too?" I bowed my head and prayed as best I could for him. The old man took my hand and said, "Reverend, thank you. That is the first time I ever heard anybody pray for me."

Oh, let me tell you, ladies and gentlemen, this country of ours is a sick, suffering, sad country. Somebody needs to care. There ought to be some place in every village and town and every countryside and hamlet and neighborhood in America that has a man of God behind the pulpit who knows how it is to 'weep o'er the erring one, and care for the fallen, and tell them that Jesus, the Mighty, can save.' There ought to be some institution in every village and hamlet and neighborhood and town in America that weeps o'er the erring one and cares for the fallen and the burdened and cares for those who are shut-in.

There are folks in this room this morning who have not one time in a year made one call to one of these mighty millions of aged people whom nobody seems to care about.

Oh, beloved brethren, we better not lose our heart.

I am against sin like you are. There is nothing I am not against. I am against it all. I dot every fundamental *i* and cross every fundamental *t*. But I am not concerned about a dry-eyed fundamentalism. I am concerned about a fundamentalism that has compassion, one that seems to care.

The Bus Ministry Needs Compassion

His name is Johnny. Or maybe it is Joe or Pete or Jack. His address is Ghetto, U.S.A. He is a little fellow. He did not know he was abnormal, or not normal, until he visited the home of a friend down the street. He looked in the closet and saw the friend's clothes and compared that to his clothes. And he thought he must be poor. He looked inside the cupboard and saw all the food and remembered what his cupboard looked like at home. And he decided he must be poor. He looked at the shoes on his friend, and he looked at his own bare feet. And he decided he must be poor. He noticed he was different.

Then one day his mother called him in and said, "Son, your father left home this morning. He will never come back."

The boy said, "But, mommy, where is he going?"

"Your father and I are getting a divorce."

"Well, why? Why?"

Or maybe the little fellow didn't even know who his daddy was. His mother got busy, and he hardly knew he had a mother because she had to go to work early in the morning and work until late at night to make ends meet. He is just the poor little kid in the neighborhood.

His only Christmas is what the church brings him. Somebody knocks on the door with a big Santa Claus suit on and says, "Merry Christmas! Merry Christmas!" There is a Christmas tree. That is the only Christmas he ever had.

The only Thanksgiving he ever had was when the church brought a Thanksgiving turkey to his family. He has never had a birthday cake or felt a shiny pair of new shoes on his own feet. He has never heard anybody say, "You are a cute little fellow." He sort of needs you.

I am worried about the deterioration of the bus ministry. I know they mess up the services. They make the carpet filthy. I have seen where a little kid has taken a knife and slit right down the beautiful upholstered pews that I gave my life's blood to put there. But I would rather have the cut pew and the dirty carpet, than to have a poor little fellow never hear "I love you," and nobody to pat him on the head and say, "God bless you, fellow."

Ladies and gentlemen, twenty-two years ago when I spoke to fundamentalists for the very first time, we were in storefront buildings. We were in tents. We didn't have carpets and chandeliers. And the folks I am preaching about today are the only kind who would hear us. And we better get back to them.

Our 5,000-seat auditorium is all white and gold. Gold carpet, gold pews, gold padding and white wood. Every piece of wood in the building is white. I wanted on Dedication Day to have a dignified service, not a formal one. The mayor was there. The city council was there. The bank president was there. Dignitaries from all over Hammond were there. I didn't want them to find out what we were really like. I wanted one time to have a dignified service. We were doing real, real well, I recall. I thought, *Good night! This is so good, I think I will just do this all the time.*

Like one little boy who went to the picture show, and he came home and told his Nazarene mother, "Mother, if you just went to the picture show one time you would never want to go to prayer meeting anymore."

I felt, *Boy, this is great! It is fun being dignified. I never tried it before. It is fun being proper. I never tried it before.*

In our dignified service sat the mayor, the city councilmen, the bank president, the dignitaries. The house was packed, and folks were standing outside. And right in the middle of my sermon that morning when I was trying to be dignified, way up in the balcony some little bus kid got a bulletin and began to make an airplane out of it. I knew what was coming. I thought, *Oh, I hope he won't launch that missile in this auditorium.* But down it came!

I know what such things do to a service. You have to stop and say, "Hey! You sit still while I'm preaching." Well, let me tell you something. I would rather have a service not quite as dignified and a sermon not quite as eloquent and have those little bus kids there who need Jesus and need loving. We need to care.

We have four on our deacon board right now who were once bus kids. Seven of our little bus kids have grown up and now teach in our Christian school. Thirteen of our bus kids are now wives of pastors. Twenty-seven are in full-time service for God. Over two hundred are in our Christian schools now.

We even started a new high school this year. We already had a high school, but this is our bus kids' high school. It is just for bus kids. One hundred and ten students already have signed up in our high school. Some of these are ex-hoodlums and ghetto kids and the switchblade kind.

I Once Was One of Them

I guess the reason I plead the case for these is that I once was one of them.

Thank God, when I was a little boy, nobody yet had found out it was wrong to give a poor kid a balloon in Sunday school. The first balloon I ever held in my hand, somebody gave me in Sunday school.

I am glad that I was a kid, a poor kid, when nobody had yet found out it was wrong to give a kid a hamburger because he was hungry. We thought it was feeding him to keep him from starving back in those days. The first hamburger I ever ate was given to me by my Sunday school teacher.

Down in the human heart
Crushed by the tempter,
Feelings lie buried that grace can restore;
Touched by a loving heart,
Wakened by kindness,
Cords that are broken will vibrate once more.

I can't drive down the streets of Chicago without tears. Oh, the suffering! The heartache! The sorrow!

One little girl three weeks ago came to me and said, "Brother Hyles, I don't know what to do. I am pregnant by my own father." That is the way it is. Concrete jungle of sin and sorrow! Somebody needs to care!

I am not concerned about a fundamentalist that dots the *i* and crosses the *t* and believes the virgin birth—and I do believe it with all of my soul. I'm a fundamentalist from the crown of my head to the sole of my feet. But in God's dear name, let's don't lose the moistened spot right there at the corner of the eye.

O my God in Heaven, there is a country going to Hell. Somebody said, "O Brother Hyles, sin is so bad." I know. Every time an extra tavern goes up, you have a brokenhearted wife sitting at home waiting for somebody to come and cheer her. Every time an extra tavern goes up or a nightclub, you have some orphan kids who need somebody to send a bus by their house and get them and bring them to Sunday school and feed them when they are hungry and clothe them when they are naked and love them when they are unloved and pat them on the head and say, "God bless you!" Somebody needs to care. Compassion makes a difference.

"Ain't You Even Gonna Cry?"

A little girl came to our Sunday school, seven years of age. She called me Mister Brother Hyles. She came after the service one morning and said, "Mister Brother Hyles, would you be my best friend?"

I said, "You got yourself a deal there, honey. I'll be your best friend." She kissed me on the cheek, and I tousled her hair and told her she was cute.

Beneath the dirt on her face there was a pretty face. Beneath the filth in her hair was a lovely little girl. Behind those tattered clothes was a body as precious to Jesus as the body of your child and mine.

On Sunday mornings she came up after baptism. "Mister Brother Hyles, we are best friends, ain't we?"

I said, "You better know it. We sure are good friends, and I love you. You are a pretty little girl."

Her mother was a prostitute and her dad an alcoholic. Nobody ever looked at her little story she brought home from Sunday school. Nobody asked her what it was like in Sunday school. But she had a best friend.

One morning after several months she came up and said, "Mister Brother Hyles, I have some bad news for you."

"What is it?"

"We are best friends, and my family is moving out of the state, and this is the last time we are going to get to see each other."

I said, "Oh, I'm so sorry about that because I do love you, and you are mighty pretty and sweet, and I love you very much, and we are best friends."

She said, "Mister Brother Hyles, you don't understand. This is the last time you will ever get to see me on this earth. We are moving out of the state, and we are best friends."

I said, "Honey, I understand that. And I sure will miss you."

She put her hands on her hips and looked at me with big tears as she said, "Mister Brother Hyles, ain't you even gonna cry?"

And I said, "Yes, I am."

Ain't you even gonna cry when you preach on Hell? Ain't you even gonna cry when you preach against the adult bookstores? Ain't you even gonna cry when you preach against liquor? Ain't you even gonna cry when you preach against the homosexual crowd? Ain't you even gonna cry? Compassion makes a difference.

The Case of the Retarded Baby

Her address is Anywhere, U.S.A. She is a mother. She and her husband have a new baby whom they love. He grows and learns to say "dadda" and "mama." But one day the mother notices the eyes don't focus just right. There is a strange look about the eye.

Mother and dad go to the doctor's office. The doctor gives the examination, and a few others; then the word comes. The baby is retarded.

Ain't you even gonna cry? Ain't you even gonna cry? Thousands of them across America whom nobody seems to care about.

How about the deaf? How about the blind? How about the cripple?

"For we know that the whole creation groaneth and travaileth in pain together until now."—Rom. 8:22.

Fundamentalist, ain't you even gonna cry? Preacher, ain't you even gonna cry? Ain't you gonna cry because of poor little kids and the folks in the rest homes and the maimed, the halt, the blind, the lonely, the sad, the poor, the naked, the hungry, the unloved, the unlovable? Ain't you even gonna cry?

Compassion Makes a Difference

Ladies and gentlemen, if we get to the place where we memorize this Bible and dot every fundamental *i* and cross every fundamental *t* and find out exactly who the Antichrist is and win all the battles we have to win, if we lose our tears, we have lost our right to exist! Compassion makes a difference.

Brother Coleman and I were in Ottawa, Kansas. We were asked to go eat in a lovely home. It was a wonderful meal with these sweet people. As we walked out to the car, Brother Coleman said, "Dr. Hyles, wasn't that fun?"

I wasn't smiling as I said, "Yes, but I feel as guilty as the Devil because I have thousands of church members who would give anything to have me eat one time in their home. I feel like I have been unfaithful to my people, eating with somebody else and not having time for my own folks because there are so many of them. I have hundreds of people who would give anything in the world if they could find me long enough to have me sign their Bible."

If I took thirty minutes with all of my members and spent forty hours a week doing nothing but counseling and gave each member thirty minutes, it would take me eight years.

I can't be in their homes, but I can think about them, and I can have compassion on them.

The Unsaved Need Compassion

His address is Anywhere, U.S.A., or Everywhere, U.S.A. He is an unsaved man. He has heard all the sermons on Hell, but he is still not saved. He has heard all the sermons on the judgment; he has had his wife nag at him, and soul winners come by to see him; but he is still not saved. Do you know what he needs? Compassion! It makes a difference.

Compassion in the Dentist's Office

I was in a dentist's office. I tried to win the dentist's wife, who was also his nurse, but I couldn't win her.

One day I was waiting for my appointment. A short, elderly lady walked in. You've seen her—the kind who does housework all over America. You've seen her—a big, heavy-set lady, straight hair, legs wrapped because of varicose veins. She came in holding a set of teeth in her hands. She said, "The teeth won't fit." Some blood was on her mouth.

And the wife (the nurse), said, "But, Mary, the guarantee is all up. You should have come sooner."

"I didn't have any way to come. My teeth don't fit, and I can't afford any more teeth. I've got to have them fixed."

And the nurse said, "Mary, if you had just come before the guarantee was up, we could have fixed them."

I said, "Nurse, how much would it cost to give her a new set of teeth?" She told me. I said, "Fix her up a new set and put it on my bill."

The dentist's wife said, "Are you serious?"

"Of course I'm serious. Make her a set of teeth and put it on my bill."

Within two weeks I got a call from the dentist's wife. She said, "Could I come to your office?"

She came to my office and said, "I have hardly slept since you offered to buy those teeth. Now I can listen to what you have been trying to tell me."

'Twas compassion that made a difference.

Her Tears Won Him

I was sitting in my study trying to win a man to Christ but couldn't. His wife was a faithful member of our church, and I said to him, "Won't you be saved?"

"No, sir. I am not interested."

I said, "But, sir, God loves you."

He said, "I don't want to, and I am not ready."

All of a sudden his wife threw herself on the floor and said, "Honey, you have to get saved, or I'll die!"

He looked at her, and big tears came down his cheeks. Then he looked at me and said, "Reverend, I can do it when she cries."

Compassion makes a difference.

I am a fundamentalist. I am like you. I fight my battles. I don't belong to the ministerial association, and I don't plan to join them until they decide to believe the whole Word of God is inspired. I believe in shorter hair than most of you have on this morning. I believe in longer skirts than some of you wear. I am an old-fashioned, rock-ribbed, barn-storming, Hell-fire-and-damnation, window-rattling, shingle-pulling fundamentalist. But I want to weep, and I want to care. Because one day when I was a little barefoot boy with a little white tee shirt on and a little pair of khaki britches patched at the knees, my mother and I walked into our first city church I had ever attended. It seated 400 people. A little lady walked up to me, and she said, "Good morning."

My mother said, "Good morning."

She said, "My name is Mrs. Bethel."

My mother said, "My name is Mrs. Hyles. And this is my son, Jack."

Mrs. Bethel looked at me, and she said, "Hello there, Jack. How are you?"

I dropped my head and didn't say a word.

She said, "Could I call you Jackie Boy?"

I dropped my head and didn't say a word.

"How old are you, Jackie Boy?"

I dropped my head and didn't say a word.

My mama said, "He's five."

The lady said, "I'm superintendent of the five-year-old department, the Beginner department. You come with me."

We walked down the aisle, over to that door. The first door on the right was the Beginner department. She set me on her knee. She looked out, and she said, "Boys and girls, we have a visitor this morning."

All the little boys had on white shirts and ties. All the little girls had on nice dresses. Twenty children had shoes on. I was the only barefoot kid, the only boy without a tie or a shirt. I tried to cover the holes in my trousers. I tried to put my feet behind me the best I could.

She said, "Boys and girls, we have a visitor, Jackie Boy Hyles. Aren't we glad to have him?"

Nobody said a word. They just stared at my ten toes sticking out from underneath my britches. Then that godly teacher pulled my little face to her breast and said, "Jackie Boy, did you know Jesus loves you?"

I will never forget how I felt. I looked at her, and I said, "Mrs. Bethel, does He love me as much as the other little boys and girls who have on shoes?"

She hugged me to her breast and said, "I think He loves you more than He loves anybody else in the room today."

'Twas her compassion that made a difference.

Compassion makes a difference.

For a complete list of books available from the Sword of the Lord, write to Sword of the Lord Publishers, P. O. Box 1099, Murfreesboro, Tennessee 37133.